BREAKER BOYS

Also by David Fleming

*Noah's Rainbow: A Father's Emotional Journey from
the Death of his Son to the Birth of his Daughter*

BREAKER BOYS

The NFL's Greatest Team and
the Stolen 1925 Championship

David Fleming

For my girls—Kimmy, Ally, and Kate

CONTENTS

P<u>ROLOGU</u>E

THE GHOST SPEAKS

AT THE END of the 1954 football season, Harold "Red" Grange agreed to speak at a sports banquet near his hometown of Forksville, Pennsylvania. Although it had been twenty years since he had hung up his spikes, the Galloping Ghost, an icon of the 1920s and a pillar of professional football, was still very much in demand—and every bit the crowd thriller he once was. As a packed audience of more than two hundred took their seats inside the Lycoming Hotel's grand banquet hall, the legendary running back with the flaming red hair and thick shoulders teased his audience by promising to talk about the greatest football player and the greatest team the game had ever known. Assuming that good old Red was referring to himself and his very own Chicago Bears, most of the diners just smiled politely and kept right on shoveling up their dinner.

What they didn't know was that back in 1927, at a time when a new car cost $700, Grange had once been offered $500 to play a game just down the road in Pottsville, then a prosperous mining town ninety miles northwest of Philadelphia. Over time, the Pottsville Maroons had faded into little more than Pennsylvania folklore, but to true football men like Grange they remained one of the most dominant, influential—and unforgettable—teams in NFL history.

Grange had breezed into Pottsville expecting to pick some tiny coal town clean for pocket change on his way to New York. Instead, on the morning of the game, Grange stepped off the train in his trademark raccoon coat and into a gleaming, vibrant city that fully captured the spirit of the times. In Pottsville, there was a nine-story office building under construction, eight luxury hotels, several first-class theaters that drew the biggest acts on the East Coast, row upon row of the most ostentatious mansions he had ever seen, and a burgeoning, diverse population of 27,000 that seemed to live and breathe the carefree ethos of the 1920s.

"Everybody just seemed to let their hair down a little after the First World War, and when the Twenties came along, boy, people were just ready for some entertainment," Grange once recalled. "It was a great generation. Everybody seemed to be enjoying themselves. People wore felt hats with big three-inch brims. Your clothes were big and baggy. You wore overcoats that pretty near touched your shoes. You read about players today, well shucks, drinking and sex were not just recently invented you know. That sort of thing has been going on for a long, long time, but in my day they kept it out of the papers. Prohibition made no difference. There was more drinking in Prohibition than there is today!"

What Grange quickly discovered was that nothing in Pottsville embodied the spirit of the Roaring Twenties, the "Era of Wonderful Nonsense," quite like the town's colorful, break-the-mold football team. "Yes indeed," Grange told his audience, "the Maroons were a notorious bunch."

NFL neophytes in 1925, the Maroons broke the bank, the rule book, and their opponent's backs. Their roster had a little bit of everything: rough-hewn coal miners, clean-cut college All-Americas, an ornithologist, a dentist, a city councilman, a lawyer, a pair of future millionaires, and a nut-job lineman who played with a wool baseball cap instead of a helmet. Built by an eccentric owner, molded by a visionary coach, and loaded with equal amounts of talent and personality, after just one unbelievable season the Maroons were dubbed 'The Perfect Football Machine."

The Maroons steamrolled their first seven opponents by a combined score of 179-6. They so thoroughly brutalized the boys from nearby Coaldale that angry citizens shot up the team's train as it chugged out of town. They humiliated legends like Green Bay Packers founder Curly Lambeau and bullied storied franchises like the Canton Bulldogs. After running out of competition in the fledgling NFL they risked everything to challenge Notre Dame's mighty Four Horsemen, the sport's ultimate standard of excellence, to a seminal clash described by the headline writers of the day as *The Greatest Football Game Ever Seen.*

Pottsville's team was such an instant sensation that opponents from New York volunteered to play what was designated a "home" game 150 miles west in Maroons territory in order to cash in on the Coal Crowd—the team's rabid fan base. Their home was Minersville Park, a rickety old stadium carved into the side of Sharp Mountain with a field that was more coal slag than grass. Yet crowds grew so big that Model T's sat abandoned for miles in every direction during Maroons games and late-arriving fans were forced to climb trees and sit 10 across, pocket to pocket on the sagging overburdened limbs just to get a glimpse at how their Maroons might fare against a legend like Grange.

On the first snap from scrimmage the Maroons welcomed Red to coal country by knocking him cold. The crowd went silent. After all, this was the man whose awe-inspiring talent once attracted 70,000 fans to the Polo Grounds. The man once described as "four men and a horse rolled up into one for football purposes ... Jack Dempsey, Babe Ruth, Al Jolson, Paavo Nurmi, and Man o'War." The running back who at the University of Illinois had run for touchdowns of 95, 67, 56, and 45 yards against Michigan ... *in the first 12 minutes* (a performance that actually inspired citizens in Champaign to petition to have the required age for Congress lowered to accommodate Red).

Dazed by the Maroons on that opening play, Grange got up, massaged his leather helmet back onto his head, and eased his meaty paw back into his three-point stance. On the next snap, the Maroons did it again. *Now we've done it,* Maroons fans thought, *our boys went and killed that nice Mr. Grange fella.* Then, as one eyewitness account put it, "when he comes to, he looks up at our boys. And you know what Red Grange said? 'The hell with the $500—it ain't worth it,' and he walked off the field."

That beating would haunt Red Grange for the rest of his days. Mesmerized by the memory of the Maroons, his banquet speech turned out to be almost entirely about the team that time forgot. "The Pottsville Maroons were the most ferocious and most respected players I have ever faced in football," Grange said, to what must have been a chorus of dropped forks and audible gasps. "They must have kept those Pottsville players locked up from Monday to Sunday then released them without being fed."

It was an homage that Grange repeated many times—during

interviews and speeches and even while working on air for the Chicago Bears. Nearly every time he was asked about the best team he ever faced, Grange talked about the Maroons and, in particular, their star running back, Tony Latone, the unofficial leading rusher of the 1920s who had spent most of his youth in the coal mines before trading in his pick for a pigskin. "That was one hell broth of a rugged coal miner," Grange said. "And for my money Tony was the most football player I have ever seen. I simply cannot imagine anyone who could equal this 195-pound power-playing fullback whose leg drive was so unbelievably potent he simply knocked the linemen kicking. Tony only knew two things about football: get the ball and run with it. If he was stopped at the line, he'd simply run backward and come charging back at you all over again. It didn't pay to get in his path, I know, since he came in my direction several times."

Fans who attended the banquet say that Grange seemed to be "transferring his own mantle of greatness to this son of a coal miner."

And when this happened, the room fell still. Even the waiters stood frozen, their serving platters of butter squares and sugar cubes suspended in place over the fancy linen tablecloths as they waited for Red's next revelation. Looks of bafflement shot back and forth between tables.

How? Diners mouthed to each other. How had fans in football-obsessed Pennsylvania not known the first thing about the NFL royalty located just down the road? How?

In paying tribute to Latone and the Pottsville Maroons, Grange was simply starting a chorus of voices that over the past eighty years has included Bears owner George Halas, one of the founding fathers of the NFL; former Notre Dame quarterback Harry Stuhldreher (of Four Horsemen fame); the original director of the Pro Football Hall of Fame, Dick McCann; current NFL owners Jeffrey Lurie and Dan Rooney, as well as former NFL commissioner Paul Tagliabue. "When you talk about the birthplace of professional football," Rooney says, "you're talking about Pennsylvania, you're talking about the Maroons."

Before pioneering teams like Pottsville, pro football, or the "postgraduate" game as it was called, was a ragtag collection of roughly 20 teams from New York to Kansas City dismissed as sordid, corrupt and soporific. Critics lampooned it as "paid punting." Teammates often met each other for the first time just before kickoff. And it was not unusual for pro players to barnstorm their way through four games in three days using a handful of aliases. College coaches spoke in print with utter confidence about the NFL's imminent demise. They argued that only amateur athletes who competed for honor rather than money were thought to be worthy of hero status. College ball was king. And most experts believed the pro players who could compete against a true team like Notre Dame had not even been born yet. Until then, no paid players could possibly garner the loyal following enjoyed by the universities.

In the early Twenties, the NFL's reputation was so bad the Maroons quarterback once got his face slapped by his fiancée for suggesting a pro football game as a possible social outing. Grange liked to say that he would have been held in higher esteem had he joined Al Capone's mob after college instead of the NFL. After signing with the Bears, Grange attended a White House function with Halas. When it was their turn to meet President Calvin Coolidge, they were introduced as members of the Chicago Bears, to which Coolidge replied, "Well, Mr. Grange, I'm glad to meet you, I have always enjoyed animal acts."

A few years later though, the electric Grange was more popular and many times as wealthy as the president and regularly attracting crowds of more than 50,000 to NFL contests. This is why Grange is often credited with single-handedly legitimizing the NFL. But a host of the game's greatest minds, and especially Grange himself, knew better. Pro football had floundered in obscurity and near bankruptcy for about 20 years before Grange came along, and had it not been for transcendent teams like the Maroons, the Galloping Ghost may have never had a league to save in the first place.

To men like Grange, Halas, and Tagliabue, the Maroons will forever remain one of the most important and influential teams in NFL history. And the fact that Pottsville, the smallest town to ever host an NFL team, was discarded by the very league it helped create remains an indelible black mark on the history of the game.

As Grange always argued, the Maroons were the first group to directly push pro ball past college football—on the field, at the gate, and in the national conscience. They were the first to conquer issues of skyrocketing salaries, territorial squabbles, obtuse rules, and obsessed fans. The first to field a squad with as much star power as brute strength. The first to innovate with preparation and strategy. The first to inspire the kind of civic boosterism that would one day transform the NFL into the true national pastime.

And they were the first—and only—team to be stripped of their NFL title.

"I have always believed," Grange, ever the showman, boldly declared before leaving the lectern that night, "that the Pottsville Maroons won the 1925 NFL championship but were robbed of the honor."

CHAPTER 1

BURIED ALIVE

L IKE MOST COAL MINERS at the turn of the twentieth century, Ignatius Latone began every day the same way: with his own funeral.

The sensation hit every morning like a gut punch, as he and his co-workers climbed into the rickety steel cage to begin the 1,000-foot descent into the yawning netherworld of the anthracite coal mines that honeycombed the earth under most of Eastern Pennsylvania. At 300 feet, the last available source of natural light from the shaft opening closed to the size of a pinprick before winking shut at the men. As they were engulfed by a dizzying avalanche of blackness, the rest of their senses followed a similar, and rapid, constriction. All light was gone, all sounds ceased and the air turned clammy and cold. *Hell isn't set ablaze and scorching after all*, the men would think to themselves. *It's perfectly black and a constant, bone-chilling 50 degrees.*

This was the point when most would begin to hold their breath, fighting as long as they could before allowing the unmistakable, sour bouquet of the mine to fill their nostrils: the sulfur and acidic hint of the gasses, the chalky coal dust, the mold, the mud, the manure from the mules, and the rotting stench of timbers and rats. And all the time, the steel cage continued to plummet into the inky darkness, jerking occasionally from side to side, until the walls narrowed at the bottom of the shaft, tightening around them like a boa constrictor.

The minute they began to breathe, the mine had them. There was no more light. No sound. No heat. No air. No space. And the feeling of gloom was inescapable. Coal miners started every day of their working lives like this: with the sensation of being lowered into their graves.

Oftentimes, for men like Iggy Latone, that was exactly the case. At a time before the notion of safety above profit had been born, the attitude of doom among coal miners wasn't resignation or even fatalism, it was reality. From 1900 to 1920, during coal's peak as the country's natural resource of choice, in Pennsylvania alone nearly 12,000 miners (roughly two men a day) were, in the words of industry historians, "slaughtered" while on the job. Coal mining was often the only advertised employment (with the added lure of low-cost housing) available to families like the Latones who, in 1880, emigrated from Kaunas, Lithuania, to New York and then to Edwardsville, Pennsylvania. And those who weren't blown up, suffocated, crushed, trampled, or drowned were left to die slowly, and painfully, from black lung, tuberculosis, or just plain old exhaustion.

Yet most of the men, who came from places with little opportunity and even less hope, remained grateful for the chance to swing a pick. The anthracite coal of Pottsville was special: It offered more than just an income and a way to feed and shelter a family; it also provided a unique sense of pride, culture, and social hierarchy to the men who mined it.

The Eastern Penn vein, which contained three-quarters of the world's anthracite coal, was discovered in 1790 by Necho Allen. A trapper and hunter, Allen realized he was sleeping on top of a unique bed of coal near what would later become Pottsville when his campfire stayed white hot long after the wood had turned to ash. Most other coal veins ran wide but shallow, requiring miners to move frequently after each area was stripped of its resources. But the anthracite fields, Allen discovered, typically ran vertically, and this allowed miners the luxury of settling in one place where they could put down roots and become part of an actually community. When the coal started to run out, they didn't have to uproot and move like their counterparts, chasing the cheaper, more common bituminous coal—they just dug deeper. As a result, at 1,500 feet, the mines in Pottsville were the deepest in the country.

Anthracite is a rare and nearly pure type of carbon created by a geological anomaly some 300 million years ago. When the plates of the continent violently collided, the result was rapidly formed mountains that shot up into the sky and then folded back over onto deep caverns of swamps, forests, and other organic matter. The speed and totality of the coverage acted as a purification process for the organic matter, the by-product of which was anthracite, a rock that burned cleaner and longer than any other type of coal. Cheaper and virtually smoke free compared with common coal, it quickly became the fuel of choice for businesses and homes in the early 1900s. And because of anthracite's hard, shiny, jet-black surface and the labor-intense excavation required to bring it to the surface, its miners boasted to their counterparts in the industry that they weren't merely scratching around in the dark looking for just any kind of rock—they were mining for "black diamonds." Many in the mining industry also saw something heroic about miners repeatedly risking their lives in order to provide the raw materials required to fuel the greatest industrial revolution the world had ever known.

Iggy Latone just wasn't one of them.

He saw nothing special or lucky about working in unspeakably horrid conditions for less than two dollars a day. Even that was a lie, he soon found out, since no one on a crew got paid until a coal car was filled to the foreman's liking—meaning that on many days you labored for free. And when you did manage to get paid, much of those wages were already owed back to the coal company (or colliery) for food, supplies, housing, and tool rentals, leaving most miners little more than indentured servants with fancy lamps on their caps.

Iggy's rapid descent was a familiar tale of a disillusioned immigrant. Like so many before him, he had come to America as a young man in search of adventure and wealth. He was a dreamer, a schemer, and, above all, a drinker. Given enough time and whiskey, Iggy could talk almost anyone into just about anything. All you had to do was ask his wife, Elizabeth, a Lithuanian girl with raven hair and mysterious, heavy eyes. Iggy had seen her in Edwardsville one day, flashed his large, ruby ring at her, and boasted of his plans to become a traveling salesman—and the next thing anyone knew, she had agreed to marry him.

But when prospects and proceeds diminished and his family continued to grow, a defeated Iggy lowered himself into the mines like everyone else, mainly because the Kingston Coal Company in Edwardsville provided its workers with housing—if you could call it that. Many of the coal patches, as they were known, were built next to the company's culm piles and garbage dumps and were made up of wood-plank tenement shacks that looked, and smelled, more like stockades. They had dirt floors, paper-thin walls, and a single water hydrant that was controlled by the colliery. Patches were strictly divided by religion or ethnicity, and each one usually had a makeshift pub that doubled as a general store, bank, phone company, post office, and social hall. All of it was owned by the colliery, of course, and like everything else inside the patch, the bar was covered in a thick blanket of coal slag and the soot that was continuously belched out by the massive coal breaker houses nearby.

For Iggy, days inside the mines were a wet, dank, horrid existence surrounded by imminent danger, rats the size of cats, and coal dust piled up all around like gunpowder snowdrifts. Some days he'd work on his hands and knees in chambers no more than three feet high. Here he could feel the boa constrictor squeezing him even more as he clawed the "monkey" coal out through his legs. On days when Iggy was lucky enough to be working in a chamber where he could stand and swing a pick, he had to constantly check his safety lamp for signs of dangerous gases while listening for the telltale crackling of the support timbers that were supposed to warn miners of a collapse. (After a while he learned to watch the rats. If they started to scurry, the miners would race them to the exit tunnels.)

Some days, Iggy did nothing but drill holes for the dynamite that would blast the anthracite out of its prehistoric resting place. It was an exhausting and backbreaking task that Iggy started by placing a thick wood board across his chest. Then Iggy would lift his four-foot steel drill to the wall of the chamber, and while leaning in with all his weight (sometimes two members of his crew would help by pushing on his back), Iggy would crank his butterflied bit into the rock—over and over, around and around, for hours at a time—until he had 10 deep holes ready to be packed with explosives. Because dynamite was expensive, however, many miners were blown to dust—or if they were lucky, just rendered deaf or blind—while checking on a slow-charging stick of TNT that ended up going off in their faces. If anyone survived those poorly timed blasts, he was taken home by the colliery's black wagon and dropped on the kitchen table. The very sight of the dreaded black wagon sent mothers and wives all over the patch into fits of crying, certain that it was their husband or father lying in the back. Dead miners were often left in a heap in their front yard, with no explanation. Although if a death resulted in the destruction of equipment or one of the coal company's mules, a bill might be pinned to the corpse's shirt.

Inside the mine, where the men couldn't see two inches in front of their faces, their dreams disappeared quickly into the darkness. When he came to America, Iggy was certain that in no time he'd be putting ruby rings on every one of Elizabeth's fingers, and a few of her toes. Instead, the reality in his new homeland was that a donkey's life was more valuable than his own. He hated how bits of blasted coal dust tattooed his face. He hated the sandy, gritty sensation of coal dust that he could never get out of his mouth. He hated having to spend 10 hours a day soaked from leg to lamp in thick, wet mud. He hated his ghoulish appearance after a shift, when the only things not covered in soot were the twin blinking beacons of white in his eyes. He hated bathing in a tin wash bucket each night. He hated how his back constantly throbbed and how the tips of his fingers would crack open and bleed, and how his "miners asthma" left him hacking handkerchiefs full of muddy mucus all day and night.

As a treatment for this ailment—and for a man's growing

enmity of the mines—coal company doctors often prescribed alcohol. Lots and lots of alcohol. A therapy, family members say, Iggy took to wholeheartedly.

There was no shortage of "medicine" around Edwardsville, either. The town was home to Bartels, a large brewery with the popular ad line "The Professor Says: Bartels." And Iggy was an eager apprentice. Soon he was missing shifts and, unable to control his wanderlust, disappearing for days at a time, often riding the rails to see friends from the old country in Chicago. Family members say that once he was off on a brannigan, he came around Edwardsville for only two things: to borrow money and make babies. Elizabeth took in laundry and cooking to make ends meet and did her best to charm officials from the colliery. She also tried to put on a brave front for her six young children.

Her one respite each week was the movies. Every Saturday she'd pack a lunch, place a tiny clean and starched lace cap on her head and a dime in her purse, and escape for a day to Comerford's Grand Theatre in town. There she'd sit sipping a sarsaparilla drink in the exact middle seat of the exact middle row, watching the cowboy matinees, one after the other—not caring at all that the subtitles were in a language she didn't understand. Comerford's was also used for the commencement ceremonies of the local high school, and Elizabeth spent many a Saturday watching movies and daydreaming of her own children crossing the stage to pick up their diplomas—passports to a better life, the one Iggy had promised her.

One morning in 1908, before sunrise in the patch, Elizabeth and her eldest son, Tony, 11, came down to breakfast to find a plow horse standing in the middle of their kitchen. After a wild bender, Iggy had stolen the horse and brought it home, before passing out on the floor. When the confusion and humor of the scene evaporated, mother and child realized they had a four-legged dilemma standing in their kitchen. If Iggy was arrested for stealing the horse, he would be fired by the colliery and the family would get the heave-ho into the streets. Luckily, it was early enough so that no one had noticed the missing horse, or its current whereabouts. Elizabeth calmly signaled to Tony to open the wood slats on rusty hinges that passed for their front door. Then she smacked the horse on the behind and ordered it—*"Eik po velniais!"* (Go to hell!)—out of her home.

It wasn't long before she was repeating the same ritual with Iggy.

He hardly paused to look back, jumping a rail and riding it west. Weeks went by, Tony started the fifth grade, and with winter settling in and the coal company landlords hovering, the Latones waited anxiously for word from Iggy.

It came, finally, in the form of a telegraphed obituary notice. On a pleasant, sunny winter day that more than likely turned bitterly cold after dark, Ignatius Latone drank himself into a stupor, wandered out into the streets of Chicago's skid row, and passed out, freezing to death. When police discovered him the next day, he was likely blue and stiff, with long icicles extending down from his ears, nose, and mouth. In a crowded, busy city like Chicago, one frozen miner wasn't a cause for alarm. *One less immigrant* is what people likely said to themselves as they walked past him on the way to work.

When word of Iggy's death reached Edwardsville, if Elizabeth mourned at all, it was for Tony rather than her husband. The coal company's explicit policy toward "freeloading" families required that within 48 hours the Latones had to provide some-one to take Iggy's place in the mines or risk being evicted from their house. Elizabeth cried and pleaded and threw herself on the mercy of the coal company reps standing in her doorway. If the mines were enough to bring grown men like Iggy to their knees, what chance would a child have of surviving? Rules were rules, she was told, and you've got 24 hours. With six young children to support (two other infants had already died in the poorhouse hospital), Elizabeth must have agonized over what she knew was her only choice.

The next morning she took Tony aside from his siblings. With mother on bended knee and son nodding dutifully back at her, Elizabeth instructed Tony to walk past his schoolhouse and report to the colliery where, more than likely, the only thing Iggy Latone had left behind for his eldest son was a death sentence inside the mines.

CHAPTER 2

THE BREAKER BOY

B Y THE TIME TONY LATONE was forced into the mines, anthracite coal consumption had skyrocketed to about 80 million net tons a year. To meet this demand, coal companies required nearly 200,000 workers, and they used anyone they could get their hands on—even children. In the days before effective child labor laws, most coal mines employed not just a few but hundreds of boys, some as young as eight. They put them to work for 10 to 12 hours a day, six days a week, inside their breaker houses. These mountainous wood buildings sat directly on top of the mines. And just like oil wells in Texas, the dramatically sloped roofs of the breaker houses served as the landmarks of the coal region. Inside, using a series of steep chutes, the coal that was unearthed by the miners was processed and cleaned before being shipped off on barges or railcars. For 13 cents an hour, "breaker boys" like Tony Latone sat on splintery wooden planks and straddled the chutes, picking razor-sharp slate and other debris from an endless flow of coal.

The work was unspeakably bad: backbreaking, poisonous, and monotonous. Boys chewed tobacco to keep the coal dust out of their mouths, and the deafening roar of the breaker made it impossible to speak or be heard. To spot a breaker boy away from the mine, one only had to look for his telltale "red tops." After a few weeks of picking slate, the outer layer of skin on the tips of a breaker boy's fingers would simply come off like the peel of an orange, exposing the pinkish flesh underneath. Red tops were excruciatingly painful, particularly during the first few minutes of a new shift, when the scabs would crack open and begin to bleed anew. And handling the chemicals contained in the coal was like dripping lemon juice on a paper cut. The boys kept working, though, because the only thing more painful than their raw nubs was a swing to the back of the neck or across the knuckles from the foreman's wooden stick—or worse, a pink slip from the mines.

Latone rarely felt the breaker boss's wrath. He was his mother's child: quiet, steadfast, and impossible to budge from a task. The work suited him, which didn't surprise his family. You could hand Tony a 12-quart bucket and ask him to go pick a few blueberries, and he would stay out all day—battling mosquitoes, hornets, snakes, and briars—picking bushes clean until his bucket was overflowing with perfect, plump berries. Tony also loved the solitude and challenge of fishing, and he convinced himself that working in the mines was in some way similar: You simply sit still and quiet for several hours at a time, working the huge expanse under you for the chance at a small but meaningful reward. He had never been much of a talker, either, so the noise from the breaker that prevented the boys from communicating in any way other than hand signals and secret codes didn't really bother him. Truth be told, he didn't care for school all that much. Besides, most of his buddies from the coal patch were working in the mines.

It felt good to work, to be productive and proud, instead of making up stories about his old man and hiding out from coal company officials. The pain he had to endure, in his back or his fingertips, was nothing compared with watching his mother suffer all those years while Iggy was alive. For Tony, the mines became almost therapeutic. Whatever anger and resentment he had toward his father, he bore it down to the nub deep inside the mountains of coal he conquered each day. If all boys are either trying to live up to or to make up for the actions of their fathers, then what better way to prove he was a different man than to excel inside the very place that had broken and embarrassed his?

As soon as Latone grew big enough to handle heavier work, he was moved out of the breaker house and into the entrance of the mine. There, adolescent boys were given any number of jobs. "Mule boys," or "drivers," pushed and directed the beasts hauling the coal cars up and out of the mines. "Sprag boys" then stopped the cars by rushing up at the last second and placing a thick, wooden wedge behind the wheels of the three-ton cars before they could roll back down the tracks and crash violently into the mines, destroying everything and everyone in their path. Often times it was a child's arm or leg that stopped the coal car instead of the sprag. Once healed, the amputees were "rewarded" with jobs underground that required them to sit in pitch-black, cavernous chambers all day, opening and closing the massive air-lock doors that kept fresh air circulating throughout the shafts.

The isolated, intense labor of the colliery made time relative: The days were interminably long, yet the years seemed to fly by.

Almost overnight, Tony Latone had grown into a formidable young man who had earned, through his own hero's trial, the kind of inner strength, drive, and perspective that no one can ever hand to you—nor take away. When he turned 18, in 1915, Latone joined the Navy. In the service, both his training and his 18-month stint aboard a battleship seemed to breeze by compared with his work entombed in the mines. After the war, with money in his pocket and the world at his feet, Latone dutifully returned to Edwardsville to support his mother and five siblings. This time, however, he entered the mines as a man working among boys. There was something about his dark, piercing eyes—accentuated by his pale skin and heavy brow—that earned him respect far beyond his years. And at 5'11" and 195 pounds, his chiseled frame and relentless vigor allowed him to take on brutal tasks, like coal car pushing, that normally required two men.

After the miners filled railcars with two tons of coal, mules would then lurch them to the entrance of the mine. There the cars had to be unhooked from the animals, held in place, and muscled several feet down the tracks, where they would be attached to a locomotive or another mule team. Latone excelled at the job because of his unique combination of physical gifts. He had quick hands and feet, giving him the dexterity needed to unhook and harness the animals, and he also had the raw power required to get a 4,000-pound cart moving. Years of this work gave Latone arms, shoulders, and thighs that looked like they had been transplanted from a man twice his size.

"I found myself pushing coal cars around for eight or nine hours a day," he would recall years later. "I was assigned to duty at the loading cage, and it meant I had to push, push, push all day. Those little cars would hold a ton or two of coal. There was more manual labor attached to that job than any in the mines. It meant constant pressure on the legs. I pushed those coal cars through the shift for more than two years, and all the time, my leg muscles were developing."

As was the region's love affair with football. To blow off steam during breaks and after their shifts, miners often played sandlot football in the shadow of the breaker house. Occasionally, laborers from different shifts would challenge each other on the makeshift gridiron. Once money began exchanging hands, it wasn't long before organizers were scouring the mines for players to improve their teams. One of these men surely noticed that the way Latone pushed coal cars around the yard—shoulders low, just a foot or two off the ground, his body parallel to the dirt, and his legs pumping like freight pistons—mirrored the technique used by football half-backs, or line plungers, as they were called.

Sometimes, deep inside the mines of Eastern Pennsylvania, the equation of pressure over time can miraculously transform ordinary chunks of black coal into precious diamonds. When he stepped on the football field for the first time, it was clear that the mines had had the same effect on Tony Latone.

Even in the ruthless frontier days of the game, Latone could make the most notorious roughnecks step back in fear simply by dropping his fist in the dirt. When he was down in position, the skin on his brow would bunch up, casting a sinister shadow over his eyes. His crouch was tightly coiled, freakishly close to the ground, and his right foot always staggered the tiniest bit. Just before the snap, the heel of that boot would rise up like a lit fuse, causing those around him to seal up their breath.

Word about Latone spread quickly, with one caveat: Better plug your ears. The vision of Latone unleashing his inner rage on the football field was at once barbaric and breathtaking. What most spectators couldn't shake from their minds, however, were the sounds it created. Even those watching from the opaque windows of the breaker house winced and shivered at the grotesque thud of Latone ramming mercilessly into the herd of flesh at the line of scrimmage, snapping bones like dry twigs. Latone ran angry. He ran mean. The more physical the fight, the stronger he became. The better the competition, the more yards he gained. With the ball in his hands he seemed possessed, as if his father's face had been superimposed under the leather helmet of every would-be tackler. And the sound it created was like that of a spooked horse hurling itself against the side of a barn. "On the street and at home, Tony was a phlegmatic, gentle man," explained one of his friends. "But once he donned his gear and graith, he suddenly became galvanized into a mood so devilish, there was no stopping him."

For others, speed, skill, and strength were the keys to the game. For Latone it was perspective. At a time when the ability to endure pain was the main requirement of a line plunger, none of the blows he absorbed on the field could compare with what he had already plowed through in life. By 20 he had buried his father, saved his family, and survived 12 hours a day in the mines and the First World War. For a man who had outmaneuvered death every moment of his life since the fifth grade, football was as uncomplicated and comfy as life could possibly get.

As a result, those who watched Latone play the game say that no man, before or since, ever did so with such fearlessness and joy.

"Everything comes natural to me," Latone said of his football skills. "On the field, I have no trials or obstacles."

His relentless, gravity-defying, hard-driving approach defied description. He even carried the ball oddly: out in front of his body, with one hand cupped above and below the ball, like a boy trying to transport a baby chick. All in all, people just didn't know what to make of Latone, what to call him, or how to elucidate to other football fans the manner in which he played, which is probably why he inspired such a wide array of nicknames: Tony the Tiger ... Push 'Em Up Tony ... Five-Yard Tony ... The Human Howitzer ... Tony the Terrible ... The Mack Truck ... The Bulldozer ... Touchdown Tony ... and his personal favorite: Old Reliable Tony. Ten minutes and half a whiskey into a description of Latone's playing style, one football fan in Wilkes-Barre threw his hands up and said, "That guy's half Lithuanian and half nelson."

Other football men in Edwardsville tried to get Latone back into school, where they were certain he could lead any collection of players to national acclaim. But by then Latone was nearly 10 years behind in his schooling. His lack of academics doomed his attempts at enrollment and, in turn, kept him a Pennsylvania secret for at least a few more seasons. Years later, George Halas surmised that if Latone had gone to college, "he would certainly have been one of the greatest pro players of all time."

Instead, he landed in the backfield of the lowly Lithuanian Knights, a barely semipro club formed by a social fraternity in Edwardsville. In one of his first games with the ragtag Knights, when rudimentary offenses measured forward progress in inches, Latone ran for more than 100 yards and two touchdowns in a 68-0 blowout against the club from nearby Steelton. "We never kicked on fourth down," recalled one of Latone's early teammates. "We just gave Tony the ball and let him roar."

He might have lacked proper schooling, but Latone was a master of football physics: In the gruesome collisions that made up most of the game, the player moving lower and faster always won. Latone also used his combination of speed and strength to stay one step ahead of defenses. When teams like Plains A.C. in

Luzerne County loaded up the center to barricade against his line plunges, he would flash to the corner, then turn the ball upfield. "To Tony Latone, the dashing new halfback of the Lithuanian Knights, goes the individual honors of the day," wrote one paper. "This youth, rated as one of the best in this part of the country, featured continually with line smashes and end runs that kept the [Luzerne] crowd on the defensive most of the time. A feature play by Latone came in the last quarter when he dodged and shook off a half-dozen men and carried the ball 45 yards on a sensational end run."

The following season, Latone signed with the Wilkes-Barre Panthers for a whopping $75 a game. It was more than he had made for an entire month in the mines yet was still well below the poverty level. And with his mother and siblings to support, Latone continued to live at home in Edwardsville and work in the mines between games. The Panthers, meanwhile, played neighboring coal region towns like Pottsville, Coaldale, and Scranton in the ultraviolent and highly competitive Anthracite League. Fans from Philadelphia called these early coal region battles "census games"—because the two teams seemed hell-bent on exterminating each other and lowering the population by 11. Hall of Famer Fritz Pollard, the game's first black head coach, always maintained that there were three kinds of football. "You had your college and your pro," Pollard chuckled. "And then you had coal mine football."

Thanks to Latone, Wilkes-Barre made it into November 1923 without dropping a single game. But as the Panthers were to face the final and fiercest part of the schedule, their backfield was decimated by injuries. Latone reacted the way he always did: He silently lowered his shoulder and pushed the team to the finish as if it were a coal car. Against the NFL's Rochester Jeffersons, he scored the only touchdown of the game, and the Panthers prevailed 10-3. "Tony became famous as a member of the Panthers yesterday," announced the town's newspaper. "His all-around playing against the Jeffersons won him the plaudits of every fan who saw the great battle. Latone was easily the outstanding star. Time after time, on almost every other signal, he crashed through the visitors' defense for big gains."

In the season finale, the Shenandoah Yellowjackets employed the defense now known around the region as The Latone Special. Seven men packed the defensive line between the two ends, hip to hip and crammed so tightly together that if their teammate had two bits in his football pants, they'd know if it was facing heads or tails. An extra linebacker was then placed directly over center, and for good measure, the defensive backs cinched in close on either flank. The strategy worked ... for three and a half quarters. "Then Latone tore off tackle from the 15," went one account, "and three times men tackled him, but he struggled on, and the last five yards to the goal line, he traveled with two Shenandoah men hanging on his back."

Latone had always had the heart of a steely saint, like his mother. But his success on the field brought out a bit of his father's dreamer's spirit. And why not? After many years in the coal mines and 18 months at war, it was a miracle that he had even lived this long. In Wilkes-Barre, it was considered a safe year if fewer than a 100 men died in the mines. Every time he returned from the football field to the colliery, Latone knew he was pushing his luck. The mine always won. Always. Even for stalwarts like him, sooner or later it would begin to eat away at you, from the inside out, like a tapeworm.

At 27, Latone had found his true calling, and it was football. His father's death and his brutal childhood had left a hole in him, one that he discovered was the exact size of a football. And by the start of the 1924 season, he was eager to see just how far he could take it, or rather, how far the sport could take him—if he could indeed run right out of the mines, for good, with a football clasped firmly between his hands.

Fate didn't make him wait long for an answer.

When the coal region football schedules came out for the 1924 season, the Panthers were slated to face Pottsville in the season opener. The Maroons were the class of the Anthracite League, and rumor had it that their avant-garde owner, while caught up in the unbridled enthusiasm and prosperity of the Roaring Twenties, was buying up all the talent in the region for a possible run at the NFL.

The mighty Maroons were said to lack only one thing: a running back.

CHAPTER 3

THE GOLDEN GLOW

FROM THE STOOP OF HIS three-story walk-up on the
nearly vertical East Norwegian Street, Dr. John Striegel
had a front row seat as the Twenties transformed his
hometown of Pottsville, Pennsylvania, from hill town to boom-
town. On most mornings, but particularly on game days in the
fall, Doc Striegel liked to pause for a moment on his porch to
breathe in the crisp mountain air and take in the magnificent
panorama of change that was engulfing the city below.

Geographically and economically, Pottsville had always rested
in the muddy, cupped, and callused palms of Sharp Mountain, a
steep range that ran rich with anthracite coal. The town was
also divided by the brown, bubbly water of the Schuylkill River.
For most of Doc Striegel's life, these were the only two points of
interest in Pottsville. Now, though, it seemed like every time the
sun crested the pointy pines atop the mountain behind his home,

half a dozen new projects were under way. Anyone from the Victorian old guard who still didn't believe in the social and economic revolution that was occurring in America only needed to view the world from Doc's perch, where monuments to new-found wealth and prosperity dotted the landscape.

There, on the south side of town: a magnificent, 60-foot cast-iron and marble statue of the great statesman Henry Clay. Clay was actually a native of Virginia, but his taxes on iron helped guarantee high coal prices, and the steady demand lined nearby Mahantongo Street with mansions, the kind that drew people all the way up from Harrisburg to wander and gaze skyward at the steep, multitiered, etched-stone pathways that led to the breath-taking homes, each one impossibly bigger and more ornate than the last.

There, just across the way from the Striegels: the city's brand-new Queen Anne-style railroad station. As the county seat and the self-proclaimed Queen City of the Anthracite, Pottsville was the first major town in the region to get rail service, and now it had two different lines that could speed passengers east to New York and south to Philadelphia 20 times a day. Over there, on Centre Street, the town's main north-to-south boulevard: an eight-story steel skeleton of the under-construction Schuylkill Trust skyscraper, located just in front of the city's new $100,000 YMCA with an actual indoor swimming pool. Farther north stood the grand new town hall designed by architect Philip Knobloch and a monolithic county courthouse with a pillared clock tower that, at dusk, would cut the setting sun into perfect, golden wedges.

If it is possible for a town to be both quaint and vibrant, then that was Pottsville. Since the end of the Great War, Pottsville had grown so fast that two of its biggest landmarks— St. Patrick's Catholic Church and the Yuengling family brewery—

wound up having to share a single wall on Mahantango. A church sharing its foundation with a brewery? To Doc, there couldn't be a more perfect metaphor for the 1920s, an era when sweeping social transformations were butting up against every conventional tenet of American life, when people had the time of their lives and then retired for the day, certain that tomorrow would be infinitely better.

It was a time of "miracles and excess," according to F. Scott Fitzgerald, and Doc Striegel was proud to be a man of the times. By the fall of 1924, Doc had risen to a place in Pottsville society that required every man in town to tip his hat to him when they passed on the street. As the town's leading doctor, he sat atop the social hierarchy, just above an attorney, a Protestant priest, and even the top-ranking board member of the largest coal company.

At 39, Doc was an imposing figure: a loud, confidant, rich, and rotund man with jowls that spilled over the collar of his custom-tailored shirt and onto the lapels of his cashmere coat. He had thinning black hair that was usually hidden under a fedora in the winter or a straw skimmer hat in the summer, and the dark circles under his eyes were softened a bit by his wire-rim glasses and the expanding, circular nature of his face. In his prime, Doc had been considered one of the finest all-around athletes Pottsville High had ever produced, starting at center for both the football and basketball teams. But when a leg injury ended his collegiate athletic career, Doc poured his endless (some might say manic) energy into his studies and earned a medical degree from the University of Pennsylvania. Using his skills as an Army surgeon, he rose quickly to the rank of major during World War I, then returned home to Pottsville, where he founded the A.C. Milliken Hospital.

Within a few years, his family owned most of East Norwegian

Street, including the expansive home at No. 324 where he ran his private practice, entertained dignitaries from all over the East Coast, and made a home with his wife, Neva, and their four children, John, Elizabeth, Karl, and Richard. The Striegels also owned a large country estate in the foothills outside of town that Doc named Aven ("Neva" spelled backward.) The son of working-class German immigrants, Doc Striegel required an entire page for his first entry into the renowned Who's Who annual.

Standing on his porch just a few hours before his now-famous Maroons were to open the 1924 season, Doc thought of himself as a giant, one of the imposing landmarks of the town and the times. He enjoyed prodigious amounts of whiskey, cigars, and cards. And he took on new challenges in the fashion that had become popular in the 1920s: without doubt, hesitation, or even the slightest consideration of cost or consequence. Doc didn't simply want to work in a hospital; he founded one. He didn't just love to gamble; he traveled all the way to Monte Carlo for card games. He didn't just own a pro football team; he had built one without rival. "No one ever met a man so sure of himself," said one family member. "Doc loved being the big man out in front of everything, and no matter what he was doing—cards, football, building a hospital—he loved to win, to be the best, more than he loved anything else ... maybe even his family."

And like the rest of the Striegels, he never backed down from a challenge. Doc's brother, George, once sparred with Jack Dempsey in New York, and his bar-owner uncle once took on the notorious Molly Maguires. In the late 1800s, the Molly Maguires were a powerful and ruthless gang of Irish immigrants who ran most things in and around the mining patches of Schuylkill County. One day, according to family legend, they ordered Doc's uncle to stop serving certain customers, most likely German immigrants. They asked him nicely. He refused. They asked him again, presumably while patting blackjacks and billy clubs in the palms of their hands ... and he refused again. A week later, customers came in after their shifts in the mine to find Doc's uncle swinging from a rafter above the bar.

It was part of the Striegel family DNA, this need to poke sleeping giants, and Doc was no exception. His slingshot was already aimed at the National Football League. Organized pro ball in Pottsville predated the NFL by a year when, in 1919, members of the 103rd Engineers formed an All-Service team after the war. The corporeal nature of football appealed to the town's soldiers and the rugged men of the region, much more so than the gentlemanly pace and subtle forms of baseball. Sandlot football games played for fun in the shadows of the coal mines quickly grew into a smattering of semipro club teams in each town that played each other on the weekends. These clubs then joined forces and finances and morphed again into fairly respectable and well-run teams that played for bragging rights against neighboring towns. Soon, fierce competition in the Anthracite region pushed even the smallest cities to raise funds, hire coaches, and begin signing ringers. By 1922 Pottsville's team, under the direction of three prominent local businessmen, was made up of a handful of local boys, and the rest were what coal region football fans called "imports."

Doc had bored quickly with running a hospital, and on a whim in 1922 he volunteered to be the team's physician. After one game he was hooked. The sport made him instantly nostalgic for his own athletic career. The visceral violence and regional rivalries also stoked his competitive nature and civic pride, which is to say, more or less, his insatiable ego. He had been a well-respected civic leader before then, but the success and popularity of the team meant Doc couldn't walk into Schneider's Drugstore, his barbershop—located in the basement of the Y—or within a city block of Zacko's Sporting Goods without being surrounded by well-wishers and fans inquiring about the schedule, a player acquisition, or a strategy for the next game. Invites for dinner, drinks, and conversation from the Moose and Elks clubs, as well as the upper-crust crowd at the Schuylkill Country Club, poured in endlessly—quite a coup for a second-generation American. Doc protested all the attention and inquiries, but not too terribly much.

Neither did the fans. Because the more Doc became involved with the team, the better the Maroons performed. Certainly it had something to do with his deep pockets and his fierce appetite for competition, but it went beyond that. Doc had a knack for finding players—whether due to his own athletic background, his understanding of the human body, or his time spent reading men at the poker table, he wasn't sure. But he was well ahead of his time when it came to understanding the importance of team-work and the complicated intrapersonal jigsaw of team building, where each player's size, talent, and temperament had to snap perfectly into place next to his teammate's. This had long been the case at the collegiate level of football, but for some reason Doc was one of the first to apply the idea of camaraderie and teamwork to the pro game.

With little objection from the town, Doc bought out the other owners over time, took control of the club, and began luring players to Pottsville any way that he could.

At the time, the benchmark of pro football was the Canton Bulldogs, who won back-to-back NFL titles in 1922-23, going 24 games without a loss. The pro game had yet to fully catch on, though, even in its stronghold of Ohio, and in the summer of 1924, the fledgling franchise folded. NFL president Joe Carr, a

pragmatic former newspaperman who was trying desperately to clean up the league's mercenary image, ordered Canton's players to report to the Cleveland franchise at once. The players scoffed, and Striegel held firm after signing several of them to exorbitant, season-long contracts (another concept he pioneered) for $150 or more a game. (The gem of this group was future Hall of Fame lineman Pete "Fats" Henry, a giant who, it was said, could take on an entire offensive line by himself while gnawing on a drumstick with one hand.) Prompted by Carr's hectoring, the Cleveland owners sued Striegel just weeks before the season was to begin. The petition for an injunction and damages never stood a chance since it was to be heard by a Schuylkill County judge, who laughed it out of court.

With that episode behind him and the 1924 season opener against Wilkes-Barre approaching fast, Doc turned his attention to more pressing matters. He rang up Joe Zacko, of Zacko's Sporting Goods, and asked for 25 new uniforms.

"What color ya want, Doc?" asked Zacko.

"Color's not important, Joe," replied Doc.

Zacko shrugged his bony shoulders. It was Friday—much too late to order new uniforms for a Sunday game. Zacko rummaged around in the back of his store. He found a box of reddish-purple wool jerseys, and shipped them over. Just like that, the Maroons were born.

At the time, though, the decision carried with it almost no fanfare whatsoever. There was just no way of knowing the significance of the team or the extraordinary serendipity that had been involved in its creation: how the Maroons, a team that would go on to change the course of professional football, could have only been run by a man like Doc Striegel in a town like Pottsville during an era like the Twenties.

As he jauntily stepped off his porch, letting his momentum carry him down into town and toward the trolley station that would take him to Minersville Park, Doc could see that Pottsville was no longer a simple valley of Sharp Mountain but rather a petri dish of cultural transformation. Norwegian Street took him past the thick-as-tar gray smoke of the refinery, past the fragrant air of the farmer's market, and toward the thundering clock chimes of the courthouse. Saturday morning was shopping day for most families. Every café and saloon offered a "free" lunch with the purchase of a soda or another drink. And this transformed the streets into a pulsating mix of people, activity, smells, and sounds, most of it painted in shades of brown: the muddy streets, the khaki-color river, the horse-drawn carriages, the permanently stained faces of the men and children who worked at the colliery, even the brown-brick mansions of the coal bosses.

Doc could see that the people of Pottsville were also changing, almost as fast as the landscape. The coal boom had brought a wave of immigration from Poland, Germany, Lithuania, and Ireland. And now almost 30% of Pottsville's population was made up of first- and second-generation Americans. This created rich new subcommunities of ethnic and religious diversity that cracked open the town's prewar homogeny. At the same time, the rest of Pottsville's mostly white, middle-class residents were undergoing what historians called a "revolution in manners and morals."

Pottsville's metamorphosis mirrored the rest of the country's postwar population shift. According to the 1920 U.S. Census, for the first time in history, half of America's 105 million residents were living in urban areas rather than on farms. Over time, this urban conquest had transformed American society from isolated and old-fashioned to a more pluralistic and, some would argue, hedonistic existence. The novelist Willa Cather wrote that "the world broke in two in 1922 or thereabouts." It started with soldiers returning from the war. Their "eat, drink, and be merry, for tomorrow we may die" credo of alienation and joyous release had infected the entire country. "Here was a new generation," declared F. Scott Fitzgerald, " ... grown up to find all gods dead, all wars fought, all faiths in man shaken." That attitude, meanwhile, had coalesced with the unique socioeconomic triad of industrialization, urbanization, and immigration to create an entirely new and completely modern American culture—whether the Victorian old guard was ready for it or not.

Wartime advances in technology and efficiency that had peaked with the Industrial Revolution now made it possible for a larger workforce to earn significantly more money in far less time. The Ford Miracle, for example, had made it possible to produce a complete Model T not every 10 days or even 10 hours, but every 10 seconds. From 1922 to 1929, a time often referred to as the Golden Glow, the United States became a dominant world economic power, piling up 40% of the world's wealth while most European economies remained in a state of postwar devastation. As a result, by the mid-1920s, 40% of Americans were earning $2,000 a year or more—enough money to comfortably support a family of four. As Americans had more cash and freedom, their spending on movies, fashion, dances, and sports rose by 300%. Out of this growth a new culture emerged, based largely on consumerism and leisure. There were dance marathons, pole sitting, yo-yo contests, roller skating, and endless games of mahjong. Gossip and fashion became national pastimes. In 1924, it was arguably easier to get a drink in Pottsville than it had been before the 18th Amendment passed. One needed only a dime and a password to get a shot of rye or a mason jar full of hot hooch at speakeasies with names like Club Four, Logan's Alley, and

Sloppy Joe's. "This country has gone mad," said one writer. "There is always something crazy to do."

Almost overnight, America had become more urban, more diverse, and far more cosmopolitan. Outward definitions of success and status—wearing the right baggy, oxford-style pants or raccoon coat, driving the newest style of car, or having the best football team—became the only kinds that mattered. Movies, radios, ball games, vacations, fancy cloche hats—Americans wanted it all, and they wanted it all right now, even if that meant they had to mortgage their futures to afford it. In this era, radio sales rose 1400% to $852 million a year. Movie-ticket sales skyrocketed to 100 million a week, a staggering amount considering that the entire U.S. population was only 123 million. And car purchases raced from 8 to 23 million. Ford described the machine as the new messiah, and nothing symbolized the spirit and attitude of the times quite like the country's newfound love of the automobile. So great was it that a new method of payment—installment purchasing—was invented just to accommodate the craze, despite the dangerous implications of the get it now, pay later mentality.

Downtown Pottsville was a testament to this new way of thinking. Pomeroy's gigantic department store used the slogan "Bigger Than Ever. Better Than Ever" while selling wingtips, fedoras, irons, radios, and the new Hoover Electric Suction Sweeper faster than they could stock them. The opulent Hippodrome Theatre hosted all the famous acts of the time under its massive arched ceiling. Across town, the newly remodeled American Theater was renamed the Hollywood, an appropriate switch considering the mentality of the times: Hollywood wasn't part of America, Hollywood *was* America. Plans were already under way for the nine-story Necho Allen luxury hotel on the corner of

Centre and Mahantongo. From S.S. Kresge's and Woolworth's to Clawson's Jewelry to Frank Hause's tobacco store to Bushnar's Café and Ginley's furniture showroom, Centre Street extended out before Doc in a tightly packed kaleidoscope of storefronts, awnings, neon signs, display cases, and red, white, and blue bunting that rivaled the busiest blocks in Manhattan.

If the war had made Americans restless, discontented, and introspective, this conspicuous consumption gave them time and opportunity not just to question but also to change the world they occupied. The importance of self-sacrifice as preached by Doc's parents had morphed into a focus on self-realization. It was a grand time, one of frenzied metamorphosis, endless optimism, and wild experimentation. And it gave birth to a dizzying array of new thinkers and heroes, most of whom embodied the independent, sky's-the-limit spirit of the times. Sigmund Freud, Charles Darwin, and Albert Einstein became household names. Al Capone ruled Chicago. Duke Ellington and Louis Armstrong scored the country's jazz soundtrack. Ford owned the streets, and Charles Lindbergh the sky. Babe Ruth dominated the diamond, Bobby Jones was the king of the greens, and Jack Dempsey was the lord of the ring. "This remarkable 10 years saw the most fabulous set of champions arise in every game, not only from the point of view of performance, but of character, as well," surmised sportswriter Paul Gallico. "Every one was a colorful extrovert of one kind or another. Each had a romance connected with them and these legends themselves were reflections of our age of innocence, for they were all success stories, the great American fairy tale, the rise from rags to riches, the first such actually dramatized before our very eyes."

That's what Doc needed: a star—a homegrown player to build his team around. Someone who would unite the community and embody the spirit of the town while drawing fan support from the dusty coal miners in overalls and financial backing from the bankers in three-piece suits. Striegel, in fact, was on his way to scout just such a player: a coal miner/halfback from nearby Wilkes-Barre who was the talk of the anthracite region. And as he stepped aboard the Market Street Trolley, heading west up the tree-lined street and out of the valley that contained Pottsville, Doc was eager to see if this so-called Human Howitzer could live up to his legend.

The trolley clacked past the block-long, red-brick Silk Mill factory and the town's large, detailed marble Civil War Memorial. (Men from Pottsville were part of the group known as the First Defenders, who had rushed down to protect Washington, D.C., from Southern rebels after the war broke out. Less-celebrated were the Pottsvillians who were part of the ignominious plan during the Civil War to tunnel under a Confederate stronghold outside of Petersburg, Virginia. The tunnel famously collapsed, and the Union soldiers were trapped in the crater and summarily slaughtered.)

After cresting the hill, Doc saw the now-telltale game day sight of abandoned Model T's clogging up both sides of the road. This was Doc's first indication that Minersville Park was once again sold out. "Fine weather brought out a capacity crowd, every seat being taken. [There was] even a deep fringe [of fans] around the standing-room sections," wrote *The Pottsville Republican*.

During games, Doc usually sat on the bench with the team, and from the first series of plays, the stadium was abuzz with talk of the bulldozer from Wilkes-Barre. He ran close to the ground, defying both the laws of physics and common sense. Most would-be tacklers calculated the recovery time of two broken kneecaps and simply stepped out of his way. "Tony Latone, Wilkes-Barre's home product, put up a splendid game for the visitors, hitting the great Pottsville line for substantial gains on several occasions," said one eye witness. "Few backs were able to do that against Pottsville last year, and few backs, if any, will do it this year."

The game was over by halftime, with Pottsville holding a commanding 24-0 lead. Yet what caught Doc's eye was that even with the game out of reach and his blockers outmanned and out-muscled on every play, the back from Wilkes-Barre continued to ram the line with a total disregard for his own well-being that seemed to escalate with each attempt. The violent collisions could be felt deep into the stands.

The day before the game, a heavy rain had flooded the field with a thick layer of coal culm. While the additional weight of the muck slowed Striegel's players, the extra coating seemed to make Tony Latone better. He appeared transfixed by the smell, texture, and taste of the coal slag smeared all over his uniform. As he continued his assault on the normally impenetrable Maroons defensive front, Pottsville's partisan crowd began to roar its approval. All the critics of the pro game, all the pontificating college coaches who hissed at the way money was eroding the true spirit of the gridiron, they needed to see this back from Wilkes-Barre: down by 24 points and with no hope of victory, attacking men who outweighed him by 30 pounds as if his very life depended on one or two extra yards.

Of course, in many ways it did.

After the game, Doc made a beeline through the muck, ignoring the damage to his own perfectly buffed wingtip shoes and bumping past his own players and well-wishers until he reached Latone. He introduced himself, and skipping past the small talk of lesser men, Doc made a generous offer for the halfback's services. Although it was exactly what he had been hoping for, out of instinct and humility Latone balked, snorted something dismissive, and began walking toward the locker room. With every step Latone took toward the sidelines, however, Striegel seemed to increase his salary. And when they approached the end zone and the tin-roof structure that housed the locker rooms, Striegel made one last plea, planted his feet, and extended his hand.

Latone paused for a moment in the doorway of the Panthers' locker room. He looked in at his teammates. He looked out at the wild scene of Minersville Park, with the entire town of Pottsville staring at their feet, kicking dirt, whistling in the wind, pretending not to be waiting for his reply.

Latone took a deep breath.

In doing so, he inhaled the pungent stench of the coal culm that had soaked his jersey, the front of his brain, and every other part of his life for the last 15 years.

Latone exhaled, squeezing the smell out of his body one last time.

Then he wiped his muddy palm on his pants, reached out, and shook Doc's hand, sealing the deal that would forever change the course of professional football.

CHAPTER 4

A
NEW
FAITH

LOCATED IN THE HEART OF downtown Pottsville, just down the street from the mansions on Mahantongo and next door to the Yuengling Brewery, St. Patrick's Roman Catholic Church was nearly as old as Pottsville itself. Construction on the original chapel began in 1828 on land donated by town founder John Pott. Nearly a century later, after countless upgrades and additions, the cut-stone cathedral and its 500-foot conical brass spire had become an architectural and cultural landmark of the town. Fittingly, its congregation had also grown into something of a who's who of Catholic society in Pottsville. Yet midway through the 8 a.m. Sunday Mass on November 9, 1924, when Father William Sullivan climbed to the top of his marble and brass pulpit to deliver his weekly sermon, he noticed his flock thinning considerably with each passing moment.

Father Sullivan was himself a great supporter of the Maroons and therefore was well aware of the importance of the game in Atlantic City later that day. For that very reason he had promised to finish the morning Mass with plenty of time to spare before the special trains provided by the Reading Lines were scheduled to depart for the game. When it came to the safekeeping of their eternal souls, the members of St. Pat's had the utmost confidence in Father Sullivan. Apparently the Maroons were an entirely different matter. Because halfway through the homily, parishioners, or at least the ones who were not being detained by the shirt collar or earlobe by their dutiful wives, began leaking out of the pews—one by one, two at a time, and then in wild droves, as if the bell at the fire station were ringing.

When Father Sullivan's patience finally ran out, he paused midsentence, smacked his thick, righteous palm down onto the banister of the pulpit, and roared at what remained of his congregation. "SIT DOWN UNTIL MASS IS OVER!" he shouted before composing himself. "It won't take long … I'm catching the same train to the same game as all of you are!"

Sparked by Doc's discovery of Latone, by the end of the 1924 football season the popularity of the Maroons had reached a higher plane than anyone could have imagined. Armed with the region's best talent and its most devout fans, the Maroons had obliterated the Anthracite League, going 12-1-1 while outscoring their competition 288 to 17. (Pottsville had battled hated rival and NFL front-runner Frankford to a scoreless tie a year earlier but had fallen, 10-7, to the NFL's last-place team, the Rochester Jeffersons.) With the coal region championship all but locked up and interest in the team reaching a crescendo, Doc decided to drop his bombshell.

"I can get this team into the National Football League if the patrons so desire it," he announced to supporters.

All that was left to do, according to Doc, was to put up a strong show of support for the Maroons at their game in Atlantic City, and the NFL would be on bended knee. To everyone in Pottsville, the National Football League represented their best, and maybe only, chance to shine on a national stage. Football was the only way they could compete with the big-city boys who consumed trainloads of Pottsville coal, depended on it for their livelihood and comfort, yet still looked down at the people who provided it for them.

For the proud Pottsvillians, football was the great equalizer. And if a chance at getting even meant a few extra Hail Marys from Father Sullivan, then so be it.

By the time the 9 a.m. train pushed back for Atlantic City, more than 4,000 football fans of every denomination had crammed into the special cars that had been requisitioned for the game. People rode between cars, hung out windows, and stood for the entire two-hour trip. Upon arrival, as had become their custom, Maroons fans paraded from the station to the stadium, where the stunned Atlantic City mayor, Edward Bader, scrambled to find a key to the city for Doc before ordering the east side of the stadium evacuated to make room for the Pottsville contingent.

Within minutes, the wood-plank bleachers resembled the train cars they had just arrived in, with the Maroons crowd packed in 20 rows high and stretched from goal line to goal line. It was an impressive sight, an expansive sea of spit-shined shoes and toothy, ear-to-ear grins. Every man present was wearing a suit and tie with a cashmere overcoat and either a derby or fedora. Most lapels were decorated with small metal footballs dangling from purple ribbons. Women made up about a tenth of the crowd, and they too were decked out in their Sunday best: tilted cloche hats and heavy overcoats with collars made of thick, luxurious pelts of fur. Everyone was beaming with pride and was giddy with nervous energy. Men smoked their last cigarettes before kickoff or packed their cheeks with chaw. Others tested their megaphones, studied their 10-cent game programs, or unfurled purple, rectangular Pottsville banners. The enthusiasm and anticipation of the crowd gave off the feeling of 11:59 p.m. on New Year's Eve: a tidal wave of human spirit that felt as if it was about to spill out of the bleachers, over the chicken-wire fence surrounding the stands, and down onto the field.

Moments before kickoff, the Maroons gathered at the 50-yard line with their backs nearly touching the mass of humanity behind them. The noise from their own crowd forced them to huddle up close on the bench and scream into one another's ears just to be heard. The metal spikes of their cleats hung off the edges of the wood benches that were softened and splintered by the ocean air, and their grave game faces peeked out from underneath the thick wool hoods of their warmup sweaters. Doc squatted down in the middle of the team, dropping his black leather medical bag at his feet, unopened. He wouldn't need it. Not today. The Maroons would have little trouble clipping the A.C. Roses, who usually wilted with barely a fight. The game was inconsequential anyway. What mattered most was the town's show of support and the effect it was having on the people who would ultimately decide the Maroons' fate: potential investors from the town, NFL president Joe Carr, and the prize recruits Doc had invited to the game as his guests.

The Maroons' difficulty with the two teams from the NFL convinced Doc that he would have to overhaul his roster as well as his coaching staff just to compete on the next level. The Maroons finished as one of the best non-NFL teams in the region and probably would have done fine as is, but in Doc's mind, the only thing more tragic than not getting into the NFL in the first place would be to gain admission and then get blown off the field. As a football owner, Doc lived his life as if there were a loaded derringer pressed against his temple. To him, the NFL was an all-or-nothing proposition: If he was going to enter his beloved hometown into the league, he was going to dominate or ruin himself trying.

And so the real story of the 1924 Atlantic City game was not on the field or in the stands but sitting there next to Doc on the Maroons sideline. Watching the game from the bench was the insatiable Striegel's latest, greatest coup: Herb and Russ Stein. The boys had grown up on a farm in Niles, Ohio, and had become the first pair of brothers ever to be named to Walter Camp's college football All-America first team. That honor would have never been possible had it not been for a legendary standoff on the front porch of their family's farmhouse between two of the most powerful men in Niles.

In 1911, the local high school team was on the verge of forfeiting the entire season due to a lack of players. So the team's coach, the eminent judge W.W. Giffen, gathered his 11 players at the high school field and, instead of practice, marched them over Mosquito Creek and up Vienna Street to Frank Stein's farmhouse on the northwest outskirts of town. The team and the judge properly introduced themselves and then went about begging Mr. Stein to let his two giant sons play prep ball. His initial reply was a flat, dismissive no. There was simply far too much work to be done in the fields to make time for such folly as football.

The judge was determined. He parked the team on the front porch, and the stalemate continued for the better part of the day until a compromise was struck through the screen door: Herb and Russ would play for Niles as long as the rest of the team would come out and help the Stein family bring in their crops. It was a brilliant trade. Working 12 hours a day in the fields since they were small children had given the Stein brothers broad shoulders, thick necks, wiry and deceptively strong arms, and legs that could plow through four men at once and never tire. The thick, coffee-color soil of northern Ohio had made the Steins what is commonly referred to as "farm strong," and no amount of weight training, football practice, or secret elixir could build a man half as powerful.

A year after adding both Steins, the Niles High football team was a state power, so explosive and unstoppable that it finished 9-1 and outscored its opponents 325-26. That year, rather than face certain humiliation as well as extreme medical trauma, Niles' main rival, Warren High, canceled their traditional season-ending game.

At a strapping 6'1" and 186 pounds, Herb Stein went on to play center and was captain of legendary coach Pop Warner's team at Pitt. He had chiseled facial features, with a glare in his eyes that made him appear to be frowning even when he wasn't. Russ had softer, thicker cheeks and a friendlier disposition. About 25 pounds heavier than his brother, he played tackle and linebacker at Washington & Jefferson University, leading the 1921 team to a 10-0-1 record and a scoreless tie against California in the Rose Bowl, in which he was the MVP.

The word in Frankford, a northeast section of Philadelphia, was that you could put a mule and a scarecrow on either side of the Steins and still run for three touchdowns a game. And according to the Yellow Jackets' garrulous owner, Shep Royle, the boys also had a bit of a mean streak, which served them well in the slaughterhouse on the defensive line.

Strategy in the early days of the NFL was quite simple: Control the line, win the game. And with the Canton Bulldogs likely to reorganize for the 1925 season, Doc was already anticipating losing his quarterback, Harry Robb, and his best lineman, Pete "Fats" Henry, back to Ohio. (Robb was more of an extra halfback than a passing threat, and because Doc wanted to open things up on offense, Robb's departure was no great loss.) By contrast, Striegel saw the immense potential of the Steins, not just as a way to solidify the foundation of his own team but also as a way to severely weaken Shep Royle's club.

There was no question in Doc's mind: He had to have them.

At the time, though, few owners ever considered signing players a whole year in advance. In such a barbaric sport, where careers ended on almost every snap, it made no business sense—which is exactly why Doc loved it so much. With Royle believing he still had several months to renegotiate with the Steins (right up until kickoff of the 1925 season opener, if need be), Doc strolled into town, took out his checkbook, and lured Frankford's two best linemen north to Pottsville. When he heard the news, Royle must have flown into a murderous rage. Doc Striegel seemed to have that effect on a lot of people. Long before the NFL even had a chance to consider the Maroons for admittance, Doc had already made mortal enemies of the league's two most powerful men: president Joe Carr and Shep Royle.

These men were only beginning to understand—or as was more often the case, loathe—the mad genius of Doc Striegel, a man whose methods of player procurement flew in the face of the gentlemanly acquiescence of the time. A few months earlier, Doc had attended a game at his alma mater, Penn, with the hopes of finding another player or two for his 1925 roster. After one series, he realized he was on the wrong side of the field. The two best players in the game were actually lined up for Penn's opponent, Lafayette College, an eastern football power located in Easton, on the New Jersey-Pennsylvania border. After the game, Doc strolled down to the Lafayette locker room and struck up a conversation with quarterback Jack Ernst and the team's All-America receiver and captain, Charlie Berry. After a few minutes, he invited them on an all-expense-paid trip down to the Jersey Shore as his guests for the game against the Roses later that month.

Berry was a natural leader and a gifted athlete. The only problem was that he had already signed with Connie Mack to become a catcher for the 1925 Philadelphia Athletics. That meant he wouldn't be able to join the Maroons until he was granted his release by the A's in early October—or later still if Mack had them back in contention for the pennant. Doc signed Berry anyway. Why wait? He knew it was a gamble, but he believed Berry was good enough to wait for. Until then, he could only hope that his hunch was correct and that this Ernst fellow was talented enough to get by on his own.

Raised not too far from the Steins in Ohio, Ernst epitomized the first generation of quarterbacks to emerge in the dawning era of the forward pass. He was a bold, confident field general, a tremendous open-field runner, and he had a cannon arm that he was not afraid to use. Ernst had developed such a strong, accurate arm that he would ask friends to pick an open window in a nearby house or garage, and then, from 50 feet away, he would deposit the pigskin through whichever window they preferred.

At the turn of the century, Ernst's father, Jack Sr., had been something of a local football legend, starting all four years on the line at Lafayette (the national champions in 1896) and then jumping in from time to time with the Canton Bulldogs in the days before the NFL. The plan had always been for his son to follow in his footsteps at Lafayette. But late in the summer of 1918, just a few weeks before Jack Jr. was supposed to enroll at the college, his father fell ill with the Spanish flu. (The pandemic was ravaging the entire planet claiming 675,000 lives in the U.S. alone and another estimated 30 million worldwide.) Less than two weeks after his father first complained of a sore throat, Jack Jr. watched helplessly from the doorway of the hospital room, breathing along with his father, as this once-vibrant, stout man took his final breath, his chest slowly sinking under the white hospital sheets, never to rise again.

To support his mother and siblings, Jack Jr. gave up on college and reported to the local steel mills, where the hellacious, white-hot heat of the blast furnace quickly melted away his eyebrows as well as the dreams of gridiron glory deposited behind them. Without his beloved father around to watch, it hardly seemed to matter to Jack Jr. anymore. And then, in the summer of 1921, the Ernst family received a telegram from the Lafayette alumni office: Jack Sr.'s college teammates had set up a scholarship fund to pay for Jack Jr. to get out of the steel mill and attend Lafayette.

By the time he arrived on the picturesque campus, located on the shores of the Lehigh River, Ernst was three years older and far more mature than most of his teammates. During the first week of football practice, Jersey cardsharps were spotted on campus trying to clean up on a new crop of rich, naïve college kids. When the mobsters set up craps games with loaded dice and three-card monte tables just outside the Lafayette locker room, Ernst recognized the scam right away—the same kind of crew used to appear at the steel mill on paydays . Without considering the risk to his own personal well-being, not to mention his throwing arm, Ernst reached across the table and slapped the top of the roller's fist. When the third die he was hiding in his palm fell to the ground, the students gasped and snatched their money off the makeshift table.

"Scram," Ernst growled at the men.

When threats didn't work, the gangsters tried offering Ernst a cut of the action. All he had to do was keep his mouth shut, and he'd have beer money for the entire school year. Ernst just shook his head and pointed to the exit gate, and the men reluctantly agreed to leave. (Luckily for Ernst, Lehigh University was close by and teeming with rich kids.) Grateful teammates were impressed by Ernst's unflinching bravery, until they realized that he dealt with everyone, including his receivers, in the same straightforward manner. "Ernst was a very good passer, a beautiful passer," recalled one of his Maroons teammates, George Kenneally. "You could go 40 to 50 yards downfield, and he would lay one up for you out there, nice and soft. But if you dropped it, oh boy, when you got back to the huddle, he'd bawl you out pretty good. He'd say, 'What are you doing? You gotta catch that ball, you son of a bitch!'"

The more time and distance he was able to put between himself and his father's death, the more Ernst began to feel like his old self, the wily kid quarterback who confidently chucked the ball through the garage window without fail. Back on the football field at Lafayette, Ernst became inspired, rather than haunted, by the death of his father. And eventually, his larger-than-life presence and his booming, guttural laugh, so powerful it bent his body backward at the waist, earned him the nickname The Bear. By his senior year, Ernst had developed a preternatural pocket poise and a silky-smooth throwing motion while leading Lafayette to a 7-2 record, including a clutch 7-0 win over rival Lehigh in his final college game.

"Jack was about as cool on the battlefield as an iceberg in Greenland," is how one acquaintance put it. Forged by the steel mill and motivated by the memory of his football-loving father, Ernst was impossible to rattle, impossible to slow down, and impossible to satisfy—the three things Doc wanted most from the quarterback who would hold his NFL dreams in his hands.

Ernst was not well-known, even in the tight circles of Pennsylvania football, nor did he earn many athletic accolades in college. But Doc sensed that Ernst had unfinished business with football, and his hunch was that the quarterback's best football was still ahead of him. Beyond that, there was an intangible allure to Ernst that Striegel didn't quite grasp until he saw his future quarterback sitting on the Maroons' bench that day in Atlantic City. As the Maroons played out the final few meaningless moments of their 1924 season, Striegel looked up at the sea of 4,000 rabid fans behind him and then over at Ernst, who looked like he was itching to shed his suit and bring that crowd to its feet. With his sinewy frame, thick, black hair, and intense, dark gaze, Doc figured Ernst could pass for a poor man's Rudolph Valentino.

And that's when it hit him. When the NFL beckoned, and it surely would after the kind of show Pottsville put on in Atlantic City, Doc and his team would be ready. To what many people had already considered the best non-NFL team in the nation, he had already added the Steins, the two best linemen in the game; Berry, an All-America end; and Ernst, a good player with a great arm who, like Doc, had a hunger for more.

"A football regime cannot stand still. It must either decline or move up," Doc shouted to supporters after the game. "We might go on beating Coaldale, Gilberton, and Shenandoah indefinitely, and it wouldn't mean anything more than it means right now.

Pottsville has been invited to enter the National League in 1925, and I am favorable of the idea. We may lose, but we will give a stiff battle, and even to lose would bring credit to our community. We will put our team in line to meet the best teams in the world and will show this region the best football in the world.

"We must go after the big stuff—and we are going after it next year."

CHAPTER 5

"WE'RE IN."

BASED ON THE WAY THEY were flying off the shelves at Pomeroy's Department Store, by the summer of 1925 it wouldn't be long before every homeowner in Pottsville possessed a radio. Until then, Maroons fans could still pop into Zacko's Sporting Goods on Centre Street for all the latest scores and sports gossip. At any moment during the day, a handful of Pottsville's power brokers could be found leaning over the glass showcase at Zacko's as if it were a bar railing, or standing in a circle on his cement stoop yelling, laughing, and carrying on about the latest exploits of Jack Dempsey, Babe Ruth, or their very own Doc Striegel.

Most arguments ended the minute *The Pottsville Journal*'s esteemed sports editor Walter Farquhar creaked in from the newspaper's pressroom around the corner. Farquhar was a peculiar looking fellow, a birdlike man, with bony cheeks and shoulders. He was also something of a Pottsville legend: an Army sergeant, the former coach of the Pottsville High School football team, and an amateur thespian known for his uncanny portrayal of Abe Lincoln. He constantly had his thick glasses with the heavy black rims aimed at the Congressional Record and he had a penchant for the kind of dewy, overdramatic prose of the times made famous by sportswriter Grantland Rice. His writing, which sometimes consisted of long, wandering and hopelessly sappy sports poems, was intensely loyal to all things Pottsville. Hometown players who inhaled cigarettes never had to worry about being described as tobacco fiends in print. To the contrary, they were "always in good physical condition" because, reporters like Farquhar promised, "they smoked very little … during football season." As the dean of Schuylkill County sports scribes, Farquhar was mentoring the paper's talented young cub reporter, John O'Hara, a gifted writer with a keen eye and a wry wit (when he could curb his whiskey intake) who was to assist him on the Maroons' NFL beat.

O'Hara, the son of a prominent local physician, lived on Mahantongo and had held out hope of attending Yale even after his expulsion for drinking on the eve of commencement from Niagara Prep. But while biding his time as a cub reporter, those plans were scuttled forever when his father died suddenly from kidney failure in the spring of 1925.

Despite the tragedy, and the precipitous dive in social standing, O'Hara remained cocky. He wore a raccoon coat, was constantly using the pressroom of the paper to practice the Charleston with female staffers, and actually reminded readers to clip his work since "there's no telling how soon I'll be famous or notorious."

He had earned Farquhar's respect for his coverage of a mining accident in 1924 and the stark way he described how rescuers were only able to unearth "a human foot in a miner's Pac boot." That fall, after a rain-soaked game in Providence, the two-man reporting team of O'Hara and Farquhar splashed back to the Biltmore and banged out their stories for *The Journal* in their underwear while their suits dried atop a nearby radiator. In a rare moment of humility, O'Hara once said his football stories suffered by comparison because they were only separated from Walter's work by, at most, three columns.

Farquhar secretly wanted to test his own talents with something other than sports. "The ultra-conservative character of Pottsville makes anybody occupied in sportswriting as an ignoramus and illiterate," he once wrote in a letter. "It burns me up and I would give almost anything to get away from it."

O'Hara, meanwhile, openly longed for bigger and better things outside of Pottsville—a "God awful town" full of "patronizing cheap bastards," he said—and the NFL was to be his ticket out of Sharp Mountain.

It was a terrific plan that lacked just one tiny detail: With two months to go before the 1925 season there *was* no Maroons team, no NFL plan, and no great national beat for O'Hara and Farquhar to cover. Since the game in Atlantic City the previous fall, there had been very little word from Doc regarding the NFL. With time running out, Farquhar decided to take matters into his own hand. He crafted a column for the next day's *Journal* prodding Doc Striegel and the city's leaders to make good on their pledge to take the Maroons, and the city of Pottsville, to the next level by signing up for the NFL.

Upon reading the column, Zacko, not wanting anyone to think him less connected or civic-minded, dispatched a few of his cronies to Striegel's mountain resort to gauge the good doctor's intentions. When the men arrived, they were a bit shocked to find Doc packing his suitcase.

Whatever are you leaving town for? The men inquired.

For the NFL meetings in Chicago, you idiots! came Doc's reply.

Striegel didn't take kindly to people who doubted him. Unless, of course, he could work the angle to his advantage, which was exactly his plan regarding the fledgling NFL and its president, Joe Carr.

The National Football League was born on September 17, 1920, on the floor of the auto dealership showroom owned by Ralph E. Hay in Canton, Ohio. A month earlier, with the Ohio League in disarray, Hay, who was also the owner and manager of the Canton Bulldogs, had extended invitations to every pro team he knew of to join the new American Professional Football Association. (Fourteen teams accepted for that inaugural season.) There wasn't enough room in Hay's office to accommodate everyone who attended the meeting, so the men met in the showroom, sitting on running boards and bumpers while cooling themselves with large buckets of beer. A $100 entry fee was agreed upon (although no one ever paid) and Olympic legend Jim Thorpe was named president of the APFA, even though he was steadfastly opposed to the idea. When the beer ran out, the meeting was adjourned, and a few weeks later Lou Partlow of the Dayton Triangles scampered seven yards for the league's first touchdown. Eventually the 8-0-3 Akron Pros were declared the first APFA champions, although by season's end three of the charter members had already folded.

At the APFA's next meeting, to help ensure the league's survival, a consensus of owners agreed that Thorpe should be replaced by Columbus Panhandle manager Joe Carr. Carr had only a fifth-grade education and next to no executive experience, but he had voiced clear-cut ideas and a refreshing enthusiasm about the growth and direction of pro football. His timing needed a little work, though. Because when he made the mistake of excusing himself, presumably to use the bathroom, the owners quickly elected him their new president.

At 13, Carr had begun work as an apprentice in a machine shop. At 20, he became a machinist in the Panhandle Division of the Pennsylvania Railroad in Columbus, Ohio. And using Panhandle employees, he had organized one of the country's finest semipro baseball teams while working nights as a sports-writer for the *Ohio State Journal.* Carr applied his love of sports and the pragmatic approach of journalism to running the Panhandle football team and then the APFA, which he simplified to the National Football League. ("National" being something of a stretch since Kansas City was the league's western-most franchise.)

Carr had silver hair, circular wire-rimmed glasses, and yellow corn-niblet teeth from years of smoking cigars. He looked much older than his 40 years and he ran the young league the same way, insisting that order and strict adherence to the rules were the only way to clean up the NFL's mercenary image. In private, Carr was said to have a "gentle countenance," but in his public role as president of the NFL he was stiff, strict, and stubborn. As H.L. Mencken once observed, the pall of Puritanism hung on men like Carr who carried it like a heavy overcoat—a "haunting fear that someone, somewhere, may be happy."

To his credit, Carr proposed the creation of the league's first constitution and bylaws, the first official standings, and a stan-dard player's contract. He was adamant that his owners not employ college players and that they respect the home "territory" of each franchise. In 1922, when the Green Bay Packers were caught using college players, Carr unceremoniously kicked them out of the league. The Packers reformed under Curly Lambeau and were reinstated several months later, but even then Carr had made no secret of his desire to wean all the small towns, bumpkin franchises, and barnstormers out of his league.

In fact, the only reason Carr was even considering Pottsville for the NFL was as a service to the league's bigger clubs. To Carr, the Maroons were little more than a sucker bet. Blue laws forbidding games on Sunday made it cost prohibitive for most NFL teams to travel to the East Coast for just one game. Pottsville simply ignored those laws. The town didn't particularly care for Prohibition. And no politician, prosecutor, or sheriff had the clout or the guts to tell a town full of coal miners what they could do—or consume—on a precious day off. Carr figured with a pushover like Pottsville in the mix, teams could play a Saturday game in New York or Philadelphia and pick up another W and some additional gate receipts from the coal crowd while traveling home on Sunday.

From the beginning, Carr and Doc Striegel were natural enemies, men who represented the two sides of the social revolution occurring in the 1920s—a go-for-broke dreamer from a small city and a rigid, conventional big-city bureaucrat. Ever since Doc had "stolen" those Canton players from the Cleveland Bulldogs, Carr and the rest of the league's Ohio stronghold had been looking for a way to put Pottsville in its place. If nothing else, admitting the Maroons into the NFL would surely give them that chance. They were giddy with the prospect of pounding Pottsville into submission every week during the fall. Neither Carr nor his cohorts could conceive of a scenario where little old Pottsville would be able to compete in their league.

Of course, Doc had been counting on this. As a Pottsvillian, he had always been able to rely on the condescension of strangers. Only this time he was going to parlay it into fame and fortune; for his team, for his town, and especially for himself.

Doc made it to Chicago without incident, and once he produced two checks—$500 for the franchise, $1,200 as a guarantee—Carr approved his application. Just like that, the Maroons were an NFL franchise. In six years they had grown from a sandlot team of soldiers looking for a postwar release all the way to full membership in the NFL. Doc excused himself, trying very hard to contain his pride and joy. He phoned Farquhar and Zacko, who were hovering over the receiver inside the *Journal's* pressroom.

Upon Doc's departure, the two men began frantically trying to raise money for the team—it had never been Doc's intention to be the sole financier of the Maroons. Since the semipro days after the war, the Pottsville team had always been run by an association, with a board of directors that included Striegel and several other town dignitaries. The NFL was a nickel-and-dime operation in those days—with a bank balance that regularly dipped below $2,000—and an almost certain losing business proposition. While the lure of pro football was strong, the payoff was not. In Chicago, George Halas's 1921 team played an entire season and turned a profit of $7. He was one of the lucky ones. In the league's first dozen years, 40 NFL teams went belly up. A start-up team in New York suffered $40,000 in losses in Year One alone. While the teams that did make money were more sideshow carnivals than football games—like the Oorang Indians in tiny LaRue, Ohio. They were owned by Walter Lingo, the founder of Oorang Kennels, the largest mail-order puppy kennel in the world, who forced his players to wrestle bears and parade with his dogs before kickoffs.

As a serious cardplayer, Doc was hoping to run his NFL team

on house money provided by the town of Pottsville. But with a coal strike looming, and the prospect of the Maroons getting blown off the field in the NFL, some of the town's leaders had backed off from their earlier pledges of support. Doc, meanwhile, had already given his word. For him it was now or never. And when he left for Chicago, team boosters back home went door-to-door soliciting donations on the team's behalf. Zacko and Farquhar also raised cash by selling large white Maroons buttons and banners that said, I'M A POTTSVILLE MAROONS BOOSTER! It was a rather inauspicious start to Pottsville's NFL franchise, but it beat wrestling bears.

Zacko and Farquhar, who, coincidentally could have passed for brothers, hadn't even had time to count their button collections when, just after 6 p.m., the phone rang inside the *Journal* pressroom.

It was Doc.

"I got it," he said. "We're in. The Pottsville Maroons are now an official member of the National Football League."

Zacko and Farquhar trembled with delight.

"Well, Doc," Zacko squawked into the receiver, "you'll be glad to know that we have the money to cover those checks you wrote."

By pounding the pavement, Maroons supporters had raised $1,500, along with an additional $900 for Striegel to begin fielding the team. Striegel figured he needed five times that amount to get the job done properly, although he didn't seem overly concerned about the significant lack of funds. The hard part was over. Pottsville was in the NFL. The money would come from somewhere. It always did. Zacko and Farquhar, meanwhile, shook hands and shot a thumbs up out the window and into the street where football fans had gathered waiting for the news.

"Sirens screamed, whistles blew, and fireworks lit the sky as bands paraded in the city streets," Zacko wrote in his diary. "To a stranger it would have appeared that Pottsville had just won the championship."

CHAPTER 6

THE MAD DOCTOR

THE CANTON BULLDOGS, one of the NFL's first dynasties, played many of their games behind a psychiatric hospital in a makeshift park nicknamed Asylum Field. That was convenient, went the joke, since anyone willing to pay to watch the NFL's brand of football had to be nuts in the first place. In 1922, the Bulldogs won the NFL title by scoring a mere 15 points per game. So it was hardly a surprise when two years later the team went bankrupt due, in part, to a lack of fan interest.

Doc Striegel and most of his contemporaries in the Twenties abhorred the kind of trench warfare that teams like Canton tried to pass off as football. "Paid punting," they called it. Doc wanted something that would even surpass the excitement of the college game; nonstop action, breakneck speed, trick plays, lots of scoring, and bone-rattling tackles. In his mind, if pro football was ever going to catch on it had to be a combination of gladiator fights and Barnum & Bailey.

To do that in Pottsville, Doc needed a coach who shared his vision, a freethinker and an innovator who approached the game with the keen eye and open mind of a college coach. In 1924, Penn State graduate Clarence Beck had done a solid job as a player/coach for the Maroons. Toward the end of the season, Striegel had noted how Beck had begun consulting with one of his linemen before nearly every snap. Curious as to why this particular player needed so much instruction, Doc mentioned the odd interaction to his coach. The player, Dick Rauch, was a fellow Penn State alum and an assistant coach at Colgate playing under an alias to earn a little extra scratch on the weekends. Beck confessed to Striegel that it was actually *he* who was constantly seeking advice from Rauch, one of the best and brightest young minds in the game.

He's the man you want to coach this club, Beck told him. *He might be a tad eccentric, Doc, but you won't do any better than Dick Rauch.* The only problem, according to Beck, would be tracking Rauch down to make an offer.

A native of Harrisburg, Pennsylvania, the 30-year-old Rauch had studied electrical engineering at Penn State and was a protégé of Hugo Bezdek, the Nittany Lions coach and legendary disciplinarian. Bezdek thought so highly of Rauch that after graduation he put him on his coaching staff and left him alone to scout, analyze, and break down all of Penn State's upcoming opponents. Rauch was a classic Twenties renaissance man, with an insatiable intellect and a wide variety of pursuits. His football strategy was often as avant-garde as his tastes. Constantly juggling several thoughts at once, Rauch often came across as aloof. But, generally, he had a quiet, calm dignity about him, so that, even though he was soft spoken, he never had difficulty being heard. Rauch's face was a perfectly balanced contrast between his rugged jaw and a pair of warm, charming eyes below a mop of soft brown hair. The first time he met Rauch, in fact, John O'Hara, blurted out, "he's the handsomest man I ever saw." Said another of Rauch's acquaintances, "Knowing him and spending time with Dick Rauch was not just an experience, it was, in fact, an education."

After a season at Penn State, Rauch moved on to Michigan State's staff and then to Colgate. Had he not disappeared into the wild every summer, certainly Rauch would have already been offered any number of head coaching jobs. Rauch, however, preferred to spend his off-seasons working as an ornithologist, traveling as far west as the Yukon to study and identify birds. While sitting for hours at a time in a marsh blind or up in a tree stand, Rauch passed the time writing poems and humorous verses. Upon returning to Pennsylvania, his poetic writings and ornithological observations would often be published simultaneously.

The previous summer, with little more than a horse, some camping gear, a notebook, and a pair of binoculars, Rauch, along with two companions and a French Cree Indian guide, worked their way 1,000 miles northwest from Alberta, Canada, in search of the Short-billed Dowitcher. *Limnodromus griseus* was something of an obsession with Rauch. A small shorebird, the Dowitcher had a narrow, elongated beak that it bobbed up and down in the mud like a sewing machine to fish out worms, insects, and small crustaceans. Its call was sharp, low, and nondistinct. Therefore, differentiating between the species and sexes of Dowitchers often came down to experts like Rauch who could read the intricate spotting and color found on the breasts of the birds, just in front of the wings. It was common for a mesmerized Rauch to spend an entire summer tracking a single flock of

Dowitchers, filling his notebooks with sketches and information along with odes to his favorite bird.

And so it wasn't until late in the summer of 1925 that Doc Striegel was finally able to track Rauch down. Before even considering the job, however, Rauch insisted on several non-negotiable rules that would later prove to be monumental. He told Doc that he would not stand for the traditional method of barnstorming, in which pro players met on the morning of the game, created aliases for themselves, knocked heads for a few hours and then took their game checks to the pub. On this they agreed. Rauch also wanted the Maroons to live in town, to attend daily practice, and become a part of the community. It was a concept that was just taking hold in the NFL and something that actually worked against the Maroons. When given the choice, most players would naturally sign with a team that didn't require them to practice all week. Rauch inquired about the roster and Doc proudly explained that he had already secured the services of half-back Tony Latone, quarterback Jack Ernst, end Charlie Berry, center Herb Stein, and his brother, fellow two-way lineman Russ Stein. Impressed as he was by this foundation, Rauch made it clear that he expected autonomy when it came to the rest of the roster, as well as the play calling.

Doc agreed, and with less than a month to prepare before the 1925 NFL season opener, Rauch accepted the job and immediately moved to Pottsville, taking a room on the third floor of Doc and Neva's house on the east side of town. Together, with a mixture of cash incentives, a unique eye for talent, plain old hard work (canvassing most of Eastern Pennsylvania), and far more than their fair share of serendipity, Rauch and Striegel rounded out the Maroons roster.

Outwardly, the coach and owner seemed like polar opposites,

but as football men they complemented each other rather well. The professorial Rauch, who had served in Army intelligence during the war, appealed to the players' respect for the game, and he certainly understood and accepted their idiosyncrasies. Doc played off their Twenties sensitivities: vanity, greed, and dreams of NFL stardom in news reels shown across the country. Striegel was almost manic in the way he would wake up one day and decide he had to have more size or speed on his roster—no matter the cost. Doc had no qualms about throwing around money he didn't have, privately leveraging himself well beyond the point of no return. It was the Twenties, after all, a time of miracle and excess, and Doc was all in, counting on a football miracle to pay for all his excess.

The result was an all-star collection of talent that heretofore had been unimaginable to the typical fan of the ragtag NFL. The Maroons roster was packed with eye-popping talent and speed, a perfect mixture of brawn and brains—a host of colorful characters united, as strange as it might seem, by their eccentricities.

To add more beef up front, Doc shelled out $350 to the Dayton Triangles for the rights to 238-pound former All-Big Ten lineman and Indiana scholar-athlete Russ Hathaway—then he tripled his original salary to $150 a game. News of Striegel's generosity (or stupidity, depending on whom you queried) spread quickly across the league, drawing in the likes of end Frank Bucher from the University of Detroit Mercy and speedy tailback Hoot Flanagan from Martinsburg, West Virginia. Flanagan had played under Pop Warner at Pittsburgh, and after graduating from the Pitt School of Dentistry, was looking to make some quick cash to help stake his practice. Hoot had ears the size of gramophones, curly strawberry blond tresses that no leather helmet could contain, and a wild, flailing, open-field running style that, folks said, resembled someone getting a root canal without a dose of Novocain.

To complement Hoot's speed and plow a path for Latone, Striegel signed Schuylkill County native and former Penn State fullback Barney Wentz. Built like a tree stump, Wentz grew up in the nearby coal-mining town of Shenandoah, where his proper, professional father locked him in his room on Saturdays to keep him from playing sandlot football. "This did not stop Barney," recalled one reporter. "It just meant that he had to jump out, and he did. After the game, Barney climbed up over the rear of the house and got into his room. Thus when his father opened the door at suppertime he found his big boy peacefully reading a book."

His father acquiesced, temporarily, when Barney reached high school weighing a rotund 200 pounds. In 1918, Wentz single-handedly beat Pottsville High School after picking up a fumble and returning it 85 yards for a score, moving like a boulder crashing down from the peaks of Sharp Mountain. The elder Wentz believed that Barney had gotten his football follies out of his system and threatened to cut off his finances should he be tempted while at Penn State. By his junior year, however, the itch for the game was too much to take. His father kept his word and Barney had to work odd jobs and as a fraternity house caterer to pay for school.

Wentz, who had a perfectly round, plump face that made his eyes, nose, and mouth appear too small, smashed linebackers as easily as stereotypes: When Striegel and Rauch signed him, in 1925, he was a suit-wearing insurance salesman who had gotten engaged to his hometown sweetheart, and had just been elected to Shenandoah's city council.

Wentz ran his campaign on the simple platform of fiscal responsibility and more parks and playing fields. This was to his own benefit since he coached a semipro football team in Shenandoah with his good friend Frankie Racis, a coal miner and famed sandlot player. Racis had an impossibly thick, sturdy frame for someone who stood just over six feet. His hands were as big and heavy as concrete trowels and he had the telltale "red tops" from his years spent as a breaker boy at the Maple Hill Colliery. He had a leathery face, jet-black hair parted dramatically right down the middle of his skull, and the kind of steely stare that made strangers wonder if they owed someone money. Racis also had a temper and a wicked sense of humor, and he often displayed them at the same time. In a parochial school basketball game, after getting called for his fifth foul, a referee tapped him on the shoulder and said, "You're out, Frankie." Racis turned, snapped his meaty paw into the man's temple, dropping the guy with one punch, and without missing a beat said, "Now you are too, mister."

That was his last basketball game and the beginning of his football career, something the school's administrators wisely concluded Frankie was much better suited for. Racis became the coal region's original 60-Minute Man, famous for playing every minute of every game he entered. He hit so hard that at least once a game a woozy Racis reported to the wrong bench or huddle. "I was determined and conditioned," he said. "And boy oh boy, I liked to give it and I liked to take it." In game programs Racis gave himself a different college alma mater each week, a long list that included Vassar (then a women's college), Harvard, and a school that Frankie listed as "Da Mines." He worked in the mines during the week and on the weekends played for several semipro teams in and around Shenandoah, receiving as little as $7 a game while absorbing tremendous beatings, particularly from the smug, cold-blooded Frankford Yellow Jackets down in Philadelphia, who were notorious for running up scores. Racis had heard about the team Doc was building but he didn't think he had a chance to make a "real" franchise like Pottsville. "I realized that they were all college men, with a lot of football knowledge," he said. "I did not think I had a chance."

Wentz, however, convinced him to try out, and once Doc saw his size and relentless style, and heard of his one ambition in life—"to defeat Frankford"—he inked Racis for the bargain price of $75 a week. With only one homegrown player on the roster—end and punter Fungy Lebengood, who captained the Pottsville High School team in 1916—Doc knew it didn't hurt from a promotional standpoint to add another Schuylkill County native. On top of that, like all great coaches, Rauch thought of himself as a teacher. And he saw Racis as a raw, eager block of granite who he could mold into the Maroons' left guard, sandwiched between the Stein brothers. It was a strategic decision, first and foremost. Rauch must have also realized that Frankie was probably the only guy around big and crazy enough to get in between the Steins should a skirmish erupt between the highly competitive siblings.

Rauch understood that controlling the line of scrimmage was still the best way to win football games. He had Hathaway, the Steins, and Racis. Rauch's line lacked only one crucial element: a running guard. It just so happened that the best in the game at that position was Duke Osborn, Rauch's former teammate at Penn State. Fast, scrappy, and tireless in the trenches, Osborn had just petitioned Joe Carr to become a free agent after becoming the first man ever to captain three NFL championship teams in a row in Canton and Cleveland. And when word got to Pottsville that Osborn was on the verge of signing with Frankford for the 1925 NFL season, Rauch cabled him with a request that he come up to Pottsville for a look around before signing with the Yellow Jackets.

The odd couple was at it again. Rauch lured him in and Doc did the rest.

Striegel offered a $25 bump per game from what the Yellow Jackets had proposed and Osborn signed, even though he knew that Royle and his coach, Guy Chamberlin, whom he had played for in Canton, would "never get over that I went to Pottsville." Each of Doc's signings for 1925 had been better than the last, culminating with Osborn. (And losing his best three linemen to Doc Striegel must have pushed Royle halfway to the loony bin.)

Running guards like Osborn were a different breed, since their main responsibility was to seek out the often much larger defensive end and eliminate him from the play; the football equivalent of pawing your way across a crowded bar to start a fight with the big ugly fella holding a pool cue in his hands.

Osborn, though, was born to play the part. He had a thick thatch of wild black hair atop his head, a crooked smile to match, and fiendish eyes. He grew up in Falls Creek, Pennsylvania, 65 miles northwest of State College, where football, he said, "looked like a good game to either get socked or sock the other fella." The other fellas were wearing helmets, of course, while Osborn preferred to play wearing his trusty wool baseball cap. He chewed tobacco during games and seemed shocked and puzzled when tacklers complained that the spit had somehow ended up in their eyes. Players like future Hall of Fame running back Fritz Pollard said they always kept their cleats chugging long after the whistle to guard against the late licks Osborn had become famous for. "Duke played the game to the hilt," said one eyewitness. "And he was not a fella known for his fair play."

What others called "dirty," Osborn considered shrewd and cunning. If he was across the line of scrimmage, you hated his guts. If he was on your team, you loved him to death. Having played on three straight NFL-championship teams, Osborn knew the game so well that he often called out opponents' plays before the snap. He wasn't big and there wasn't any kind of physical presence to him, but Osborn dominated play with his relentless style: a bloodthirsty frenzy that caused former opponents, many years later, to want to attack him on sight. "I loved to play," Osborn once cackled. "I could run interference better than anyone who ever played football. And people liked to see me play because I was always getting in a fight or something. Nope. They didn't come any tougher than me."

Or crazier, according to most of his contemporaries. While playing in Canton, Osborn had become friends with Jim Thorpe. After a game in Cleveland, Osborn was hanging out in Thorpe's hotel room when he tried to order a bottle of alcohol from the bellhop. Thorpe walked over, picked him up by the scruff of the neck, and tossed him ten feet across the room. "Listen, kid, nobody buys anything in Old Jim's room," Thorpe roared, unfolding the bills needed to buy the bottle himself. By the time the booze was finished Osborn and Thorpe were fast friends and the next day they skipped practice and went raccoon hunting. From then on, Duke was known as The Kid.

Rauch named Osborn his team captain and set him up in an apartment on Centre Street with Ernst. The rest of the team boarded with families around town or in one of the Striegel's many properties. Doc's house was only two blocks west of Centre Street and the heart of downtown Pottsville. From the intersection of Norwegian and Centre, the players were minutes away, by foot, from everything they could want or need: the railroad station, the YMCA, the Hippodrome Theatre, the Schuylkill Trust building, which housed the team's offices, Schneider's drugstore, which doubled as the Maroons ticket office, Zacko's

Sporting Goods, Rabenau's cigar store, and a host of restaurants.

The players never did seem to wander too far from Doc's house, though. Next door to the Striegels was the Phoenix Hook & Ladder Fire Company, where Duke had sniffed out a working beer tap for the volunteers in the long narrow basement bar below the fire trucks. While waiting for the rest of the players to trickle into town, Osborn and some of his new teammates prepared for Rauch's preseason "camp" with some intense training underneath the Phoenix. They played cards, lifted an occasional medicine ball, and tossed the football around a bit. But mostly they helped themselves to a river of beers while keeping a constant eye out for the two most dangerous things in town: a four-alarm fire and Mother Striegel.

Rauch had scouted out the castlelike armory in Pottsville to use for occasional team meetings, indoor practices, and chalkboard, or skull, sessions. Daily practice would take place inside Minersville Park, which was a short trolley ride up Market Street, although once the team's preseason regimen began—two-hour practices in the stifling late-summer heat—fans emptied out the coal from the back of their colliery trucks, set up benches for the players to sit on, and drove them all to practice. It was an honor to be connected to the town's new NFL team, even in the slightest way. Beyond that, the reward for transporting the players was an excuse to hang around on the perimeter of the field, smoke a stogie and take part in what had become the town's most-popular pastime: speculating about their new coach and how the Queen City of the Anthracite, the smallest city in the league, might fare in the NFL.

During the first few light practices, fans stood on their bumpers and gazed into Minersville Park at the eclectic and largely unknown roster of the Maroons. Then they passed around copies of the team's just-released NFL schedule. It was loaded with powerhouses like Canton and Green Bay, as well as a home and away series against the always formidable Frankford. Rumors then jumped from one running board to the next about how Striegel's first choice for coach, Penn State grad and Pittsburgh native Harry Robb, had turned him down to sign with Canton, as did Pete "Fats" Henry, the Maroons best lineman from 1924. Word on the street was that Henry's replacement, husky lineman Dick Stahlman, had arrived in town from Chicago earlier that week, took one look around, mumbled something about Pottsville being "a dump" that wouldn't have enough money to pay the water boy, and promptly left town on the next train.

People knew of Latone and Wentz, and had probably read about the Stein brothers and Osborn. But who was this rookie quarterback, they wondered. Who was this skinny, carrot-topped ball carrier with his nose buried in a book about bicuspids? Who was going to catch the ball and kick the ball? Our line is so dang small, they muttered, we'd get pushed around by Pottsville High.

"Doc Striegel is being swamped with requests to dismiss the unknown Rauch," Zacko jotted down in his diary. This news began a fit of wagering among football fans throughout Pottsville—not on the record or the success of the team, but on the longevity of Dick Rauch's tenure as coach of the Maroons. Just two weeks remained before the start of the 1925 NFL season, and the odds were running 2-to-1 against the bird-watcher and the mad doctor keeping their NFL dream alive past Halloween.

CHAPTER 7

IODINE
AND
WHISKEY

IN THE FRONTIER DAYS of the NFL, the game literally oozed gore. During the horrific college football season of 1905, 150 serious injuries and 18 fatalities were recorded. Football itself had evolved in the late nineteenth century from the European sport of rugby (where the original ball was a Danish soldier's skull). By 1906, the American version was so barbaric that at a conference of college educators representing 13 universities, six voted to abolish the sport. Instead, spurred on by President Theodore Roosevelt, rule changes were instituted to make the game less brutal. A neutral zone at the line of scrimmage was established while dangerous mass plays and formations like the Flying Wedge were outlawed. A follow-up study in 1923 found that another 20 football players had died and 43 had been seriously injured during the previous season, but this was hailed as tremendous progress by the sport's advocates, since the number of football players had nearly doubled.

While a smaller percentage of players were now expiring on the field each fall, every set of downs still produced a hideous cornucopia of carnage: splintered bones, digits mangled beyond recognition, hemorrhages galore, noses pushed flat, and ears torn half off. "Bloody, brutal, disgraceful affairs," said one critic of the pro game. And for each of these injuries, trainers often recommended the same remedy: a splash of iodine and four fingers of whiskey. Speed, strength, and smarts were important, but in the early days of the NFL the primary requirement of a prospective player was the ability to absorb tremendous amounts of pain.

Although the legendary college coach Pop Warner had once famously discouraged the use of leather helmets—or "head harnesses" as they were called—most Pottsville players wore them. They provided slightly more cushion than a large dollop of hair grease. The material was so flimsy players could crease their helmets and cart them home in their shirt pockets. By contrast, their heavy wool jerseys often doubled in weight after soaking up water, mud, and sweat during games. Most players also wore wool socks and high-top black leather cleats that featured nine large (and lethal) metal spikes. Football pants were made of thick canvas or moleskin that rose above the hips and were held in place by a belt, presenting a distinct hayseed appearance. For extra protection, players often stacked newspapers and magazines on the bench, and as the game progressed they would tear off pages and stuff them into their trousers and sweaters. Osborn insisted on *The Philadelphia Inquirer* because he believed it to be the "thickest" paper printed. One good collision, however, could leave the field looking like a ticker-tape parade.

The average player of the era was around 5'10", 185 pounds,

and saw action on both sides of the ball for the full 60 minutes, as players were not allowed to reenter the game once they left. Most teams carried 16 players, while maintaining another half dozen to combat the inevitable injury attrition during the course of the season. During the NFL's first 13 years, the league followed the rules established by college football. The field was 100 yards long and 53⅓ yards wide with goal posts situated at the front of two 10-yard-deep end zones. The idea of using hash marks to keep the ball in the center of the field was still many years off. Until then, each play of a drive would begin from the exact spot where the previous play had ended. If a ball carrier ran out of bounds, officials (dressed like golf caddies in white button-down shirts, bow ties, and knickers) placed the ball on the sideline. Teams were then forced to line up with all 11 men left of center and "waste" a play in order to get the ball back to the middle of the field. Games were sixty minutes long, divided into four 15-minute quarters, with a brief halftime. There were 11 players to a side, seven of whom were required to remain on the line of scrimmage. Teams were given four downs to gain 10 yards. Touchdowns scored six with the chance to add one more with the point after kick. Field goals were worth three, but they were extremely rare. The average team made less than four placement kicks during an entire season.

The forward pass was perfectly legal but was still considered by many older coaches as an act of desperation, and so it was rare. The ball had to be thrown from at least five yards behind the line of scrimmage, and incomplete passes into the end zone resulted in a touchback with the ball awarded to the defense at the 20. With the proliferation of the forward pass, the football became more streamlined but still more closely resembled the shape and weight of a medicine ball. At 28 inches long, 23 inches around, and 15 ounces in weight, it was better suited for the kicking of a rugby match than the throwing or carrying that was supposed to be done on the football field. Zacko, the self-proclaimed official outfitter of the Maroons, provided the game balls, which took several hours to inflate and stitch up. For good luck he would drop-kick each finished ball through a small opening in the giant glass display case near the back door of his store, a ritual that no doubt helped the local glass man put his children through college.

Strategically, pro football's evolution from the game of rugby was still very much evident. In 1924, Pottsville had won most of its games by controlling the line with a massive front seven. Defensive formations could not have been simpler: They consisted of seven to nine men at the line of scrimmage, along with a few defensive "halfbacks" who played three to four yards off the line, one roving "center," and one "safety" (often the quarterback) who played several yards deep and acted as the last line of defense and punt returner.

The run-dominant offenses of the era had but one goal in mind: to overwhelm defenses by funneling the highest possible number of bodies to the point of attack. The most popular way to do that was the single-wing offense developed by Pop Warner. In the single wing, if the play was headed to the right, only a tackle and an end would line up to the left of the center. To the right of the center would be two guards, a tackle, and an end. The team's best athlete, the halfback, would then line up three to five yards behind the line of scrimmage and directly behind the ball. The rest of the team's backfield would stagger diagonally toward the right end of the line. The fullback would be one step forward and one step to the halfback's right, then the quarterback, and then the wingback.

Since instruction from the sideline wasn't permitted in the Twenties, and substitutes were not allowed to speak to other players before the snap, most coaches, including Rauch, doubled as players. If not, they used hand signals from the sideline or simply relied upon the quarterback to act as their on-field generals. To signal plays, Ernst called out a rudimentary code in which a number was designated for each gap between blockers and another was assigned to each potential ball carrier. "Red, right, 63 on one" simply meant a single-wing formation, unbalanced to the right, with the "three" back running through the "six" hole, between the guard and the tackle. There was no real "snap." Instead, the center, Herb Stein, who was arguably the second-best athlete on the team, hiked the balloon-shape pigskin directly to Wentz, Latone, or Flanagan. On passing plays he sent it straight back to Ernst, although in Rauch's scheme, any of the backs could be called upon to attempt a forward pass.

While college ball had begun to evolve through better coaching and daily practice, pro games often still devolved into a grotesque series of pileups at the line of scrimmage where players seemed far more interested in socking each other in the puss than gaining or protecting ground. Offenses were so conservative that it wasn't at all strange to see a team on its own 20-yard line punt the ball away on first down. At the time, this was what passed for strategy.

During their first week of practice, the Maroons quickly discovered that Rauch's approach to the game flew in the face of most conventional coaching methods, but particularly so when it came to offensive strategy. In many ways, Rauch was heavily influenced by his summertime passion of bird watching. He stressed pregame scouting, relentless attention to detail, and note taking, the study of movement as it related to escape and pursuit, the importance of a daily regimen, the ideas of adapting and evolving, as well as the use of camouflage, decoys, and mis-direction. Rauch was a strong proponent of the forward pass and in one practice he sent Ernst, Bucher, and Eddie Doyle, a skinny, fast kid from Army, off to work on their own and develop the kind of passing rapport Ernst and Berry had had at Lafayette. "In one corner of the field, and for fully an hour, they practiced catching forward passes which they threw to each other," reported the local paper. "Later, just Jack Ernst took the ball and threw to each of them. Judging from the practice of this trio, the Maroons are going to use the air route against Buffalo in the season opener."

Wentz and Latone had reported to camp in the best shape of their lives, inspiring Rauch to experiment with the new "double wing" offense to maximize the diverse talents of his backfield. In the past, strictly power running offenses like the single wing had lost what little element of surprise they had by being utterly predictable; and, in turn, the games dissolved into an endless, inevitable string of pileups. In Rauch's version of the double wing, Wentz moved to the "weak" side of the field. What the formation lost in power at the point of attack, Rauch gained back in strategy and surprise with the ability to run plays in either direction. Occasionally, Rauch also liked to back up his weak-side full-back a few yards, forming a funnel, or a V, which allowed the Maroons to run a power-plunging ground game out of a scheme known for sweeps and end-arounds. It was clear that to Rauch the game was more about speed, deception, and execution than about just raw power and brawn. The Maroons, though, had plenty of all of the above.

All the horizontal movement at the line of scrimmage explained why Rauch and Doc Striegel had signed so many smaller, athletic linemen rather than the typical wall of giant, sedentary bears that fans had grown accustomed to seeing. Right away, Farquhar and others scolded the skeptical masses: "The Maroons showed one thing and that one little thing is that the line will do. There were folks who were all bent up about the light line. They said the line could not compete against the line of last year. This year's line shows up just as well as last year's line ever did. If anything, Pottsville has a better offensive line this year than they had last year. Defensively, it is good."

As a way to combat the usual injury attrition in the gruesome NFL, Rauch announced that his backs would occasionally rotate playing time. Rather than play Latone on every snap until he was reduced to a bruised and bloody pulp before the season's midway point, Rauch would play him for three quarters one week and then sit him for three quarters the following Sunday. Every other week, Latone or Flanagan would come in off the bench as a "reliever" and, with fresh legs and the pent-up frustration of a caged animal, would run wild on defenses for the final 15 minutes of play.

Rauch was perfectly aware that, at the time, getting pulled from a pro game for any reason other than death or paralysis was considered a disgrace, one that players often reacted to violently. "You took your own life in your hands pulling a player off the field," warned George Halas. The year before, prior to a Chicago Bears game, the team's part owner Dutch Sternaman had told center George Trafton he was not going to start. Trafton didn't say a word. He just stood up and attacked Sternaman, knocking him through a plate-glass window in the dressing room and out onto the field.

Announcing that he was rotating his skill players was one of the many gutsy, brilliant moves by Rauch. It immediately established his authority over the team, particularly the high-paid college stars, while making it clear to everyone else that the

Maroons were going to operate less like a pro team and more like the college squads of the day in which each man set aside his ego for the benefit of the team. Nevertheless, as the team's roster took shape during the short preseason, Rauch worried that the Maroons were split in half between the "bought-in" college players and the local coal-region roughnecks. From a football standpoint it was ideal: The Maroons would have the brawn and physical presence to play old-school NFL trench ball when needed and the speed, skill, and smarts to keep up with the more progressive teams in the league.

Still, the question remained: Could these two groups of players, different in every imaginable way, coexist on the same team? Could people from vastly different walks of life set aside their differences and work together toward a common goal beyond just a fat paycheck? College football coaches had always maintained that this was an impossible obstacle for the pros to overcome. What hope did the NFL have, they argued, when society as a whole in the Twenties was struggling with the exact same issue?

It left Rauch and Striegel to wonder: *Have we just amassed the greatest collection of professional football talent the sport has ever known, or have we compiled a combustible mix of men with absolutely nothing in common and no will to work together?*

Only time would tell.

When Osborn, the team captain, didn't step forward to bridge the gap between the two sides of the team, Rauch came up with his own solution: a "players-only" fraternity room where teammates could hang out and get to know one another off the field. Striegel asked around town and Jack Ginley, the owner of Ginley's furniture store just off Centre, volunteered to clear out the large space above his showroom for the team. Ginley, Rauch, and Striegel then filled it with enough cots to accommodate up to 12 players overnight, along with couches, chairs, and card tables to host the entire team.

The Maroons were under intense local and regional scrutiny as well as a hellacious time constraint. Yet between the daily two-hour practices in the smothering September heat, the nightly blackboard tutorials inside the Armory, and the time spent under the Phoenix and above Ginley's they managed to coalesce into something resembling a functioning team in time for their first preseason exhibition.

An NFL warmup game was arranged against the respectable coal-region team of Colwyn-Darby. And from the moment the team stepped onto the field the roster upgrades over the 1924 Pottsville Maroons team as well as Rauch's magic touch were obvious to local fans. The "new" Maroons—explosive and organized, flashbulb fast on offense and merciless on defense—rolled to an easy 48-0 whitewash behind a combined five touchdowns from Latone and Wentz.

After another week of tight drill practices and conditioning, *The Republican* gleefully reported that on the eve of Pottsville's NFL debut, "the Maroons are fit and fine ... and all pepped up over the opening game of the NFL season. At signal practice, the boys got the plays off with a lot of snap and pep, and in this department they loomed up very big. A high spirit is running through the ranks, and there is almost as much enthusiasm shown as is to be found on the college campus the night before the opening game."

CHAPTER 8

BISON HUNTING

OR THE MAROONS' NFL DEBUT, nearly 5,000 fans crammed into Minersville Park, a converted baseball stadium nestled into a crescent-moon-shape foothill a few miles west of town. To accommodate the coal crowd, wood-plank bleachers had been extended from the covered grandstand and down the length of the visitor's foul line. Past the outfield and behind the far end zone, closer to the road and a small creek, was a square, two-story tin-roofed structure—covered in billboards for car dealerships and haberdasheries—that housed the ticket booth, concession stands, and locker rooms. The town had upgraded the park after the Maroons were admitted into the NFL, but it still wasn't much to look at, and the patrons joked that the gravel parking lot might have been more forgiving than the turf inside the stadium.

Covered bench seating went for $2.20, and general admission

was set at $1.65. To avoid the ticket prices, kids would wait for the sheriff to walk past on his rounds then sneak under, or through holes in, the outfield fence. When this didn't work, they'd pay 10 cents for a program and sit with the miners and other working-class fans up in the steep hills surrounding the field, where the view was actually better than in the grandstand. It was not unusual to see a quarter of the total crowd, in this case more than a thousand fans, up in the pine trees, watching the game for free—a quirk of geography that Doc was certain would drive him bankrupt or mad. Or both.

No matter where they were sitting, the nervous coal crowd was subdued before kickoff. Buffalo had something the Maroons didn't: a proven marquee star in halfback Walter Koppisch. A Buffalo legend, Koppisch had led Masten Park High School to three city titles before starring at Columbia in a backfield that featured Lou Gehrig. Known for his upright running style and speed, Koppisch captained the Ivy League team for three seasons, earning All-America honors, and later, induction into the College Football Hall of Fame. At 23, Koppisch became the youngest coach in NFL history when he signed with the Bisons to manage, coach, and star for Buffalo's franchise. Whereas the Maroons were regional stars at best, Koppisch had been anointed by the fawning New York media as one of the pro game's next great young talents. The New York Giants had planned on signing Koppisch for the 1925 football season but stepped aside at the request of the Bisons management, who desperately needed the draw of a hometown hero. (This kind of cooperation between competitors simply baffled Doc.)

Koppisch was young but he was no pushover. Before the season began, a newspaper reporter in Buffalo had published what Koppisch believed to be secret information about his roster.

When he saw the writer the next day at practice, Koppisch physically removed him from the field by the seat of his pants while using what was reported to be "foul verbiage." In retaliation, the rest of the season the paper published only short accounts of Bisons games.

The season opener, at least, required very few words to describe. The day before, Rauch had traveled down to Frankford to scout Buffalo. By applying his bird-watching skills to the football field, Rauch had established himself as a pioneer in football scouting. When he arrived back in Pottsville with a notebook full of data, the Maroons knew Buffalo's game plan better than Koppisch himself. Armed with this information, the following afternoon Osborn and the rest of the underdog Maroons bullied and battered the skinny young star from the big city of Buffalo, while Latone and Ernst produced the offensive fireworks that Doc Striegel had been promising since the Fourth of July.

On the third play of the season, Ernst dropped back to pass, and, after using his left hand to push the giant football down into his right paw for a better grip, the Bear let it fly to Bucher, who caught it for a first down. The Steins' dominance up front gave Ernst plenty of time to throw and, more important, it seemed, to strike his trademark pose: a swashbuckling follow-through in which his right arm would glide across his body, float for a moment with his fingers tautly extended, then plunge gracefully to his left hip. "Pottsville will soon be feared throughout the league for its air attack," wrote one of Ernst's converts. Prone to athletic improvisation, Ernst excelled at punt returns for the same reason he had grown to love being in the pocket. In the chaotic open field, the thought of having every eye in the stadium transfixed upon him always brought out his best.

If Ernst and Latone were the razor-sharp tip to Rauch's new offensive weapon, it was clear right away that the Stein brothers were the power behind the plow. What set them apart in the Buffalo game was the telepathy the brothers shared in the trenches, where one seemed to understand, instinctively, where the other was going or what he was trying to accomplish. Playing hand-in-hand like this allowed the Steins to do the work of an entire line by themselves. This, in turn, freed up Osborn and Racis to make plays and wreak havoc. Against Buffalo, the Steins also opened huge holes for Flanagan—Rauch kept Latone in "reserve" this game—and Wentz, who, on the Maroons' first drive, smashed through from the 5-yard line to make it 7-0. After this touchdown, Walter Farquhar began referring to Wentz in print as The Councilman.

In the second quarter, Ernst got off a booming punt. With the ball in the air and the Bison coverage flatfooted, Bucher raced downfield and fell on the ball at the 1-yard line, trapping Buffalo deep in its own territory. During the Twenties, a major swing in field position like this was the equivalent of a checkmate in chess. Koppisch may have been young, but he followed the anti-quated thinking of the times, and on first down he punted the ball right back to Pottsville.

"The exchange of punts gained Pottsville more than 30 yards," reported *The Republican*. It also kept the ball in Buffalo territory for the rest of the half. Several plays later, with the ball on the Buffalo 9, "one of the prettiest and most neatly executed plays was pulled when Ernst threw a high forward over the goal line to Doyle," wrote the paper. "Doyle caught it above his head as he was speeding over the line. He reached high into the air and pulled it down. It was a sensational catch."

A 14-point lead was more than enough for the Maroons

defense, which continued to smother Koppisch, allowing the Bisons only two first downs the entire game. A fresh Latone came in during the second half and, using his freakishly low-to-the-ground running style, ran the Bison's ragged while pushing the final score to 28-0.

With their first NFL victory secured, Pottsville fans exhaled a collective sigh of relief, and Minersville Park quickly turned into a coal-crowd carnival. The party trickled from the field into Pottsville, rising out of the Phoenix and spreading across town to all the impromptu parties. The celebration lasted into the wee hours. (Buffalo players were spotted the next day groggily making their way back to the train station.) In the afterglow of Pottsville's first NFL triumph, opponents, fans, and media alike began to wonder the same thing: Could the Maroons actually be for real?

"The Buffalo game was to apply the acid test to the Maroons," concluded one local reporter. "And if the results of the game are to mean anything, then Pottsville is going to have a bright future."

CHAPTER 9

DARK SKIES

WITHOUT WARNING, DARK CLOUDS began forming over Pottsville. *The Republican* reported it as "the first bit of bad luck that Pottsville has had [although] it could be much worse." Not likely. Word had quickly spread across the league about the little coal-mining team's fast start. And so, in preparation for their upcoming game against the Maroons, the Providence Steam Roller announced they were holding back six starters from their Saturday game just so they would be fresh and rested for Pottsville. The Maroons, meanwhile, were anything but. Flanagan had spent most of the week following the Buffalo game in bed with an infected arm. To make matters worse, Frankie Racis had gone AWOL and "management is at a loss to know why" the paper said.

The loss of Flanagan's end runs meant the Maroons no longer had the ability to use misdirection and outside speed. Therefore,

Rauch had no choice but to aim the Howitzer right at the Steam Roller's formidable interior line. Besides a bevy of former college players, Providence boasted a line that featured the three top amateur heavyweight wrestlers in the country. Guard Bert Shurtleff had won the New England intercollegiate heavyweight title while at Brown. Lined up next to him at center was Dolph Eckstein, a fellow Brown grad, who had lost in the finals of the 1924 Olympic trials to Jack Spellman, the man now stationed as a tackle on the Providence line. A year earlier, Spellman, a 5'10", 200-pound earthmover, had won gold at the Paris Olympics. In 1924, this trio led Providence to the professional football championship of New England, and in their first game of 1925 Spellman and his cohorts mauled a team of former West Point players 127-0.

Zacko announced to the men gathered in his store that his sources in the East claimed Providence wanted the honor of being the first team to defeat the Maroons. While there was no way to know for sure if by "sources in the East" Zacko meant the other side of his store, Maroons fans didn't seem to care. It made for great theater, far more compelling than anything they were showing at The Hipp. By Thursday, Pottsville was a 3-1 underdog. Newspapers fueled the hype by previewing the impending clash of the titans, Latone vs. Spellman, who posed for his pregame publicity shots in his three-point stance with his tongue hanging out like a junkyard dog waiting on a juicy steak bone.

The dark skies overhead only added to an ominous atmosphere that even seemed to affect Rauch. Late in the week, the local papers reported that he "put the big Maroon squad through a stiff practice. Rauch had them display football in all its departments. Every angle of the game, both offensively and defensively, were gone into, and it is thought the afternoon was the most strenuous since the boys reported."

On the morning of the game, the gunmetal-grey clouds above Pottsville finally triggered a torrential rainstorm. Because of its topography—situated between a soft-banked creek and the foothills of Sharp Mountain, which acted as a natural dam—by game time the thin grass and coal-slag field at Minersville Park was a muddy mess. Normally, volunteers would gather at the park several hours before the game and clear the field by hand using their own shovels, brooms, and rakes. The worst spots would be filled in with sawdust. But the lateness of the storm prevented any significant pregame cleanup. Nevertheless, a few thousand fans still showed up for the game, which, from the stands, looked to be taking place in the middle of a swamp.

The game began like most of the Maroons' contests: with Latone handing out a brutal baptism that left the grapplers from Providence longing for the comfort of the Olympic mats and a cuddly Russian headlock. On his first two carries, Latone ripped through the middle for 18 yards. It wasn't the power of his legs or his keen eye for slivers of space at the line of scrimmage that was so amazing but the ease with which he was able to impose his will on men twice his size. It was mesmerizing to watch, even though it didn't seem physically possible. Shurtleff, Eckstein, and Spellman outweighed Latone by nearly 400 pounds and were schooled, on a world-class level, in corralling and punishing large men. But they were helpless against Latone.

The Howitzer hit them for five. Then he tore off five more.

The crowd began to pity the three giant wrestlers. The opening quarter of the so-called clash of the titans had turned into a Waterloo for the Steam Roller. With Latone averaging seven yards per carry, the Maroons splashed down to the 15-yard line where, on fourth down, Rauch elected to kick a field goal.

Fans yelled for the coach to reload Latone. Rauch, however, could sense how quickly the playing conditions were deteriorating. Waterlogged players were slipping and sliding in the shin-deep mud, barely able to hold the smooth leather ball that was now as slick as a greased anvil. The coach figured one score might just win the game, and without Flanagan he couldn't be certain Pottsville would ever get this close again. The only problem was the Maroons did not yet have a reliable kicker. Russ Stein volunteered, but his placement kick was low and Providence end Joe Kozlowsky was able to get a hand up and deflect the ball.

After a scoreless first half, the Maroons were backed up near their own goal line when Denny Hughes, subbing at center for Herb Stein, got his signals crossed with Ernst and hiked the ball before the Pottsville backfield was in position. The ball sailed backward, untouched, and splashed down near the end zone, where it floated like a leaf on the surface of a pond. There was a mad scramble. Rooster tails of mud and rainwater splashed everywhere, causing both teams, as well as the fans, to crane their necks and squint their eyes nearly shut trying to make out what, exactly, was happening. A sodden Ernst gallantly raced Steam Roller end Red Maloney toward the ball. The two men moved in slow motion, as if trapped in a nightmare, exerting tremendous force and energy and still not covering any ground, clawing, pawing, and elbowing each other as they dove into the drink.

"As the mud-spattered oval bounded over the muck, Maloney scooped up the ball, took a short gallop, and planted it behind the goal post for a touchdown," wrote the *Republican*. "And that was all there was to it."

The enraged Maroons blocked the extra-point attempt. And Latone continued to tear off huge chunks of real estate as the Maroons maintained an amazing first-down advantage of 15 to 0. But a series of fumbles and interceptions near the goal line conspired to keep Pottsville from tying the game. The longer the game progressed at 6-0, the fewer chances the Steam Roller took. Instead, they played a conservative stall tactic of field position and ball control. Eventually, the frustrated and rudderless Maroons began to unravel in the rain. With time running out, Latone mustered one more drive downfield. When it stalled at the 14, rather than hand the ball to Latone, Ernst inexplicably called his own number. He shot-putted the leather brick over the goal line to a wide-open Bucher, who cradled it for a split second before letting the season-saving touchdown slip through his arms and into the watery abyss below. Ernst's final two pass attempts were intercepted, and the Steam Roller floated out of town with a shocking 6-0 victory.

"That Pottsville should have won, there is no doubt," concluded *The Republican.* "The Maroons outplayed them in almost every department; it was just the one break of the game that gave the Rhode Island guys a victory."

There was more to the win than just poor weather and dumb luck, though. Besides being a huge financial flop for Pottsville's already strapped football association, the Providence game exposed the Maroons in three key areas: They lacked a kicker, for starters; they needed to upgrade their receiving corps; and unless a leader stepped forward to curb things like Ernst's ego and Racis's wanderlust, Pottsville was in for either a very long, or a very short, season. The two likeliest candidates, Osborn and Latone, were men who led by deed, not word. Therefore, the team lacked the calming influence and uniting force of a leader who could help them ride out the inevitable peaks and valleys of their first NFL season.

The Maroons were a supremely talented group. There was no doubt. But they were not a team. Not by a long shot. It was the same thing that plagued most other NFL franchises. Unlike college teams that played for the love and honor of their university, pro players like the Maroons weren't necessarily committed to one another or the town they played in. And the lackluster response from fans was merely a rejoinder to the lack of emotion and commitment they perceived from the players.

And so a few hours later, when a solemn Striegel appeared inside the fraternity room above Ginley's, the players sat up in their chairs and steadied themselves for their first real tongue-lashing of the season.

They didn't know the half of it.

Doc Striegel didn't waste time with pleasantries, cigars, or long, fancy speeches. Although the news would not become public for another 10 days, he told the players simply, "We're going broke, fellas."

The Maroons had planned on taking the NFL by storm. Instead, a storm was conspiring to take them out of the league. Striegel was getting by week to week on gate receipts. But the rain had cut their anticipated ticket sales by 70%. The latest news on the coal strike had also just come in from Harrisburg, and it wasn't good. The miners were going to ignore the union's decree to get back to work. No one could blame them. Miner representative John Lewis said that since 1870 more than a million miners had been "butchered" by the anthracite industry. "Every day, two of our men die and sixty are carried home injured on stretchers," Lewis screamed to reporters. "The wages paid are pitifully small in view of the extreme hazard of the work."

This kind of angry rhetoric signaled a long stalemate in the negotiations and caused local businesses and most of the rich men on Mahantongo to hold on to their cash, drying up a major source of funding for the team. A week earlier, the Pottsville Football Association had begun a public offering for shares of the Maroons at $5 for common stock and $24 for preferred. There were very few takers. In fact, the stock sold so poorly that a public statement was issued reminding fans that the football association was *not* a private corporation but a publicly owned trust.

"Had the association wished to make a closed corporation, they could have done so long ago," the posting said, "as the fans have been very slow in the purchase of the stock and the directors could have gobbled it all up had they wished to and the fans would really have no excuse because ample time had been given them." Even after this strangely condescending and openly desperate announcement, fans did not respond. Pro football was still a luxury item, an indulgence, and Pottsville was far from smitten with its new NFL team. Regardless, a large turnout for the Providence game would have kept the team afloat for another month or so, but the rain washed away that plan. And after the loss, the association informed the town's papers that if $5,000 was not raised in the next two weeks, the Maroons would be finished.

Unfortunately, this was not the extent of Striegel's bad news. Since the 1925 NFL championship would be awarded on the basis of overall winning percentage, one more early-season loss would essentially take the Maroons out of the running for a title. Depending on the kind of late-season schedule juggling and barnstorming events that were common at the time, Pottsville had at least 10 games left to play. It just so happened that the toughest of those opponents—the Canton Bulldogs—was up next on the schedule and set to arrive in less than a week.

With the way things were going, it figured. Having reformed under new management and the hopeful eye of NFL president Joe Carr, Canton was now back in the NFL and supposedly stronger than ever. Their all-star caliber roster featured two future Hall of Fame tackles in Fats Henry and Link Lyman. And to make matters worse, Henry and Harry Robb had both turned down contract offers from Doc Striegel after playing in Pottsville in 1924.

"These Canton boys are tough, I know. I played with most of them, and they are up this year with some very good material in that lineup," added the always brutally honest Osborn during a team meeting attended by Zacko. "I feel they have the best players in the league and are headed for the championship again this year."

Striegel let the dire situation sink in for a moment—in the next week they could get blown out and go bankrupt, perhaps at the same time—before offering an unconditional release to any player who wanted to leave town and try to sign with another team. This was the height of the Twenties, an era during which material possessions and financial gain were said to rule man's every whim. If you listened to college football coaches, the worst of the lot were pro football players, a group of men who whored themselves out to the highest bidder with no regard for loyalty, camaraderie, or civic pride. So it would not have surprised anyone, really, if a mad dash for the door ensued and the Maroons simply ceased to exist.

Instead, not a single player took Doc up on his offer.

The players pledged to stick it out for another week; to rededicate themselves to practice and game preparation and to curb their time spent in the belly of the Phoenix. Perhaps they had gotten just a little ahead of themselves. It was the curse of dreamers like Striegel and Ernst: focusing on the giant glory of the finish while ignoring the day-to-day training needed to run the race. In that way, at least, Canton was the perfect opponent. Everything involving the Maroons had now been condensed to one game. In a week, the situation would be over. One way or another they'd know for sure exactly where they stood in the hierarchy of the league as well as the association's balance sheet.

"The players' first consideration was for Doc Striegel," Zacko explained, regarding the team's decision to stick it out for one more week. "He had gone all out and had staked his all to make good with the team. The next consideration was for coach Rauch, whom all the players adored. The final consideration was for the very nice people of Pottsville who had received the boys with arms wide open.

"Pottsville was their alma mater," Zacko concluded, "and they are determined to stick by her."

CHAPTER 10

IN BERRY'S HANDS

ALTHOUGH HE WAS NOT a big baseball fan, for most of the summer of 1925 Doc Striegel had been keeping a keen eye on the American League standings and, in particular, his new favorite team, the Washington Senators. By October, their season was over: Despite the work of pitcher Lefty Grove and slugger Al Simmons, who led the league with 253 hits, the Philadelphia Athletics had been unable to overtake the Senators in the race for the AL pennant. Just as Connie Mack had promised, a few days after the washout against Providence, Striegel received word that A's catcher Charlie Berry, the former All-America end and a teammate of Jack Ernst's at Lafayette, had been given his full release by the club and would be joining the Maroons as they prepared to face the mighty Canton Bulldogs.

The timing could not have been better for the Maroons, a team in desperate need of good news. And no one was happier to see Berry in town than Ernst. In 1921, they had arrived together on campus in Easton, Pennsylvania, and during their four years at Lafayette, Ernst and Berry had become inseparable friends off the field and an unstoppable combo on it. While they couldn't match the school's national championship of 1921, as seniors in 1924 they won seven of nine games and were years ahead of their time when it came to route running, communication, and synchronization. Together they created an explosive, entertaining high-wire act that often brought out the worst in opponents who felt humiliated by their considerable aerial skills.

Early in the 1924 college season, Berry had snatched one of Ernst's passes out of the sky and raced it to within inches of the goal line. Slowed by the rain-soaked field, Berry was caught by an angry mob of defenders, who piled on and elbowed his head into the soggy turf until his face was completely submerged. Berry believed they would have held him there until he drowned had Ernst and the officials not arrived quickly and begun pulling bodies off the heap. Later in the year, at the Lafayette game Doc attended, there were only a few seconds remaining on the clock when Ernst heaved up a long forward in Berry's direction. This time, however, Berry had every intention of drowning—in beer. He caught the ball, galloped into the end zone, through the end line, out the stadium tunnel—his metal spikes *clack-clack-clacking* on the sidewalk—and down into Easton, where he bartered the ball with a local speakeasy for free postgame ales for the entire team.

In one beautiful act, Berry had invented a way to exploit his extraordinary football talents for both a touchdown and free suds for his teammates. This was Doc Striegel's kind of kid. And now, sprung loose by the Senators' stellar play down the stretch,

Berry's arrival in Pottsville turned out to be just what the doctor ordered for the ailing Maroons.

Berry grew up poor in Phillipsburg, New Jersey, where, like Ernst, he worshipped his hard-nosed but fair and gentle father. Berry's mother had emigrated from Germany. His Irish immigrant father took shifts at the Ingersoll Rand plant in town whenever he could. To help make ends meet, as a child Charlie would rise each morning at 5 a.m. to deliver milk in glass bottles on a wagon throughout the neighborhood. The fact that he never complained about the predawn work impressed his parents until they realized, some years later, that Charlie appreciated the early hours because the cover of darkness prevented his classmates from seeing what he was doing. Charlie was smart and accomplished enough to gain admittance to Princeton but attended Lafayette because it was considerably less expensive and right across the river from his family, in Phillipsburg.

At first glance, Berry appeared to be a nondescript 6'0" fellow with black hair, green eyes, and a soft but heavy countenance that gave him a gravitas beyond his years. After college, he had planned on attending dental school. He certainly had the grades, and a season with the A's would have given him decent money toward tuition. But at the first school he applied to, the dean came out from behind his desk, grasped Berry's wrists and held his hands up to his face. One look at those meaty hands and his sausage-size fingers—Berry's class ring from Lafayette was the size of a napkin holder—and the dean shook his head. Unless Berry were going to operate on hippos, his hands were just too big for dentistry. Charlie Berry embraced his fate with his usual magnanimity and humor: His massive paws simply belonged inside a catcher's mitt or wrapped around the huge, egg-shape footballs of the day. Certainly, there were far worse fates than being a professional athlete during the Golden Age of Sports. At least he was no longer delivering milk.

All those mornings spent handling the expensive and heavy glass bottles, slick with morning dew, had turned Berry into a quarterback's dream: Anything his giant mitts touched, they caught. Milk bottles or footballs, he never dropped a thing, and by the time Berry was a senior, Walter Camp had honored him as a first-team selection on his college All-America team. Yet even with his tremendous success, Berry did not suffer from the kind of overly inflated sense of self-worth that plagued most young men of the times.

For him it all went back to the milk. One drink, one sight of the stuff, or just the simple sound of the empty bottles clinking together was enough to remind him of where he came from and what he was about. This created in Berry an unmistakable gravitational pull, an energy and goodness that caused even new acquaintances to begin measuring themselves by their standing in his eyes. If you were okay in Berry's book, it meant something. At Lafayette, *This guy's friends with Berry* was a passport into just about every club, party, or meeting on campus.

In high school and then again in college, Berry was elected captain or president of everything he ever joined or just happened to wander by at the right time. He captained both the football and the baseball teams all four years, was the officer of the Phi Delts, and was president of his class as a senior. "As successful as he was, he didn't have a condescending bone in his body," said one family member. "He had a way of making everyone in a room feel equal. I don't know how, but he did. It was magical almost, the way people just felt better with him around."

Berry was a man equally at ease in a drawing room or a saloon. Educated, well-spoken, and personable, he had an immediate connection to his college cohorts in Pottsville. But it was his self-deprecating style and his working-class upbringing that also allowed him to bond with the Maroons' coal-region veterans and leatherheads like Latone and Racis. And when Berry warmed up before his first practice in Pottsville by repeatedly drop-kicking the ball through the uprights from 30 yards away, Rauch was as smitten as everyone else. Like a math genius who sees the answer while the equation is still being written on the blackboard, the Maroons coach knew it before anyone else: Berry's leadership and myriad football talents had the potential to radiate out and improve every aspect of the Maroons.

To begin with, the Maroons now had a reliable placement kicker. Berry also added another athletic end to the team's stout, but underappreciated, defense. Most important, his speed, height, and hands created a true passing threat that would not only produce yards and scoring opportunities but would also help satiate Ernst, who tended to get into trouble by trying to win games all by himself. Once they reconnected through the air, it would spread defenses out and open things up for Latone in the trenches.

Right away, Berry and Ernst began perfecting the early version of a screen pass they had begun developing while at Lafayette. Lined up at right end, Berry would offer just enough interference to convince the defensive linemen they were making progress into the Maroons' backfield. At the precise moment he felt them surge upfield, Berry would step aside like the ticket taker unlatching the velvet rope outside The Hipp. Their eyes as big as saucers, the defenders would roar past him to get to the elusive and mouthy Ernst, whom they were dying to hit. Berry would then watch them pass by, turn around, and calmly wait for his teammate to loft the ball over their head.

Ernst loved the drama of the play, of course, and always waited until the last possible moment to release the ball in order to maximize the whiplash effect—players called it the *"Oh, crap"* moment—on the poor, unsuspecting defenders. By then, the rest of the Pottsville blockers would have left their posts at the line of scrimmage and formed a wall around Berry several yards downfield.

"Then we have ourselves a picnic, boys," Berry exclaimed.

By completing more passes and becoming more balanced on offense, the Maroons could keep defenses from loading up the line of scrimmage with run-stuffing formations like the Latone Special. Now they would have to play the Maroons honest. This would severely reduce the wear and tear on the Howitzer, while simultaneously making him far more effective as a line plunger. Rauch suddenly had a pick-your-poison plan: If you stuffed the line to stop Latone, Ernst would kill you with forwards, and if you backed off to cover Berry downfield, Latone would gut you right up the middle.

As an added bonus, Berry had brought Walter French with him to Pottsville for a tryout. After starring at Army as a wiry, elusive halfback, French had joined the A's as a pinch hitter and utility outfielder. It had been several seasons since he last played the game, and French was small, just 5'7", 155 pounds—he was immediately dubbed Little Walter (a name that, more than likely, he despised)—but his lateral explosiveness and water-bug moves in the open field were exactly what Rauch needed now that Flanagan was slowed by injuries. (A student of the human psyche as it pertained to football, Striegel also knew the arrival of another halfback would dramatically speed Hoot's recovery.)

The use of French or Flanagan to the outside added yet another dimension to the Maroons' attack. In an era when most teams could barely hike the ball and plunge forward for a yard or two, Pottsville could now beat opponents straight up with power, stretch them vertically down the field with aerials, and dash around end—on consecutive plays. Out of breath from being run ragged all over the field, defenses wouldn't know what had hit them.

And in the infant days of the NFL offense, unpredictable meant unstoppable.

All of this inspired the mad scientist in Rauch, who immediately began scratching out new formations and plays to incorporate Berry and French. If Canton was beefing up its interior defense in preparation for Latone's line-plunging barrage, it would be completely helpless against end runs and downfield passes. The most difficult task for Rauch was that he had just five days to reprogram the mentality of his lineman—from the straightforward-mauler technique of drive blocking to the more intricate and patient angular interference required for end runs.

Once considered the Maroons' Achilles' heel, Rauch's decision to sign smaller, more athletic linemen had turned out to be prescient. Osborn, the Steins, and Racis picked up the changes quickly and adapted with ease to the new style of play. "An excellent offensive interference is being developed for French's fast end runs," *The Republican* reported from practice by midweek. "The plays were pulled off nicely in the first practice. A few more days and we will see the machine well lubricated and working smoothly."

As the countdown to Canton's arrival ticked away like a doomsday clock, what Berry provided, more than anything, was a glimmer of hope where there had been none. A few days earlier, the Maroons' demise had seemed imminent. Now Berry had given them a chance, a sense of "maybe."

"Maybe" we can hang with Canton after all, they thought.

"Maybe" we won't go out of business.

"Maybe" the fans will give us one more chance.

"Maybe" we've got something special here.

All they needed was a spark to reignite the fire of the team and the passion of the town.

By the end of Berry's first week, Osborn knew what he had to do—and there was no "maybe" about it. He had to provide that spark. So when the team met above Ginley's on the eve of the Canton game, Duke boldly stood up, moved to the front of the room, and asked for everyone's attention.

Players stopped talking. They sat up in their cots. They cinched up their cards and placed them face down on the table.

Osborn cleared his throat and with little explanation and the fewest possible words, he did something unthinkable: He resigned his captaincy.

The news caused quite a stir. Was he quitting on them? Was the bastard jumping back to Canton? Was he leveraging Doc for more money? Who was better suited to lead them than Duke? What else was going to go wrong with this team? Were they doomed?

With his accomplishments, talent, and temperament, Duke Osborn answered to no one on the football field. Besides the honor of it, there were significant monetary benefits to consider. The team captain earned up to $50 extra per game, plus whatever cash bonuses miners and other overly excited fans stuffed into his pockets after victories.

Duke held up a hand, asking for quiet. He rang the bottom of the brass spittoon with a long, thick stream of tobacco juice. Then he calmly recommended that Charlie Berry take his place at the head of the team. This was what Duke had been getting at all along. Suddenly, outrage turned to understanding, and then empathy turned to respect for Osborn's sacrifice. It was the kind of gesture that made every man in the room, even Latone, silently question his own commitment to the cause.

When Osborn sat back down, Latone and the rest of the players nodded their heads in unison. Of course. *Charlie.* It made perfect sense.

Although he hadn't played in a single pro football game, the 22-year-old Berry—the youngest man on the team—was then unanimously elected the new captain of the Pottsville Maroons. And in honor of both captains, the room burst out into a wild round of cheers.

From the street below it sounded as if a revival meeting were taking place in the Maroons' fraternity room. In a sense, that's exactly what was happening. Their financial outlook hadn't changed. If something wasn't done, and soon, the Maroons would be broke in under a week. The best team in pro football was, at this very moment, still bearing down on them from train tracks to the west. Yet Duke's decision to relinquish his captaincy to Berry signified a major transformation within the Maroons. Faced with the decision to either play for free or cancel the entire season, the men who had started as strangers less than six weeks earlier had now chosen to stick together and literally go for broke.

The money mattered to them but not more than the game.

By definition, the Maroons were professional football players, but in their hearts—and now in the minds of their fans—they had proven themselves every bit as honorable and pure as amateurs. In doing so, the Maroons had been reborn—as an actual team, a true band of brothers. And in this incarnation they believed they could not be defeated.

The next day, the mighty Canton Bulldogs offered little evidence to the contrary.

Using a type size and font normally reserved for wars, election results, and possibly the return of the Messiah, the headline across the top of the *Journal* said it all:

CANTON SUSTAINS WORST DEFEAT IN HISTORY AT HAND OF MAROONS

No one outside the team had seen this coming. Attendance was not reported, a sign that it was embarrassingly low, perhaps even fewer than 1,000. Thus, the responsibility of reporting the Maroons' astonishing turnaround fell to the town's two newspapers. And they were fully expecting to eulogize the team's brief NFL existence, not record the greatest upset in Pottsville history. Below its banner headline, the *Journal* included game statistics—as if readers needed proof that the reported result wasn't a hoax. The numbers told the same story. Touchdowns: Pottsville 4, Canton 0. Totals yards: Pottsville 267 (105 by Latone), Canton 49. Yards per play: Pottsville 3½, Canton 1. First downs: Pottsville 19, Canton 1.

The Republican went even further than a 72-point headline. Their writers dared to compare the Maroons to Knute Rockne's Notre Dame Fighting Irish—a team not only considered the best football squad on the planet but a seminal team in the history of American sports. "Those who attended the game were privileged to look upon one hour's real football," stated *The Republican*. "The game was a classic and will go down in local grid history as one of the best played in the county. The Maroons looked like a Notre Dame squad in action. They moved about like one big machine, well oiled and tuned up to the minute. Pete Henry, et al., were hopelessly outclassed in every department. The Maroons' interference was perfect. It swept up and down the field like a huge mowing machine, having the same effect on the Bulldogs as the reaper does to ripe grain."

Berry had proven himself worthy of Osborn's trust by volunteering to start the game across from Henry. The baby-faced, 245-pound Henry moved like a halfback and hit like a billy club. "Oh boy, did Henry really give it to me," Berry said about the game. "Anything you've read or heard about Pete Henry is true. He's a great one. Hitting him was like hitting a rubber sponge. I could get in, but I couldn't get out."

With Berry neutralizing Henry, the Maroons were able to wring the power out of the Canton attack. Without having to worry about Fats, Osborn, Herb Stein, and Racis roamed free and suffocated Canton's offense so completely that the Bulldogs managed to cross midfield only once the entire game. Latone and Ernst may have enjoyed a majority of the headlines, but the Maroons defense, which had yet to surrender a single rushing first down, was the real story in Pottsville. "It was evident that Dick Rauch's coaching has developed results," concluded one reporter. "Canton used the same stuff they always did ... while Pottsville's attack puzzled them throughout."

When the Maroons had the ball, Rauch bracketed Fats with a tag team of Russ Stein and Hathaway. This allowed Ernst to complete a whopping seven passes (more than some NFL teams completed in half a season). Meanwhile, it was reported that Latone and a suddenly cured Flanagan "outgained Canton by so many yards that it is useless to recount them." Flanagan's rather miraculous recovery kept Walter French out of the starting lineup. And when Rauch did finally insert him as a sub in the second half, the untouchable speed demon from practice was nowhere to be found. Little Walter loved running with the ball. He just didn't like getting hit.

By then, though, the game that had held so many grave consequences for the Maroons had turned into a laugher.

Afterward, Berry howled as he recalled how "in the second half, Ernst asked me if I wanted to try a field goal. I agreed to try because it was a chance to back off the line of scrimmage and get away from Big Pete. I dubbed the kick. It hardly got off the ground and sailed into some of the players. Later, the same thing happened. Then I decided to try for the third time, and as we lined up for the kick, Pete stood up and yelled, "Duck, you guys, he's gonna try another one!"

Berry did manage to connect on all four of his extra-point kicks. He also recovered a blocked punt in the end zone for a score, kept several of the Maroons' drives alive with clutch catches on third down, and even managed to pick off a pass. Berry's play had inspired the Maroons and, more than likely, kept the franchise afloat for at least another week. "Every man on the Pottsville team played wonderful football against the heavier Canton line," said the paper. "The Maroons threatened to score on at least 10 occasions. The results were not considered possible, even by the Maroons' staunchest supporters."

CHAPTER 11

A MILLION RUMORS

THE CANTON MIRACLE, as it was now known, made
believers out of the town. As the football association's
two-week financial deadline loomed, rumors about the
Maroons' financial standing swirled from Schneider's to Zacko's
to the Phoenix and back around again.

On the Tuesday following the defeat of the Bulldogs, Captain
Berry's boys were looking sharp at practice, and the talk of the
town was that it was a shame such little money had been raised
because after the rematch with Providence, "the dream of
football supporters in Pottsville will come to a rude ending."

On Tuesday night, the team's supporters were said to be
canvassing the town for more donations, that the team had been
informed of the dire financial situation, and that a promoter from
a more prosperous and organized town up north—Scranton,
perhaps—was considering taking over the club if indeed the city

of Pottsville was not up to the task.

By Thursday, the whole debate had shifted again. "DO NOT BELIEVE MAROONS WILL LEAVE POTTSVILLE," read the headline. "That the Maroons will not be lost to Pottsville, there is little doubt. This was the statement made by several prominent sports followers late Wednesday night," *The Republican* reported. "The announcement of the directors of the Pottsville Football Association that $5,000 was necessary to keep football here was met on many sides by surprise and as a result the city is chock full of a million and one rumors."

By Friday the most prominent theory was that the Pottsville Football Association had but one key board member—Dr. John G. Striegel—and that all this talk of bankruptcy and canceling the season was Doc's way of bluffing a poor early draw into more chips. Certainly, many of the association's tactics resembled the work of Striegel, who was quite adept at manipulating the media to use the crow bar of civic pride to pry open wallets for his team.

No matter who was behind the strategy, one thing was certain: It worked, particularly the rumor about Scranton. By the time the deadline hit, the town had raised another $2,500 for the Maroons. Coincidentally (or not), Doc Striegel then announced his bid to buy the franchise outright. Striegel's plan was to reimburse the city for the original NFL franchise fee and league guarantee, and then finance the rest of the season with the newly donated $2,500 by providing a return for all investors at the end of the season.

This did little to end the question of ownership about the team, however, and rumors persisted for the rest of the season. First, that the players owned the team, then that the Football Association had bought it back and, finally, that Striegel had owned it all along. While no clear declaration of ownership was ever made to the public, Doc was privately guaranteeing salaries against his personal assets—like his medical practice, cars, and country estate—to keep worried players from jumping ship. In the end, knowing who owned the team wasn't entirely necessary. After the Canton Miracle, the Maroons had become solvent and would remain so for the rest of the season. And that's all that mattered. "Striegel's offer was received and accepted," wrote *The Republican*. "And all the players were paid their full salary Friday afternoon."

To celebrate their windfall, most of the players went to Providence a day early, taking in the Yale-Penn game along the way. Relieved and revived Maroons fans followed them in droves, by train and in an auto caravan that snaked for miles up the curvy highway heading east over Sharp Mountain. Providence had followed its win against the Maroons with an impressive 14-0 victory against the New York Giants. Yet on their way, the stogie-chomping crowd from Zacko's surmised that if Latone's end-arounds in Providence were anywhere near as slippery as Doc's financial dealings, the Steam Roller wouldn't get within a 100 points of the Maroons.

They weren't that far off.

Even the Associated Press, an unbiased news-gathering agency with no ties to Pottsville or Schuylkill County, could barely contain itself after witnessing the wrath of the Maroons.

"Baring a powerful line plunging attack with an aerial system that was well nigh invincible," the AP report began, "the Pottsville Maroons gained a sweet revenge over the steam rolling team of this city by trouncing the Juggernauts by a 34-0 score. A crowd of more than 10,000 witnessed the struggle, including a large delegation of Pottsville rooters. The outcome of the game was never in doubt.

"From beginning to end it was a series of gains by Latone, Wentz, and Flanagan with touchdowns the ultimate result in nearly every case. The Steam Roller line, which in its last game turned back time and the array of All-America talent on the New York Giants, failed miserably against the flashing tactics of the Pennsylvania backs. Pottsville's crushing backfield ripped the Roller line to pieces while the Providence backs could do nothing against the defense put up by the Maroons. The Rollers made only two first downs, both by forward passes.

"The Maroons showed the best football that has been displayed on the local gridiron this year and with a continuation of this kind of play will be among the leaders at the close of the NFL series."

Fans had lined up outside the team's hotel in Providence, chanting Latone's name until he rewarded them with a curtain call. By noon Monday, the AP's glowing review had made its way around every store, barbershop, and hotel lobby in Pottsville. And at 1:27 p.m., when the Reading Line deposited the Maroons back home, the Pottsville Drum Corps was waiting for them on the train platform, along with most of the town's hook-and-ladder trucks and several hundred fans who had "gathered at the station to meet the conquering heroes." Shocked, embarrassed, and a bit skeptical of the town's fickle affections, at first the team flatly refused to join the celebration, "scattering in all directions" according to *The Republican*.

"However," the same account said, "a little later someone captured Frankie Racis and he was held a prisoner by admiring fans in the hope of getting other players. Not a one could be found until it was learned that Tony Latone was up at Dr. Striegel's office. A crowd went in and got him down. Both were placed on the front seat of the [fire]truck and the parade was underway. As the parade was marching up Centre Street it was ascertained that Duke Osborn was eating in a restaurant. The crowd ran in after him and stuck him on the truck with Latone and Racis.

"If there is any doubt that Pottsville is football mad, Monday afternoon it was settled for good and for all."

The town hadn't seen anything yet.

Canton and Providence were just the beginning. The Maroons were now in the middle of the most dominant, game-changing stretch of football the NFL would ever know.

Chapter 12

A TOWN'S SOUL

THE BALL EXPLODED OFF THE FOOT of Fungy Lebengood and all the return man could do was remain flatfooted at the 15-yard line, tilt his face skyward, and watch as it shot by, past the goal post, and into the crowded stands beyond the end zone. At 23, Harold 'Fungy' Lebengood was one of the youngest players on the Maroons' roster and the only native Pottsvillian. After starring for Pottsville High in 1916 and 1917, he played for Villanova before returning home to Schuylkill County. By local standards, Lebengood was a talented back and kicker. But the caliber of the Maroons' roster had turned him into little more than a role player. Besides, Ernst handled most of the punting duties himself, which meant anytime the overeager Lebengood was given the chance to kick, he would swing hard enough to punt the ball all the way down to his backyard on West Market.

This time, Fungy's prodigious punt cleared the entire playing field, landing high up in the stands where it struck a young, pretty Maroons supporter on the head, knocking her out cold. Lebengood saw the commotion and climbed into the stands to see what had happened. But by the time he reached the ball and spotted the stricken Miss Mary Jane Reed, it was Fungy who was in need of smelling salts. He tore off his helmet, bent down to be closer to her, and began to apologize profusely. Several minutes later, after play had resumed on the field, the suddenly smitten pair continued right on talking, oblivious to their surroundings.

An errant punt had turned into love at first sight.

By this point in the season, even Cupid had become a Maroons fan.

After settling the score in Providence—with compounded interest, according to Farquhar—the Maroons notched back-to-back home shutouts against Columbus (20-0) and Akron (21-0). They were now 5-1 and sitting atop the league, having outscored their first six opponents 131-6, thanks to the mind of Rauch, the merciless line-plunging of Latone, and the Steins' swarming defense, which maintained a nearly unfathomable 8-1 advantage in first downs. "As the situation now looks," reported *The Republican,* "Pottsville has a wonderful chance to end up in front in the national pro football fight."

Akron had come into Pennsylvania undefeated, and afterward even Joe Carr himself was forced to admit that the Maroons were the best team he had ever seen. The little Queen City of the Anthracite was fast becoming the king of the NFL. Seemingly overnight, the town's initial indifference had been transformed beyond the infatuation shown at the end of 1924 to something resembling religious zealotry.

For most Maroons fans, the games themselves had become extensions of their Sunday worship. As church services ended and the bells chimed—the tones bouncing off the cliffs of Sharp Mountain and reverberating against each other—congregations from across the city and every religious, ethnic, and economic stratum exited their houses of worship to converge on Market Street and climb toward a common goal.

The Protestants came from West Market; the Catholic crowd at St. Pat's was on Fourth; the Lutherans were on Arch; the Episcopalians on Centre; St. Joe's on Fourth was known as the Italian church; the Presbyterians were on Third; and the Baptists were on Tenth. At the same time each week, men, women, and children from every denomination—some in expensive flapper skirts or Oxford baggies, some in denim overalls and some in three-piece suits; some with 75 cents to their name and some with 75 grand in the stock market; immigrants, natives, educated, and illiterate, of every race and creed—headed toward Minersville Park to see their beloved Maroons. And when Model T and trolley traffic stirred up so much road dirt and coal dust that it was difficult to see, fans would cover their faces with handkerchiefs and hats, clasp hands, and help each other up the steep trail. There was something beautiful and hopeful about the communal pageantry of football fans climbing to the games together each week. And once Doc Striegel made admission to Minersville Park a flat $1.65 for every seat, the throng heading up Market Street each Sunday grew to several thousand strong.

Pottsville had always had a strong base of German, English, and Welsh in its community. But the Industrial Revolution's insatiable need for carbon fuel had created a coal boom that lured huge numbers of immigrants from Eastern and southern Europe, as well as Ireland. In nearby Shenandoah, for example, almost a third of the town's population was made up of immigrants from countries such as Poland and Lithuania. This added yet another ingredient to an already tense atmosphere. There was a polarizing social battle being waged for the country's soul, between the strict Victorian vanguard and the youthful, consumer-based progressives of the booming middle class. On top of that, Schuylkill County and the rest of coal country faced ugly ethnic and religious divisions, as well as class conflicts between coal barons and miners, brought on by the never-ending series of miners' strikes that threatened to bankrupt the city.

At best, Pottsville was a peaceful and prosperous melting pot of political, ethnic, and social diversity. At worst, it was a powder keg of jingoism and xenophobia waiting for a match. In the late 1800s, the same tensions gave birth to the Molly Maguires, who ruled coal country until the town was forced to intervene. Funded by the coal companies, a Pinkerton detective, James McParlan, was able to infiltrate the Mollies' hangout on Centre Street. As a result of his private investigation, 10 Molly Maguires were sentenced to death. Six were hung outside Pottsville's hilltop prison—though not at the same time, since there was some question as to whether the town's gallows were sturdy enough to hold them all.

Feeding off the same anxieties and pressures of the changing times, the Ku Klux Klan had since become a presence in the coal region and beyond. The 1924 Democratic National Convention, in fact, had disintegrated into a fistfight on the hall floor while representatives raged over whether to condemn the Klan. (A vote to denounce them lost by the slimmest of margins.) Large marches, with numbers in the tens of thousands, took place in towns throughout the North. It was nothing to see a grandmother, daughter, and grandchild featured on the front page of a paper all proudly decked out in their white robes and hoods. Some coal cities chose to field several separate teams, perhaps as a way to keep from mixing rosters. Restaurants regularly refused to serve immigrants. A Catholic rosary was often reason enough to deny someone a job. Eastern Europeans in Pottsville were derided as "schwackies." A union between parishioners from St. Pat's and St. John's was said to be a mixed marriage.

Meanwhile, the town's upper crust was so obsessed with the subtle yet vicious rituals of ambition and exclusion that by the time John O'Hara began his prolific career in fiction, he had stored up a lifetime's worth of characters and conflicts from which to mine (for which Pottsville never forgave him).

All of these new ethnoreligious communities were brought together in Pottsville by the economics of coal. But in the end, it was a universal love of competition and sports—and more specifically the suddenly unbeatable Maroons—that transcended the boundaries of social class and transformed Pottsville from what would have been a dozen different enclaves into one community, if only for a few hours each week.

During a time of such national tumult, passion for football was one of the few things that was capable of moving the tectonic plates of a divided society toward each other. As the team continued to win, Pottsville merchants began to place banners and posters in support of the Maroons in the front windows of their establishments, covering up signs that might otherwise have read *Immigrants enter in back* or *Irish need not apply*. The message this sent was simple but profound: The things the town shared, like a love of and passion for the Maroons, eclipsed the things that drove them apart. The concept was called civic boosterism, the fundamental principle that would not only save the fledgling NFL but one day turn it into the true national pastime. And the

Maroons were the first pro football team to inspire something so noble and fervent from their fans.

This team had done far more than win games and acclaim for Pottsville.

The Maroons had given the town a soul.

In the past, Pottsville's rich Protestant elite had segregated itself from the working class, Catholic or otherwise, through country club sports like tennis, cricket, and golf. Pro football had long been considered a beastly event better suited for the poor, ignorant, and unsophisticated masses. But the Maroons were different. They were run by the preeminent Doc Striegel, the scholarly, handsome Dick Rauch, and their All-America captain, Charlie Berry. They were a professional, first-rate outfit that brought honor and national praise to Pottsville.

It didn't hurt either that their dominant, fast-paced, and violent product was simply too exciting to pass up. By now, the incorrigible Racis had gotten so good at pinballing his way through kickoff coverage that he would wager an ice-cold beer to all takers that he would be the one to make the ensuing tackle. Ernst had become so capable and confident in the pocket, he once tucked himself into the Maroons' huddle and laughed, "Better be a bit conservative this time and only make it a 30-yard pattern."

Fans were also drawn together around the team because the Maroons' roster mirrored the town and the ethos of the transitional times they played in. As a man of the times, Doc Striegel cared for two things: winning and gate receipts. Therefore he wasn't inclined to limit his roster or his fan base by excluding talented players based on ethnicity or religion. With the possible exception of Mussolini, Doc would sign any man he thought could help him win on Sunday. And so in Pottsville, college All-Americas happily blocked for coal miners, Protestants passed to Catholics, and pileups in the end zone featured a Pole on top of a German next to a Welshman behind a Lithuanian. The stands were filled the exact same way. Men born with silver spoons in their mouths cheered next to fans still trying to get the tinny taste of coal dust off their tongues. People from divergent backgrounds who once stared at their feet while riding the trolleys, standing in the aisles of Pomeroy's, or visiting the coal mine washrooms, soon discovered they had something in common to talk about besides the weather and the price of anthracite. "The players were like folk heroes in Pottsville," said a member of Lebengood's family. "And when the Maroons played, it was like a holiday for everyone in town."

In the Every Man for Himself decade, there was also something reassuring about the way the Maroons had succeeded by coalescing as a team. Accepting diversity was one thing. Having proof, in the form of a football team, that there was a tangible value to the concept was nothing short of monumental. Jack Dempsey and Bobby Jones worked alone. Babe Ruth was starring in the Bronx. Even the most die-hard fans would have a difficult time naming a single teammate of Red Grange's. From week to week with the Maroons, however, no one knew who might lead the team to victory. Would it be Latone's line-plunging? Flanagan's speed? The strength of the Steins? The relentlessness of Osborn? Ernst's arm? Berry's hands? Or Rauch's strategy?

In late October, an editorial lauding the Maroons and calling for more civic support of the team stated: "Many clubs would have thrown up the sponge [at the threat of bankruptcy], but please remember after these rumors were afloat, the Maroons turned out and played the best game of their career. A Boston paper came forward with the statement that the Maroons are the best team in the country. A college official, after seeing the teamwork in two games, said the Pottsville Maroons could defeat any college team, present or past.

"Let us show ourselves worthy to have a combination of this kind and, above all, stick to the players as they are sticking to you."

Maroons fans followed this advice—literally. Whoever the hero of the game turned out to be, by the time that player had made it from the field to the Maroons' locker room, wealthy fans had filled their ears with invitations to private parties all over town while the miners stuffed their uniforms full of cash. These were the team's poorest fans, men who likely had to choose between meat in their stew and a ticket to the game. For them, the games acted as a temporary escape from their 12-hour entombment in the mines, the worry of another strike, and the inevitable threat of a cave-in. For a few hours each week, they ceased to be coal crackers and were fans of the smartest, toughest, professional club in all the land. Supporting the Maroons was the one time they could rise above their existence, literally, and take an active part in the community.

What's more, while the mines were out on strike, gambling on the Maroons with the ignorant and overconfident visiting fans was also a nice way for miners to maintain their income. And for this they were grateful beyond words. "After games, the miners would be pushing ones and fives at you—passing you a cut of the money they had just won by betting on the Maroons," a player later recalled. "These were not men with a suit of clothes on. They would be in rubber knee boots, dungarees, a heavy jacket, and a miner's cap without the lamp. Their hands would be clean and their face would be clean and their clothes would be clean, but they would be wearing the very clothes they had worn down in the mines from day to day. It was an extraordinary sight, I tell you. Extraordinary."

Following the Columbus victory on November 1, by the time Walter French made it back to the Maroons quarters, he looked like a scarecrow stuffed with greenbacks. Early in the game, another bad snap near the Columbus goal line had threatened to doom a Maroons drive. With all of Pottsville sickened by a bout of déjà vu from the Providence loss, Little Walter darted backward, snatched up the ball, and returned it back to the goal line. From a psychological standpoint, it was the most important no-yard gain of the entire season. As he always seemed to do, on the very next play, Latone crashed in for six. " … in an instant, Little Walter had scooped up the ball and ran far to the opposite side of the field, cutting in at every step, and when he stopped, he had the ball on the 1-yard line, on the opposite side of the field," wrote one reporter. "It was about as pretty a run as seen locally this season, as the fleet-footed Army star put the ball back in position to score."

French broke off several more long runs, including a 30-yard touchdown in the third to ice the victory. When he had first arrived in town with Berry, French had been fast but rusty, and after a few good licks, he had begun to run timidly, like a weak-kneed fawn. His skinny build and decent speed had always seemed better suited for his summer job as a pinch hitter for the Philadelphia Athletics. Before joining the Maroons, French's only other NFL football experience had been one game with Rochester, in 1922. "He's a quiet little fellow," said a reporter for *The Republican.* "One of those men who sits in a room full of people, generally back in a corner, and who does not say but a half-dozen words all night."

Before attending West Point, French played college ball for Rutgers. In 1919, during a game against Lehigh, he suffered a severe neck injury that kept him out for an entire year. He recovered physically. Mentally it was another story. Understandably, at 155 pounds and with a fragile spine, Little Walter didn't have the stomach for the kind of line-plunging that Latone had made famous. In the open field, though, he was magnificent and harder to lock down than Al Capone. "The back who is to cover the eligible Mr. French," said one fan, "usually ends up growling to the manager on the sidelines, 'Gimme a gun.' "

The following week, it was Russ Hathaway's turn at the post-game till. His interception thwarted a late comeback by Akron, and in the eyes of the Maroons' adoring public, Hathaway was no longer just a big, gristly lineman. Now, according to one Philadelphia reporter, the hefty tackle from Indiana was "built on the slim, Grecian lines of a packing case, works faster than four aces in a poker game, and covers more territory than the dew."

As the wins piled up, so too did the Maroons' cult of personality. Ernst no longer threw passes; he was now "pitching forwards like a twirler with Chief Bender's control," stated one press clipping. "He romps around the backfield, cool and collected. He sights the eligible man—this isn't as hard as it seems, as Berry and French are so far ahead of the covering backs that you couldn't miss 'em— and shoots it. The cow skin then nestles and purrs contently in the arms of the receiver after Jack, of the family Ernst, completes his end of the play. Oberlander of Dartmouth, the All-America, may be all right but we'll bet any part of a million dollars, except $999,999, that he isn't one wit better than Mr. Jack Ernst of Pottsville, Pennsylvania."

Berry was privy to the same treatment. He wasn't just a good player and a great leader, reporters trying to make up for lost time now claimed he was "the best end in the United States of America. He tosses interference on its spine and often nails the ball-toter, as well. He is down the field under kicks so splendidly that rarely does the runner advance a punt. He takes forward passes as a child absorbs confectionary. He is just about the cat's syllables when it comes to anything that resembles an end. Berry's work on any field is worth the admission alone."

Latone's mythical hold on the region also continued to grow with every carry. By mid-season, there were rumors that Tony was so feared that he left the cash he received for each game sitting on the bench, daring someone to rob him. No one ever did. A picture ran in the paper of him dressed to the nines in a three-piece suit, silk-lined cashmere overcoat, and fedora, with his Italian-leather shoes up on the running board of a new streamlined REO Speedwagon. Pottsville named chewing gum, cigars, cigarettes, toothpaste, and even football shoes after him.

Growing legions of coal country fans felt a solidarity with Latone, this battering ram of a man who hit so hard and spoke so softly, and they enjoyed not having to share him with the world. Fans barely recognized Latone after games once his sinister, twisted visage had been replaced by the warm, boyish smile that seemed to overinflate his cheeks. To the few people he opened up to, there was a powerful, animal warmth to him. "We remember seeing him beat a team almost single-handed, and after the game we sought to praise him," one local paper wrote. "But his warm, glowing modesty caused him to recoil from the encomium as the cold beads of embarrassment oozed out of his forehead. He left us with a feeble wafture of his arm, and soon this unfeigned man was lost in the covert and sconce of the locker room."

Little boys started carrying the ball with both hands out in front of their bodies, just like the Human Howitzer. Tailors in town competed over who would get to sew his custom pants, since his massive legs wouldn't fit into the normal sizes. And grown men spoke breathlessly about him. "He could never make a mistake, and he was never criticized," Zacko opined. "He was quiet and unassuming. He was loyal to the core. He was the personification of honesty. He was fearless in play, but in private life, he was the picture of humility. I have never met anyone who disliked him or spoke ill of him. I don't believe he ever had an enemy in the world."

Latone's performances even inspired Farquhar to verse:

You can teach a man to play the game with skill and
fighting zeal,
But you cannot give him deer-like speed nor legs of
supple steel;
It's natural ability, that rarest gift of all,
That marks the truly greatest star in any game of ball;
Who gave Jim Thorpe his speed and weight, Babe Ruth
his eagle eye?
Who taught Ty Cobb to swing a bat, or Grange to
"phantom" by?
So when you find a willing boy, who'd crack a wall
of stone,
And getting through pick up rare speed, that man is
T. Latone.

During the 1920s, athletes were iconic, larger-than-life heroes, and it was no different in Pottsville. By the midpoint of the season, the Maroons had to employ a security agency to maintain calm at home games. According to Zacko, "Theaters refused the players' money and admitted them for free. Restaurants accepted them as guests, they were praised in schools and churches, businesses regarded them as special people—all were proud in Pottsville to claim the Maroons as their boys. To the young and old, the Maroons were idols."

Doc Striegel's daughter, Betty, was the envy of her peers, because occasionally players from the team would escort her to Sweetland, the confectionary store on Centre Street. On the city's main drag, every fan had a Maroons button on his lapel or a banner across the back of his automobile. And as they passed each other in public, fans would yell, "Fight! Fight!" and another group of supporters would reply, "Anthracite!" Men fought over who would pick up the Steins' prodigious restaurant tabs. Flappers prayed a pigskin would fall out of the sky and knock them dizzy just like the one that had struck Mary Jane Reed, the lucky girl who was now dating Fungy Lebengood. Others took matters into their own hands and volunteered to tidy up the players' living quarters. The apartment shared by Ernst, Berry, Bucher, and Osborn was so clean it resembled a museum.

After the Akron blowout in early November, Rauch gave the team off until Wednesday. These were the halcyon days of the 1925 NFL season, and the Maroons drank them in fully, spending long days at the tap inside the Phoenix, or playing cards and listening to the radio in the fraternity room above Ginley's. At juke joints all over town, players could buy a jar full of liquor for a dime before heading to the ballroom at the Hotel Allan to meet girls while convulsing their way through the Charleston. Berry preached for temperance as often as he could, but these were grown men, flush with cash and admiration during the peak of the Roaring Twenties. There was only so much he could do.

In the fervor created by the Maroons' first NFL season, gossip about the team ran rampant. To Pottsvillians, these men were like their very own movie stars, and the tittle-tattle about every last detail surrounding the team never seemed to end. Questions about players, signings, and strategy soon degenerated into whispers about affairs, gambling, and too much drink. At one point the gossip got so ridiculous there was even a rumor that the proper Dick Rauch and Doc's lovely wife, Neva, had fallen madly in love, and their coupling had produced a secret love child. Decades later, townsfolk still swore that the tales of their torrid affair were true despite the fact that no proof, no baby, and certainly no confessions were ever uncovered.

Players were asked to attend everything from dinners at the Elks to business openings to student assemblies and even movie premieres. One of the year's most popular films was Harold Lloyd's *The Freshman,* a silent comedy about a nerdy college student who tries to become popular by joining his school's football team. When the movie debuted at The Hipp, the Maroons were invited as the special guests of honor on opening night.

In keeping with the theme of the show, the players kept the overflow crowd in stitches. After Doc Striegel introduced the entire team, a member of the audience presented Herb Stein with flowers. Without missing a beat, Herb's teammates remarked that he probably had them sent to himself.

One thing was certain: With the rival Frankford Yellow Jackets now 9-2 and next up on the schedule, the bouquet had most certainly not come from Shep Royle. Word inside The Hipp and around Pottsville was that the owner of the Yellow Jackets was still smoldering over losing the Steins to some hick doctor. And in private at least, he was also steamed at the way Pottsville's little coal-mining team had captured the region's fancy, thus robbing Royle of the headlines and attention that would have otherwise gone to his Yellow Jackets. The first part of the home-and-home series was set for November 14 at Yellow Jacket Field in Philadelphia, and Royle was giddy with anticipation over the chance to administer the Maroons' long-awaited comeuppance.

For football fans at The Hipp, the mere mention of Royle's name ended the pageantry of the evening. And the memory of his pedantic whine was like the foreman's steam whistle at the mines: It marked the end of the midseason party in Pottsville.

It was time for the Maroons to get back to work.

CHAPTER 13

A SAVAGE STING

I N 1854, THE CITY OF PHILADELPHIA ANNEXED THE
small borough of Frankford. The joke in Pottsville was that
Shep Royle believed it had actually been the other way
around. Royle was a wealthy president of a large textile mill who
considered himself a shrewd player in Philadelphia politics. In
1920, he and several other textile presidents from the area formed
a football conglomerate. Since then they had spent considerable
money to build a first-class stadium (it seated 15,000) and acquire
enough talent to make a run at the 1925 NFL championship.

Royle had lured to Philadelphia player/coach Guy Chamberlin,
the man behind Canton and Cleveland's three consecutive titles,
as well as a 215-pound tackle and kicker named Russ 'Bull'
Behman, and the battering-ram fullback and tackler Tex Hamer, a
star at Penn who had led the league with 12 touchdowns in 1924.
Despite the defections to Pottsville and the ridiculously packed

schedule Royle had created, by midseason this trio had managed to guide the Yellow Jackets to an impressive record of 9-2.

As the showdown with the Maroons drew closer, Royle's attitude began to echo Joe Carr's and the other big city franchises'. It was undignified to have to compete for something as grand as an NFL championship with a town as provincial as Pottsville. Royle still considered the Maroons a backward coal cracker outfit and he was not exactly shy about speaking out against the scheduling quirk that he believed was unfairly aiding the breaker boys. While Pottsville simply ignored the state's Blue Laws and played home games on Sunday, as a refined gentleman from a God-fearing, law-abiding metropolis such as Philadelphia, Royle was honor-bound by the law. Therefore, the Yellow Jackets were forced to play their home games on Saturday. The next day, the same team, bruised and battered, would travel 90 miles north to play in Pottsville. There was no denying the huge competitive advantage for the Maroons. The day before nearly every game, Rauch was able to extensively scout most of his opponents in Frankford. By the time a team arrived in Pottsville 24 hours later, they had already been tenderized by the Yellow Jackets.

In Royle's mind it was plain and simple, the Maroons were a fraud—nothing more than the beneficiary of the Yellow Jackets' dominant opening act. In Philadelphia, Yellow Jacket fans enjoyed tweaking Pottsville's inferiority complex as a former hill town. And in Pottsville, Maroons fans believed Royle was the personification of the big-city pompous ass, a stuffed suit with baby-soft hands whose next day of honest labor would be his first. He certainly looked the part: the bow tie and high, starched collar that looked like it was cutting off his oxygen; the thick wavy hair shellacked into place; and the puffy, bloated, rosy cheeks that forced his eyes into a permanent sinister squint. The Yellow

Jackets had twice as many games scheduled as the average NFL team, and Pottsville fans believed it was typical of the owner's greed and moral turpitude. *You watch, he don't care, he's gonna kill those players while stuffing his own billfold.* What's more, Royle degraded the sport with halftime games of midget football and all-female gridiron exhibitions to lure in larger crowds.

For years the two towns had been carrying on like this. Pottsville was a hick coal town. Frankford was full of rich weaklings and phonies. It had all the makings of the perfect civic rivalry: labor versus management, rural versus urban, blue collar versus white, and all the other social, class, and economic issues conflicting the rest of the country. As is often the case with such mutual enmity, the towns of Pottsville and Frankford were more than likely railing against the things they recognized in their rivals that they actually feared or loathed about themselves. "Pottsville is not little, never was little, except in the minds of unprogressive inhabitants," one columnist shot back. On some level, Pottsville desperately wanted to become a respected metropolis but knew it would never happen, while Frankford wanted to remain a small, autonomous town, knowing full well it could never go back to that.

The teams had brawled their way to a tie in 1923 and the rivalry was ratcheted up further in 1924 when Frankford bowed out of the game four days before kickoff. Royle claimed the NFL had forbidden him from playing an unsanctioned opponent that had been "outlawed" after Striegel signed players bound for Cleveland. Maroons fans saw it as Royle's petty way of preventing Pottsville from claiming something more than just the Anthracite League crown simply because his own team had lost the NFL title by mere percentage points. "You know that Pottsville planned all season to meet Frankford," wrote Farquhar. "It was the main topic of conversation not only here but in Philadelphia and it was no fault of our own that competition for higher honors was not forthcoming."

Connected by the daily business of coal, fans from both teams bickered loudly year-round, inside the region's banks, offices, mines, restaurants, and railcars. It was usually about who had the smarter coach, the tougher line plunger, the better captain, and the most handsome quarterback. This time, though, the stakes were much higher than regional bragging rights, and the good-natured ribbing began to take on a far more vitriolic tone. (As bad as it got, however, no one could have predicted the kind of venom the rivalry would bring out of Royle.) Pottsville and Frankford were about to play each other twice in the next 15 days. The team that survived the series would likely compete for the NFL title, a cross-country barnstorming tour, or the game's ultimate sweepstakes, a humongous life-changing payday against Red Grange or some other national draw.

These kinds of stakes, and the blistering intensity of the rivalry, drew more than 20,000 fans to Yellow Jacket Field, the largest professional football crowd in Pennsylvania history. "Root for your own team and let the other club alone," warned the *Journal.* "If somebody says something you don't like, laugh it off, don't go back at him, it's all in the game. If Pottsville wins, hold your joy within bounds and don't rub it into the other fellow. Let's win or lose like gentlemen."

The bad blood off the field continued right up until kickoff. Led by the Third Brigade Band, Pottsville fans who traveled with the team traditionally marched from the train station to the visitor's field. This time they were told that parading on the grounds had been banned and that the only available tickets for the game were standing room only. In the local coverage of the game by the Frankford media, every poor play by Pottsville—every interception, every defensive letdown, and every half-hearted block on offense—was reported to be the fault of Yellow Jacket turncoat, All-Pro Herb Stein.

By the end of the game, however, there would be more than enough blame to go around on the Pottsville sideline.

Because his team had played nearly twice as many games as the lads from up north, Chamberlin believed that Frankford could wear down the less conditioned Maroons. First, though, they would have to withstand the hellacious onslaught during the game's initial 30 minutes that had become Pottsville's trademark. Immediately, Latone drove the Maroons to the 7-yard line only to have an incomplete pass in the end zone turn the ball over to Frankford. Pottsville's next scoring chance began on its own 20-yard line. With trademark efficiency and brutality, the Maroons blasted their way 79½ yards straight down the field. Local accounts said it was one of "the most spectacular and most savage attacks ever witnessed on the stadium field. They reeled off first down after first down. Flanagan, Ernst, Wentz, and Latone seemed unstoppable. And it did not seem possible to halt that raging Pottsville backfield."

Near the goal line, however, the Maroons' main offensive weapon—balanced and unpredictable playcalling—was simplified into a pure battle of power by the shortened field. After a penalty and two unsuccessful line plunges, Latone bobbled a screen pass on fourth down at the goal line, and the first half ended 3-0 in Frankford's favor. "That great thrust wrecked the invaders," wrote one Philadelphia paper. "The Maroons came on [in the second half] as if they had shot their bolt. Chamberlin ordered his men to play the invaders off their feet in the second half."

The Yellow Jackets followed his instructions to the letter. This was the first time a team had the man power and fortitude to stand up to the physical fury of the Maroons. Behman, for starters, was renowned as a "5x5" man, meaning he appeared to be five feet tall and five feet wide. A shocked Maroons team reacted like a schoolyard bully who gets punched in the nose by his normally docile victim—they cowered. Frankford's bend-but-don't-break defense wore out Latone and badly frustrated Ernst, and on offense the home team hammered away at the Steins until they too cracked and surrendered.

"Fans saw a Pottsville team completely swept from the field, wilt, and fall before the onslaught of captain Russ Behman's eleven," wrote *The Philadelphia Inquirer.* "They saw a relentless Hornet, carry on in such marvelous fashion that Pottsville never loomed as a winner and in only three instances during the entire fuss even threatened to score."

When Pottsville packed its defensive line, the Yellow Jackets took a page out of Rauch's playbook and began heaving forwards over their heads. Drained, confused, or just plain intimidated, the Maroons couldn't keep up. Frankford scored two touchdowns in the second half, the first on an 18-yard forward, and Behman added his second field goal to make it 20-0. Near the end of the game Ernst sent a long forward to a wide-open Berry, only to watch as the ball missed his hands, and a sure, face-saving six points, by mere inches. For the first time all season the Maroons had been soundly defeated. There were no excuses or alibis for Pottsville and until the two teams met again 15 days later inside Minersville Park, Maroons supporters would have little to say to their hated rivals. "And so today Pottsville's hopes are blasted hopes," wrote a saddened Philadelphia columnist. "Her dreams of victory are now mere figments of the memory and Frankford assumes undisputed possession of third place in the National League of Professional Football Players."

CHAPTER 14

SHADOWS
OF
DEFEAT

IN CONTRAST TO THE shocking loss to Providence in the
second week of the season, this time the Maroons had built
up enough good will and quality wins to sustain them after
the poor showing at Frankford. An NFL neophyte, Pottsville was
a quick study in the machinations of professional sports. The
season was not over. Not yet, anyway. If the Maroons could
regroup and survive their remaining games—starting with a
visit from the Rochester Jeffersons in less than 24 hours—they
still had an outside shot at the glory that seemed certain just a
week earlier. In this regard, Royle's own insatiable appetite for
profits provided the Maroons' greatest hope. Frankford was
scheduled to play a sadistic four games in the next nine days.
The Maroons were to play three, including a Thanksgiving Day
game against the Green Bay Packers. If Pottsville won out and
the Yellow Jackets lost even one of their remaining games, their

rematch on November 29 would likely catapult the winner to an NFL title and beyond.

Dick Rauch reacted to the loss in his typical sanguine fashion. Every football season he had ever been a part of unfolded the same way as this one, with peaks and valleys. Rauch's response was that the players could learn more from this loss than from all their other games combined. For starters, he wanted his men to realize that while a football field was 100 yards long, the game in Frankford had been won and lost in the 10 yards of turf closest to the end zone. As dominant as they had been all season, the Maroons defense learned something new by seeing firsthand the tremendous momentum swing created by a goal-line stand.

At the same time, Ernst was finally beginning to realize that he had to tone down his careless, swashbuckling style in the shadow of the goal line, where turnovers were deadly. The last thing that stuck with Rauch was how the emotional lift of Behman's two field goals far outweighed the mere six points they provided. The first kick gave the Yellow Jackets an emotional edge by allowing them to lead at the half. And whatever hope the Maroons had of a miracle comeback late in the game were unceremoniously squashed by Behman's second kick.

Sitting by himself in the team's private Pullman car during the brief train ride home to Pottsville, Rauch pored over his postgame scribblings. He vowed to drive these points home with extra skull sessions inside the Armory during the final few weeks of the season. First though, he had to get his team prepared to play Rochester the next afternoon, because if the Maroons couldn't rebound with a win, there would be no need for extra skull sessions. The season would be over. In Frankford, the players had been stung by the growing notion that the Maroons were phonies, a mirage created by a scheduling quirk and weakened competition. Rauch simply reminded his team that this was their chance to prove that theory wrong. The Jeffersons hadn't played in four days. They would be fresh and rested when they took the field at Minersville Park the next afternoon, while the Maroons would be wearing uniforms still soaked in the sweat and stench of the previous day's defeat.

Physically, the Maroons had made it through the game relatively unscathed. Team trainer Eddie Gillespie did a yeoman's job on the trip home and throughout the night with rubdowns, physical therapy, and protective wraps for nearly every player. Meanwhile, the town did what it could to lift the team's spirits. A few hundred fans met the Maroons at the train station. And from the stoop of his store, Zacko preached that "the defeat should not be considered in any respect. The morale of the Maroons is what's important now. There are other days coming."

Farquhar reacted as he always did in times of stress: with poetry. "In the Shadow of the Goal Posts" ran in the next day's paper and was his way of coaxing shell-shocked fans into attending that day's game against Rochester.

While the train station rally, the storefront speeches, and Farquhar's rhymes were all thoughtful gestures, none of them proved to be necessary once Mother Striegel decided to take up the cause.

Doc's wife, Neva, was a vibrant, striking woman with short dark hair, large soft eyes, and a long slender nose that divided her heart-shaped face. Strong-willed, opinionated, and incredibly driven—but always quick to laugh—Neva ran Doc's medical practice, setting appointments, filling prescriptions, even monitoring all the bookkeeping. And it was no secret around Pottsville that Neva had become integral to the success and growth of the team. The *Journal* referred to her as "the power behind the throne on the Pottsville Maroons." And at the team banquet following the 1924 season Neva was given a solid silver cocktail set from the players, who chanted "The All-American Mother!" when she rose to accept her gift.

In Pottsville and across the country, nowhere was the explosive challenge to the status quo as noticeable as with the changing role of women. After joining the workforce during the First World War, women were now smoking their Luckies in public, sipping from flasks, voting for president, and flaunting a carefree attitude toward sex. American women weren't just letting their hair down in the 1920s—they were cutting it off, styling their tightly braided Victorian hairdos into modern bobs. They dumped their tight-fitting blouses and traded them in for short sleeves and loose, brightly colored flapper skirts. After all, it was simply impossible to dance the Charleston in a corset.

In 1920, *The New York Times* concluded that "the American woman has lifted her skirt far beyond any modest limitation." Meaning: nine whole inches above the ground. The hems continued to rise until flappers at football games could now be seen brazenly showing off their kneecaps, some even applying rouge makeup to further titillate. For Victorian-era parents and clergy, the ascending hem came to represent the insidious disintegration of values during the 1920s. So much so that after several national public awareness campaigns failed, bills were considered in Utah, Virginia, and Ohio to legislate the length and fit of women's clothing. With prohibition a complete failure, suppressing the progress and freedom of women was seen as a desperate and transparent effort by the Victorian old guard to maintain some level of control over the all-out social revolution sweeping the country.

Luckily for the Maroons this too was doomed to failure, allowing

Neva Striegel to become Doc's equal and then some. With many of the out-of-town players boarding with the Striegels, Neva had become the team's unofficial general manager, trainer, and therapist. "Mother Striegel knows more football than three-fourths of the men in Pottsville," wrote Farquhar. "Jealousies have cropped out, lads have been spoiled by hero worship; training rules have been broken by the stars. And there have been times when Dr. Striegel, the coach, and others in command could not convince a temperamental athlete the errors of his ways. Then they sent him to Mother Striegel. And after she has talked with him, if he doesn't turn in and fight like a real man, he'll never be a grade A football player."

Neva had developed a powerful Florence Nightingale hold over most of the players. And upon disembarking from Philadelphia, while Gillespie tended to the muscles, Mother Striegel went to work on the team's psyche. Her presence and perspective after the humiliating loss to Frankford immediately lightened the mood and soothed the bruised egos of the Maroons. To the discouraged she offered pats on the back and whispered encouragements. She admonished reckless or sub-par play with a single heart-stopping stare. And she challenged in a way that was so subtle and sweet that the players either didn't know, or didn't care, that they were being manipulated by her every glance.

There was no turning back now, Mother Striegel explained. After all they had been through, the town and the team were inextricably linked. The loss to their hated rival would only calcify the town's resolve, and as newly christened sons of Pottsville, the Maroons would be expected to react in a similar fashion. Exhausted and disheartened by the pummeling administered by the Yellow Jackets, the Maroons were stripped to their core and what shone through, what saved them and their season, were the coal region roots embodied by people like Neva Striegel, Tony Latone, and Frankie Racis.

After all, no self-respecting ballplayer could moan about the challenge of back-to-back games in the presence of Latone or Racis, who had started as a breaker boy at nine and often still worked a full shift in the mines before practice. When teammates bellyached about their bumps and bruises, Racis liked to say that his feet ached more from one shift tending bar than they did in all his years of football. The rest of his body parts were just as tough. Once, on a bet, Racis wore a straw derby adorned with an ad for a politician instead of a helmet. As one of eastern Penn's original iron men, he once played all 60 minutes of four pro games in a single week. "Finally I yells to the coach, 'Please, can I come out now?'" he recalled. "And he just shrugs his shoulders and says back to me, 'Nope, sorry Frankie, I just can't do it.'"

After starting out as a sandlot long shot with the Maroons, Racis had become a mainstay in the trenches, a fan favorite who now went by the nickname Champ, and one of Rauch's brightest pupils. Following his coach's instructions, Racis used the first few snaps of every game as a way to scout his opponent. "I just charge straight in there and watch what the guys across from me did," he told a reporter. "Then I figure him out and beat him the rest of the game." Late in a game, after he had turned back nearly every advance run in his direction, Racis would often stand over a flattened halfback from some fancy college and ask him, dryly, "Why don't you just go the other way?"

The original plan in Pottsville was for Racis to start for Coach Rauch on the line. In fact, Rauch wore his uniform to the first five games, but never saw a reason to take Racis out of the lineup. The next week, the coach came to the park in a suit and tie. "It was only then that I knew I had made the starting lineup," laughed Racis. Despite their lack of collegiate experience, Latone and Racis provided something every football team needed in times like these: The Unbreakable Man, a player tough (and crazy) enough to continue the attack gleefully when everyone else was begging to retreat. And with the 1925 NFL season hanging in the balance, this was the role Racis filled so admirably against Rochester.

The next afternoon, just as Mother Striegel had predicted, a throng of several thousand fans clasped hands and ventured back up Market Street to show their support for their battle-weary team. After disappearing against the physical Frankford defense, Little Walter French helped the Maroons out of their initial stupor with several spectacular gains that set up a scoring plunge for Latone. In choosing their running lanes, Pottsville's ball carriers only had to follow the path of bodies left behind by Racis's crippling downfield blocks. Clinging to a 7-6 lead in the third quarter, Ernst and Berry worked their trademark screen pass several times, moving the Maroons the length of the field for an insurance touchdown. And in the fourth quarter, when the Jeffersons began moving the ball through the air, the Maroons hung on like a dazed boxer praying for the final bell, defending their end zone and gutting out a 14-6 win.

Great teams win even when they don't play their best. Inspired by Neva Striegel and Racis, the Maroons' gallant effort was rewarded the following weekend when news came that Frankford had dropped not one but two games, creating a logjam at the top of the NFL standings among Frankford, Pottsville, Detroit, Chicago, and New York.

Just like that, the Maroons were back in the running. A week later, a rejuvenated Pottsville crushed the defending NFL champion Cleveland Bulldogs, 24-6. With their spirits boosted, the

Maroons had returned to their old wild, reckless selves, romping through another laugher while inventing new and even more fantastic ways to torture opponents every time they touched the ball. Against Cleveland, Ernst returned a punt 55 yards for a score. Latone picked off a pass and thundered 45 yards for a touchdown. And Berry bombed a 29-yard field goal to make it 17-0 before the Bulldogs had even blinked.

After a long run by Latone in the third quarter, Cleveland end Ed Loucks was down in his stance across from Berry when he whispered, *Just where in the Sam Hill did that halfback come from anyway?* "Went to Yale," Berry said while managing to keep a straight face. "You don't remember him?" Loucks, the poor guy, did not. And he spent the rest of the game wondering if he had taken one too many blows to the noggin from the Howitzer. Berry waited to confess Latone's real background until after the game when both teams were relaxing and rehydrating inside the Phoenix. Loucks was a good sport about it. And the next morning's paper reported that "it was the unanimous opinion of the Indian team that the Maroons were suffering from what is commonly known as a 'Bad Day' when they suffered defeat in Frankford … and they feel the tables will be reversed on November 29 here in Pottsville."

Whether that was just the ale talking, the Maroons would know soon enough. If their rematch with the Yellow Jackets was going to have any significance, they had one more hurdle to clear, a Thanksgiving date with Curly Lambeau's Green Bay Packers. A native of Green Bay, Lambeau was a local prep legend who played fullback for Notre Dame until an illness forced him to leave school and return home. While working in the Indian Packing Company he founded the Packers football team, becoming a pillar of the pro game as well as the father of the forward pass in the NFL.

Besides the obvious importance regarding the final NFL stand-ings, the Maroons' next game was also something of a summit between the NFL's two smallest towns. Pottsville and Green Bay had begun to mirror each other in their mutual attempt to field profitable and competitive pro football franchises in a league that no longer really wanted them in their ranks. "The Packers are known as 'The pro team with the college spirit,' " was the not-so-subtle reminder *The Republican* sent to its readers on the morning of the game. "Community support enables the Packer management to keep its head up with the big fellas. Green Bay takes its Packers as Princeton does its Tigers, and from September until December the natives do little else but talk, eat, and sleep football. Stockholders in the team include nearly every football fan in the city."

Not to be outdone, the Pottsville fans were eager to send a message back to their counterparts in Wisconsin. The day before the game, all of Eastern Pennsylvania had been blanketed by an early winter blizzard. Leaving nothing to chance, a brigade of Maroons fans draped in raccoon coats and miner's dungarees motored, hiked, and sledded to the field at 1 a.m., where, under the silver light of the moon, they spent the better part of the night shoveling off the field in sub-freezing temperatures.

The next day, with clean footing underneath, Berry put on a one-man show so grand, powerful, and shocking it nearly straightened Lambeau's corkscrew locks. In the first half, Berry scored all 24 of the Maroons' points. He caught one touchdown pass for 27 yards and hauled in another aerial from the 20. In between, a great defensive effort by Osborn forced a Green Bay punt. It was blocked, and Berry ran it in for yet another score and his third extra point. Later, he added a 28-yard field goal. In 30 minutes of play, Berry had all but wrapped up the league's scoring title while allowing Rauch the luxury of resting his starters for the Frankford game. "Berry puts such fire and spirit into his playing, such tremendous effort that he has been an inspiration for his fellows," Striegel told a reporter when asked to describe his young captain. "When they see Charlie in there playing more recklessly than he ever did before in his life, the other boys will tear loose too."

Latone had always led by his silent, indomitable spirit. That left a void in the vocal leadership of the team, one that Berry had filled admirably. From a strategic standpoint, Berry's arrival just before the Canton game had been serendipitous. Beyond his enormous talent, Berry had shown a unique ability to get the two factions of the team—the college stars and the local warriors—to work together. "Charlie gets half his salary for playing and the other half for keeping the boys pepped up," *The Republican* noted. "And seeing how he has performed on the grid we know he is earning his salary in both departments."

Under Berry's guidance and by his example, the Maroons had grown from a collection of individual talent in to an actual, living, breathing team. "Newspapermen expressed the opinion that there was as much college spirit in the play of the [Maroons] as in any college they had ever seen," said another Pottsville reporter. "But they beat college playing because every man was a star, because they were better trained, had better football sense, and played with the same spirit to win—was the way they sized up [the Maroons]."

Before the Maroons, the concept of "team" had been largely missing from professional football. In its first 20 years, pro ball had amounted to little more than a collection of mercenaries playing a brutal and boring form of the sport. Teammates often met for the first time at the train station or on the field before a game, shaking hands as they pulled on the same-colored jerseys. For the longest time there had been no visible chemistry, the kind of mystic element that elevates a group of players far beyond just the sum of its parts. The college game remained vastly more popular because it exuded a certain competitive élan: the notion that these were not merely teammates but brothers in arms. Until Pottsville came along, until the vision and cash of Doc Striegel met up with the mind of Rauch, the heart of Latone, and the leadership of Berry, no team had been able to replicate this on the pro level; to take the spirit, skill, and personalities of the "bought in" college players and blend them seamlessly with the work ethic, muscle, and vigor of the gritty coal region crew who shared the same locker room.

It was a transcendent shift, not just for the Maroons but in pro football as a whole. The NFL had been doomed because, in the public's eye, the concept of playing football for money lacked a sense of honor. "A man's a man all the time—whether he's a professional football player or not," scoffed Striegel. "And mere playing for money is not the main motive in his endeavor."

Doc's team was now shattering the myths that plagued the sport and getting people to rethink their position on the nobility of professional football. "Why shouldn't Red Grange capitalize on his name?" John O'Hara wrote, in a front page *Journal* column, defending The Ghost against a snipe from, of all people, a famed polo player. "If I were Grange and I could make a million dollars on my reputation, I'd make that million. True, he is not supposed to go to college to play football, but he learned more about football and how to play it well than many law students learn about law and how to practice it. Why, then, shouldn't Red establish a fortune when he can? It is all very well for Louis Stoddard to be sickened by the tales of fat offers made to Grange, but

Mr. Stoddard, unless I am mistaken, has enough money to play polo and a polo pony is worth almost as much as a ton of coal [in strike times]."

Against Green Bay, it was Berry who was worth his weight in coal. During performances like this one, after each score Ernst liked to march the ball back to his own sideline and place it on the ground in front of Berry as if he were offering up a gift to the football gods. Playing to the crowd, the Maroons quarterback would then throw his chest back and in his most regal tone shout, "Kindly kick off, sir." The Pottsville crowd roared with delight, devouring Ernst's act, as well as the 31-0 whitewash of the Packers, as if it were the first serving of gravy-soaked Thanksgiving bird.

There was, after all, plenty to be grateful for. The Maroons were once again doing things that weren't supposed to be possible in pro football. Even with Russ Stein out nursing a bad leg, Racis, Osborn, and Hathaway manhandled the meaty Green Bay line. Flanagan and Latone ran through the Packers defense. And in frosty weather conditions, Ernst had completed an amazing 62% of his passes while Pottsville's much improved secondary picked off the Packers (and the Father of the Forward Pass itself) an astonishing five times. "To clap the climax [of the rebound from the Frankford loss] the Maroons made the best passing team, Green Bay, look silly Thanksgiving afternoon," wrote *The Republican*.

Meanwhile, the Chicago Cardinals (8-1-1) still held a slight lead in the standings based on percentage points. But the 8-2 Maroons, who had outscored all comers 200-38, had answered every question, passed every test, and, most important, regained the swagger they had lost down in Frankford.

"In the defeat of the Packers, the home fans were favored with

the finest game the Maroons have offered this season," added
The Republican. "They were a sweet-moving machine that
mowed down all in its path and kept up a steady march up and
down the field. It appears that the defeat at the hands of
Frankford has done a lot of good for the locals, they came back
the next day with a victory, then met Cleveland's measure last
week and then they gave the Green Bay boys a trouncing that is
about the worst they have received this year. No team in the
league could have defeated them yesterday afternoon.

"And if they play the same brand of football a few days hence,
the sting is going to be removed from the Yellow Jackets."

CHAPTER 15

THE PERFECT MACHINE

THE VISITORS' SIDE OF MINERSVILLE PARK was bordered by a small western tributary of the Schuylkill River. And the soft grassy banks of the river were lined by huge pine trees with thick, bare lower limbs that extended far out over the bubbling brown waters. Nearly two hours before kickoff of the Pottsville-Frankford rematch, these trees were already filled with hundreds of fans perched precariously over the water for a glimpse inside the sold-out stadium. The scene looked like something out of a Brothers Grimm fairy tale. Under a cloudless sky and a radiant orange sun that warmed the light winter breeze, Maroons fans sat a dozen or more to a limb, pocket-to-pocket, with their feet playfully dangling above the water. Occasionally when the weight became more than the lower branches could bear, the limbs would crack, splinter, and break off with a thunderous crash, sending the occupants splashing into the brisk waters below.

When this happened, the fans would simply drag themselves to the riverbank, wring out their clothes as best they could, and scamper back up into the tree like derby-clad, oversized squirrels. The Frankford rematch was shaping up to be the biggest sporting event in Pottsville's history, and so it was going to take more than a pair of soggy trousers to keep Maroons fans from witnessing history in the making.

The buildup had been rapidly escalating since the Maroons' impressive Thanksgiving Day victory over Green Bay. Now, every lapel in town carried a Maroons ribbon or button, the windshield of every auto and the display window of every store-front was draped in purple bunting. The Hotel Allan was filled to capacity with sportswriters from all over the East Coast and VIPs like Curly Lambeau and Tim Mara, the owner of the New York Giants. The Reading Railroad company had to add 11 extra cars to a train from Philadelphia. Football fans came from as far west as Cleveland, as far north as Rochester, east from Boston, and south from Washington, D.C. Prayers for the Maroons were being offered in every church, in every language, in every denomination—and in every publication in town. "Pottsville is going to win tomorrow," stated *The Republican.* "Every Maroon player honestly believes that. The fans believe it. In fact, everybody in Frankford believes it, too. For some unknown reason, Frankford has a fear in its heart. From the lair of the Yellow Jackets comes the report that Frankford is licked before they step on the field."

At 8 a.m., when Schneider's drug store put several thousand remaining standing-room-only tickets up for sale, they were wiped out in less than an hour. All records for advance ticket sales had been shattered. By 11, when all the available parking at the stadium was filled, the roads leading to Minersville Park became clogged for miles in every direction with abandoned cars as fans simply shut them off, placed a sprag behind the back wheels, and began walking to the field. By 12:30 p.m. more than 11,000 fans had assembled in and around the park. The several hundred visitors from Philadelphia were astounded by the support, in light of the current miners' strike. But the truth of the matter was that with no work and little to do, the Maroons were all Pottsville had going for it. There were so many fans in the foothills surrounding the field that it looked like a complete upper deck had been added to Minersville Park. Closer to the field, warmups had to be halted so security could squeeze the burgeoning sea of supporters back behind the white chalk lines.

Although it was a bright and clear day, *The Republican* reported that many fans "brought big blankets in which to wrap themselves [while] others wrapped themselves around the contents of mysterious bottles guaranteed to produce internal warmth." It was "the greatest throng that has ever witnessed a football fray in the zone of the black diamond. And the noise, at times, was well nigh deafening."

As the visiting team, the Yellow Jackets were afforded the first warmup period and they bolted onto the field in brand-new gold-colored jerseys. Right away it was clear that Royle had padded his roster with new players, including former Lafayette lineman Bull Lowe and Penn assistant coach Clark Craig.

"They certainly looked like champions," recalled one fan. By contrast, the Maroons sat on benches in their dank locker room padding their tattered, torn, and dusty jerseys and restitched canvas pants with copies of the *Ladies' Home Journal* that had been donated by fans. New uniforms had been offered to the Maroons several times during the season but Berry and the others would not allow such a gratuitous expenditure in light of the debt Doc Striegel was carrying on their behalf. Latone had no choice. With his now familiar No. 6 shredded by desperate, frustrated tacklers, he was forced to switch to No. 22 for the second Frankford game. According to people who visited the locker room, many of the players now silently wished they had taken Doc up on his offer for new duds. Looking like ragamuffins, it took all of the Maroons' energy to divert their envious gaze.

As they laced up their cleats, limbered up and engaged in nervous, idle pregame chitchat, the Maroons were visited by a steady stream of dignitaries from the town.

By the end of the 1925 season, the 20 NFL teams had fallen into two natural geographic divisions—the Midwest and the East—and because of the way the standings had shaken out, the winner of Pottsville vs. Frankford II would likely capture the mythical Eastern Division. As the season wound down and the best teams separated themselves in the standings, Striegel and other owners prepared for the frenzy of barnstorming that typically swept through the league this time of year. Set up at a moment's notice, in the early days of the NFL these season-ending marquee matchups were usually the only way for franchises to get into the black before closing up shop for the winter. With the Chicago Cardinals holding steady at 8-1-1, an unofficial NFL title game between the Cards and the best team from the East seemed likely.

With the capacity crowd outside chanting for the Maroons and rattling the rafters of the locker room with their stomping feet, Rauch gathered his men near the doorway to the field. With two words he gave them all the motivation any football player could ever require.

Notre. Dame.

The rumors had been true. Promoters in Philadelphia were organizing the first-ever pro versus college football World

Championship game, between the 1925 NFL champion and the Four Horsemen and Seven Mules of the 1924 Notre Dame Fighting Irish, the undefeated national college champions and the greatest football team the sport had ever known. The game was to be played in two weeks, on December 12, inside immaculate Shibe Park, home of Charlie Berry's Philadelphia Athletics.

Rauch didn't need to explain the significance of this to his players—they knew. The payday would be enormous—a half year's wages, maybe. With that kind of money they could travel the world, put a down payment on a house, or even get rich in the stock market like everyone else. The crowd at Shibe Park would make the gatherings at Minersville look like a church picnic. The media attention would be national, perhaps even worldwide. The competition from the Four Horsemen would be like nothing they had ever faced. More than anything, though, the game was a shot at what everyone in the Twenties openly craved—the chance to make their mark on history.

The players had suspected something special was in the works based on Rauch's behavior during the past week. Concerned that Royle would send spies into town to steal the Maroons' secrets, Rauch had moved practice to a clandestine spot behind the massive brick Silk Mill on the northwest side of town. It was the kind of field only a Pottsville native would know about and word was passed around town to ring Doc Striegel immediately if strangers inquired about the team's whereabouts. When the local papers got wind of the switch, they had a field day reporting on the kind of tabloid-style espionage and intrigue no one ever thought would find its way to little old Pottsville.

"Frankford had spies in our town all week," *The Republican* reported. "According to Dick Rauch they did not get enough real dope to justify the expenditure of their carfare. It is said the

Yellow Jackets had a hot time of it one afternoon looking for the Maroons. They had traced them to the Armory but the big coal bus pulled out, slipped from view, and the scouts had lost the trail. They fled around town like wild men looking for our boys but they didn't know where they got to from there."

Hidden behind the block-long brick mill and set between the town cemetery and an entrance to the coal mine, Rauch spent the week introducing more new blocking schemes, some deeper pass plays, and a complete review of his pass defense philosophies in preparation for the Yellow Jackets. On their coffee breaks, hundreds of seamstresses who worked inside the Silk Mill gazed out the windows of the plant, fawning over Rauch, Ernst, and the rest of the boys. The team was so well hidden from the rest of the town, though, rumors flourished that the Maroons were not practicing at all in preparation for the Frankford rematch. In fact, they were working longer, and with more intensity, than they had all year long. "Rauch has a bag full of tricks he is going to attempt to slip over the Jacket," reported *The Republican*. Rauch's biggest "secret" was his innovative approach to the nuances of the game that most other teams overlooked or simply took for granted; little things like the value of a well-organized punt return; how to block a man based on the lean of his stance; or the importance of pre-snap recognition between a run and a pass.

It was as if Rauch saw the game through a colorful kaleidoscope rather than just an ordinary pair of bifocals. Where others gazed at the woods and saw nothing but trees, Rauch had been trained to see the thousands of species of birds therein.

In 1925, defense was still largely an afterthought, especially for players like Latone, Ernst, and Flanagan who played well off the line in a "safety" roll, jumping into the fray only when needed as the last line of defense. "Every man just watched his area and took anything that came that way," Racis said. All Rauch did was drill into them the idea that they could use their God-given speed and keen awareness of offensive strategy to anticipate where the ball was going long before it got there. Anticipation. It was nothing particularly fancy or complicated. It was a simple, basic adjustment of perspective. This new approach had already garnered five interceptions against Green Bay. And the coach was expecting even bigger things against the Jackets. At Royle's bidding, Frankford had played four games in the last nine days. (Pottsville, by contrast, had played three in eight days.) And Rauch anticipated that they would be far too worn out physically for anything but a stream of aerials on offense.

After the Maroons' practice on Friday, Rauch called the team back to the Armory one last time. The players thought their overly nervous coach was going to run them through more sets of drills on the gym floor. Instead, he sat them in a classroom, opened the playbook, and invited their input, or criticism, on anything relating to the team, the strategy, or the plays— all without reprisal. After a long, nervous silence, *The Republican* reported that a "lively discussion" ensued. Rauch had always been a free thinker and an innovator but this was radical, even for him. "Each play was gone over," said one witness. "[Each play was] traced from the beginning, signals to it were called and each part of it was examined in an effort to find any flaws. The advice of the players was asked on each of the various plays. Many good suggestions were made and just as soon as they were made they were employed, and if found practical by the group they were incorporated in the Pottsville system. The result was that Dick got a lot of good things and the boys did too."

Afterward, back at the frat room, the team was still floored by the gesture. Soliciting the input of the team was unheard of in the normally autocratic relationship between coach and player. They were moved, collectively, by the idea that a genius like Rauch would treat them as equals, like the true professional colleagues they had become. Of course, that had been Rauch's intention all along; to get the Maroons to see just how far they had come since September. They were pros now, true craftsmen in the field of football—and he respected them.

"Harmony now reigns supreme with the Pottsville Maroons," wrote *The Republican.*

After Rauch's last-second announcement regarding Notre Dame and a chance at a World Championship, all of the coach's methods and mental manipulations became clear to the team as they prepared to storm the field against Frankford. Yes, it had been a wild, unpredictable, and improbable season—and it was likely to get crazier the longer Doc could keep them playing. But by banding together, in a single season they had made it to the pinnacle of their profession.

An NFL title? A shot at Notre Dame? A World Championship? Immortality?

If the Maroons could beat the Yellow Jackets, every possible accolade awaited them. The players never doubted that they were talented and tough enough to earn football's highest honors. Inside the Armory on Friday night, Rauch had instilled something different in them. Something beyond confidence. They were good enough to win it all, but, more important, they were worthy of the football world's respect, as well.

Rauch had been driving that point home to his team for the last five months. And as he stepped aside and the Maroons sprang onto the field, the coach could finally be certain that he had convinced them of their potential for greatness.

The Frankford Yellow Jackets, as it turned out, were much easier to persuade.

After security pushed the crowds back behind the chalk lines and volunteers filled in the final wet spots on the field with wheelbarrows full of sawdust, Hoot Flanagan took the opening kickoff and raced 30 yards all the way to the Pottsville 40. Six plays later—including a fourth-and-one conversion by The Howitzer, as well as a 20-yard forward from Ernst to Berry—Latone slammed in from the 1 for the first score of the game. After getting shut out in Frankford, this score came with such little effort that it left the Maroons unsettled, as if they were being set up for something. It was just too easy.

"The Maroons line began in splendid fashion," explained one stunned Philadelphia reporter. "And made the famed Frankford forwards look like a band of badly frightened schoolboys. That Pottsville backfield worked like a charm. It is doubtful if a greater collection of grid stars were ever assembled into a team that had such wonderful driving power and perfect team work."

With Racis, Hathaway, Osborn, and the Steins dominating the trenches from the start, Pottsville turned Frankford back on its first possession. When the Maroons got the ball back, according to local accounts, Latone, "the burly, broad-shouldered son of the coal region, staged one of the most savage assaults this season," mercilessly mule-kicking himself into Yellow Jacket tacklers as the Maroons marched right back down to the 10-yard line. Gordon Mackay, a Philadelphia columnist, described the lopsided physical battle between Latone and the Frankford tacklers as being akin to a "quarrel between a tabby of the house and the maddened lion of the jungle, a brawl between a peashooter and a Big Bertha."

On fourth-and-3, with the lessons of the first Frankford loss still fresh in his mind, rather than predictably blasting away with The Howitzer, Rauch elected to send in Berry for a placement kick. The crowd groaned, but the Pottsville captain punched it over the crossbar with little effort and the Maroons were awarded what seemed like an insignificant three points. Rauch's decision, though, allowed his team to maintain the momentum and confidence of their fast start.

The Maroons would need every bit of it. On his next carry, after crashing into a blockade of bodies at the line of scrimmage, Latone went limp and collapsed helplessly into the mud. When the Frankford defense had finally emptied the pile, a hunched-over Latone staggered to the sideline, clutching the mangled remains of his left elbow as if he were afraid pieces of the joint would fall off and be lost in the mud.

Latone had been knocked loopy before. This was different. He was hurt. He was writhing in pain and unable to support his own weight. To his fans and teammates alike this was unfathomable and unsettling; it was like watching Jack Dempsey's knee go wobbly or a curveball causing Babe Ruth to duck out of the batter's box. Hoot Flanagan was seen getting sick on the sideline. The once raucous crowd inside Minersville Park grew still as church as the initial reports from the sideline swept through the crowd: it was a broken arm. The Howitzer's done, people whispered to one another. He's gone for the game, done for the season. And so are we.

Sensing the same thing, the Yellow Jackets began driving for a score on their next possession. Flanagan recovered quickly and took Latone's place on defense. With his back to the goal post, he tried to concentrate on all the things Rauch had drilled into him about pass defense rather than the gruesome sight of Latone's crooked elbow. The next snap went to Yellow Jackets halfback

Ralph "Two-Bits" Homan, who backpedaled and shifted the ball into his right hand. Flanagan saw this and when he glanced to his right and saw Bob Fitzke running a sideline pass pattern, he sprang into action, leaping in front the Yellow Jackets' receiver at the 10-yard line. The silenced crowd rose to its feet in one sudden and massive movement that seemed to levitate the entire structure out of the mud.

Using arms that the colorful and loquacious Mackay described as being "nine feet long," Flanagan "swept the oval into his arms a yard from the outer boundary and away he sped. He swept past one tackler, eluded another and there was the open country, a touchdown 90 yards dead ahead. Behind him thundered a pack of infuriated and outwitted Philadelphians. Flanagan, cautious and fleet, shifted the ball in front of him and then started to turn on the juice.

"He gathered speed and momentum with every leap of his fugitive feet," Mackay continued, breathlessly, "and while Fitzke was tearing after him like a demon and seemed at times about to whittle down the distance and bag his quarry, Flanagan, the former Pittsburgh nabob, kept ahead of him and went over the goal line for a great, a brilliant, a spectacular sprint after his deed of daring."

Flanagan's great-brilliant-spectacular 90-yard touchdown return gave the Maroons a 16-0 lead at the half. Back inside their locker room, Doc reconfirmed his diagnosis of Latone's shattered elbow. Rauch knew that without Latone he couldn't run out a 16-point lead—not against the Yellow Jackets—and so in a stunning and brilliant shift, the Maroons would seamlessly switch to a passing attack in the second half. The stage was set for Ernst and he responded "as cool as a cake of ice in the Polar Sea" said *The Republican*. The Maroons quarterback completed his first seven passes, racing the Maroons down the field, before elegantly faking a pass then handing the ball off to The Councilman, fullback Barney Wentz, who rolled in from the 1.

Predictably, the Yellow Jackets went back to the air and the result was nearly the same. Flanagan picked off another pass, this time racing 45 yards for a score. Midway through the third quarter it was Pottsville 28, Frankford 0. "Four minutes after the opening whistle tooted, Frankford was beaten," wrote Mackay. "Twenty minutes later she was routed, a half hour afterward she was butchered and massacred."

Hoot's first interception return had caused pandemonium in and around the stadium. After his second, witnesses recalled hearing the odd roar of "laughter." It was not a gleeful chuckle in support of the Maroons, it was, in fact, the worst of all taunts— *your team is so bad it's funny*—aimed directly at the red-faced Shep Royle. Seated on the sideline on one of the extra wood benches borrowed from pool parlors to accommodate the crowd of VIPs attending the game, Royle was left to fume in monk-like silence. In the most important game of the year, his Yellow Jackets were being humiliated by the very team of ignorant coal crackers he had been mocking since the day Carr permitted them entrance to his NFL. Someone would have to pay, that much was certain. And the first person Royle went after was his own captain Russ Behman, who would be suspended after the game for "indifferent play."

By mutual agreement before kick off among Striegel, Royle, and the Notre Dame promoters, the winner of this contest was going to take on the Four Horsemen in the Game of the Century. It was clear now that it would be the Maroons—and not the Yellow Jackets—who would battle for unmatched glory and untold gate receipts in Shibe Park, right in Royle's backyard.

There could be no greater indignity for Royle.

Or so he thought.

By the end of the third quarter, the Yellow Jackets had been so bullied and battered that one of their gun-shy players picked up a loose ball and began running the wrong way. It wasn't until he noticed the crowd howling at his mistake, and Frankie Racis and Flanagan running alongside him like an escort, that the poor fellow tried to reverse course. When he did, Racis, who had lost five times in a row to the Yellow Jackets, picked him up by his waistband and dumped him on his head out of bounds. "The longer the game progressed, the quicker the scores came," concluded *The Republican*. "The crowd was in a frenzy and the visitors were simply bewildered."

Early in the day, Latone had drawn and quartered Royle's toughest men. Then Flanagan and the Maroons' passing defense picked off six of the Yellow Jackets' passes and batted down countless others. Finally, Royle was forced to sit and watch and grind his teeth down to the nerve endings as Ernst chewed up what remained of his team in an obvious effort to run up the score. "Ernst threw touchdowns all the rest of the afternoon," wrote Mackay, "great hurls that carved their way through the air for twenty, thirty, sometimes forty yards, always to nestle in the arms of some recipient who raced over the remaining chalk marks for a touchdown." In the fourth quarter, with the Yellow Jackets barely able to offer the slightest interference, Ernst lofted touchdown passes of 30, 32, and 45 yards.

Against teams like Canton, Cleveland, and Green Bay, the Maroons followed the canon of good sportsmanship and eased up late in the game. But this was Frankford, and Shep Royle had it coming. "The Pottsville machine was simply invincible," concluded *The Republican*. "They pulled everything known to the football world. They used the air, they smashed through the line, they ran the end, they held the Jacket for downs, smeared his offense and broke through his defense."

The Maroons went for it on fourth down, they continued to send deep passes downfield while jumping in front of every one of Homan's wobbly ducks. Even with a 21 to 4 advantage in first downs, Pottsville continued to pour it on until the final gun sounded.

The scoreboard, nearly smoking from the turnover, read 49-0.

It was among the most points ever scored in the NFL, the worst defeat in Frankford history. "When the final whistle blew ending the game there was a rush onto the field of wildly dancing, excited fans," recalled one observer. "They had seen their dreams realized of not only trouncing the Philadelphia crack team by the most decisive score professional football has ever had but of ascending to the top of the pro football world."

It took several hours for the coal crowd at Minersville Park to dissipate and trickle back into Pottsville, where the throng outside the Phoenix, just trying for one glimpse at the Maroons, was 50 men deep for most of the night. In the press box after the game, Mackay decided to top his next column with the only four words he could come up with to described the Pottsville Maroons: THE PERFECT FOOTBALL MACHINE.

The next morning, Doc laughed off an urgent call from Shep Royle suggesting a rubber match. When the phone rang again, it was the local radiologist, who said that he wasn't quite sure what this Latone was actually made of, but it certainly wasn't flesh and blood. The Howitzer's elbow wasn't broken after all. In fact, if the healing went particularly well he might even be able to play in two weeks against the Four Horsemen. The entire town let out a sigh of relief.

Striegel's phone continued to ring off the hook with congratulations, well wishes, and offers from potential opponents from around the country. The one game that intrigued him the most, however, was an invite from Chris O'Brien, owner of the now 9-1-1 Chicago Cardinals, who suggested a game in Comiskey Park later that week for what would essentially be the "World Series" of pro football. The matchup appealed to Striegel since it would circumvent the NFL's arbitrary system of awarding the championship based on an owners vote following the season—a system everyone knew favored the upstanding Cardinals instead of the Maroons and their owner who didn't have a friend in the league outside Schuylkill County. The politics of the NFL meant that playing out their regular schedule of league games (against Detroit and Providence) and hoping for a fair championship vote from the owners was simply not an option for the Maroons. They would have to win out against the best possible competition and leave the league no other choice but to crown them champions.

For that reason, Striegel agreed to the game even though the setup left his team at a grave competitive disadvantage. The game was scheduled for December 6 on Chicago's South Side, which meant the Maroons would have to be on a train in a few days, giving Rauch almost no time to prepare and nowhere near enough time for Latone's arm to heal. Doc wasn't sure how his team would respond to playing in the NFL title game without The Howitzer. But they needed to know one thing: if they were to lose in Chicago, there was no guarantee Frank Schumann, the promoter of the Notre Dame game, wouldn't dump them in favor of the Frankford Yellow Jackets for the World Championship. Because of that scenario, many in Zacko's crew were convinced that the whole idea of a Cardinals-Maroons NFL title game had been brokered behind the scenes by none other than the nefarious Shep Royle.

It didn't matter. Doc had accepted the challenge. The game was set. The contracts were signed. The Maroons would control their own destiny.

Since their fluke loss to Providence in the second week of the regular season, the Maroons had clawed their way back into the race for the 1925 NFL championship. And now, less than 24 hours after accomplishing that feat, Doc Striegel was about to call the league's bluff one more time, push his chips into the center of the table, and ask his team to do the impossible all over again.

CHAPTER 16

GIANT WALTER

DECEMBER 6, 1925, WOULD ONE DAY be considered the unofficial birthday of the NFL, but for the Pottsville Maroons it began as just another raw and bitterly cold Sunday in Chicago. Back on the East Coast, the incomparable Red Grange and his wildly popular barnstorming crew had just arrived at the Polo Grounds for a game with the New York Giants. The event would draw an astonishing 70,000 fans and serve as pro football's coronation into the Golden Age of Sports. At the same time, the 9-2 Maroons had traveled in the opposite direction to face the 9-1-1 Chicago Cardinals in what newspapers had declared to be the NFL championship game.

"Pro football seems destined for another boost forward tomorrow when the Chicago Cardinals and the Pottsville, Pa., Pros gather at Sox Park to battle it out for the national professional title," wrote the *Chicago American*. "With the exception of the storm and commotion to view Grange, the tension preceding tomorrow's combat is unprecedented in professional football history."

Although the NFL did not think to create an official title game until 1933, in the public's eye the circumstances surrounding the Pottsville-Chicago matchup—a season finale between the top two teams in the league standings—clearly established it as a championship game. Years later, in trying to rewrite history to suit its needs, the NFL would say this was just an ordinary contest—a ridiculous claim, considering the coverage and consensus at the time.

CARDINALS PLAY POTTSVILLE FOR PRO TITLE TODAY, declared the *Chicago Tribune.* "The National Professional Football league championship hangs in the balance today when the Chicago Cardinals and the Pottsville, Pa., elevens clash on the gridiron at Comiskey Park," the paper wrote. "A victory for either team carries the national title, for the Cardinals have swept over all opponents in the western half of the league while the Pottsville eleven holds the eastern crown."

As the Maroons were en route to Chicago, however, a nasty snowstorm had moved up from the Illinois plains and settled on the shores of Lake Michigan. By game time, the field inside Comiskey Park would be a windswept sheet of ice with little visibility and temperatures in the teens. It was so frigid, in fact, that a wash boiler loaded with hot coals was set up in the press box so the exposed hands of the wire service's telegraph operator would not freeze to the keys during the game. The telegraph wire had been arranged by the Hippodrome Theatre back in Pottsville so Maroons fans could follow the game play by play. Live results were a revolutionary concept, and the announcement made front-page news in Pennsylvania:

Hear How Maroons Win
WORLD'S CHAMPIONSHIP!
At The HIPP
50¢
(Get tickets at Schneider's Drug Store)

Fewer than a hundred fans had made the trip to Chicago with the team. Another couple dozen transplanted Pottsvillians met the team upon their arrival at the Cooper Carlton Hotel. (As was their ritual, Schuylkill locals Herbert and Harold Wensel drove the 30 hours on their Harley Davidson motorcycles. "If the Maroons went to Europe, we'd try and follow them," the brothers said before departing.) Everyone else was invited down to the grand domed ballroom of the Hipp, where Maroons fans could listen to the telegraphed results from Chicago announced through a megaphone. A large chart onstage showed the progress of the ball, and another board displayed downs, yards to go, time, and the players' names.

There had been genuine euphoria in Pottsville following the extermination of the Yellow Jackets, and fans could sense their team was on the verge of national acclaim. As a result, tickets for the Hipp broadcast sold out in a few hours. "It was the first time that such a stunt was tried in this community and it went over big," exclaimed *The Republican*. "How nice to be comfortably seated in a warm theatre listening to the game as it progresses while those sending it will be almost frozen!"

To test the equipment prior to the game, the Kiwanis and Rotary Clubs along with the Merchants Association, paid for telegrams sent directly to the playing field, addressed to Captain Berry. The team and the town were very impressed that Major League Baseball commissioner Kenesaw Mountain Landis had been waiting to greet Berry and French upon their arrival in

Chicago. Just before kickoff, Berry halted his pregame stretching and place-kicking warmups long enough to respond: YOUR KIND MESSAGE RECEIVED. STOP. THANKS VERY MUCH. STOP. GLAD TO KNOW YOU ARE WITH US. STOP. YOU CAN DEPEND ON ME AND THE MAROONS TO DO OUR BEST. STOP. WE ARE GOING TO WIN. STOP.

After the first evening meal on the train to Chicago, Berry had stood in the aisle, steadying himself with a giant hand on each row of seat backs, and delivered a pep talk to the boys. It was something along the lines of "We have a chance for greatness, men, and we will regret it the rest of our lives if we don't join together and seize the opportunity." Berry's timing was impeccable. Rauch needed the Maroons sharp and ready to learn while on the train, not slumped in their seats with their derbies pulled down low, tucked away in their berths or off sipping from flasks, pulling on stogies, and throwing dice in the dining car.

With Latone's elbow still fragile and several other players banged up from the Frankford series, Rauch had only run the team through two light workouts in the week leading up to the Cards game. His plan was to let them recuperate physically and then use the extended time with his captive audience on the train to install the strategy he had developed to defeat the oldest, and one of the most renowned, franchises in the league.

Founded in 1899 by Chris and Pat O'Brien, two brothers living on the South Side of Chicago, the Cardinals began as a neighborhood team playing on a sandlot in the predominantly Irish section of town. Chris O'Brien, who owned a paint store and a billiard hall, was a kindred spirit of Doc Striegel's: a grand huckster at heart and another one of the larger-than-life personalities that shaped the frontier era of the game. Hitching onto the automobile craze, O'Brien drew people to Cards games by promising free parking, and he was one of the first owners to distribute game programs with pictures. (The largest photograph was always one of himself in an ornate office, dressed in a tuxedo, with spit-shined shoes, and his thick, wavy blond hair swept neatly to one side.)

Local legend had it that when the rival Chicago Tigers began cutting into O'Brien's gate, he challenged them to a winner-take-all showdown. O'Brien's club won 6-3, and the Tigers were never heard from again. Once, when he was low on cash, O'Brien purchased used jerseys for the team on the sly from the University of Chicago. When someone pointed out that his "new" jerseys were worn down and faded to an almost maroon color, the quick-thinking O'Brien shouted back, "Why, that's not maroon, it's cardinal red!"

And thus, the Cardinals were hatched. Sort of. The team disbanded in 1906, re-formed in 1913, won the Chicago Football League title in 1917, suspended operations due to the war in 1918, reorganized in 1919, and in 1920 promised to pay the $100 entry fee in order to join the NFL.

In 1921, O'Brien made Northwestern's All-America halfback Paddy Driscoll the game's first "franchise" player by paying him the then-outrageous fee of $300 a game. (Three times what O'Brien had paid to join the NFL.) O'Brien knew it was actually a bargain price since Driscoll, who was lean and strong with the dexterity of a decathlete, could do the work of six players. The future Hall of Famer was a cagey field commander who could run, pass, tackle, punt, and placekick with equal skill. With quarterback Red Dunn, who was known as the "Grange of Marquette," O'Brien was certain the Cards' aerial attack would prevail against the rubes from coal country. During practice leading up to the game, Dunn completed 50-yard bombs to Driscoll with stunning regularity.

With the Cardinals in top form, the idea of witnessing a championship game in pro football greatly appealed to fans in the Windy City. "Long lines formed all day today at Spaulding's to obtain ducats," wrote the *American*. "The White Sox Park can seat over 30,000 fans and while there is no reason to believe that this number will see the game, it appears certain that a goodly share of this capacity will be filled." To accommodate the unprecedented pregame sales, the Cards announced on Friday that the gates at Comiskey would be opened 90 minutes in advance of kickoff.

Featuring a white stucco veneer with thick, arched entryways and a wooden double-decker grandstand that horseshoed around its baseball diamond, Comiskey Park was infamous for two things: as the home of the Black Sox scandal during the 1919 World Series and for the horrific stench that emanated from the nearby stockyards and slaughter houses. For football games, the home sideline ran down the third baseline so the Cardinals could seek shelter from the brutal Chicago weather inside one of the baseball dugouts.

A day before the game, O'Brien's plan to lure the Maroons to Comiskey seemed to be working to perfection. He figured if the coal crackers could somehow manage to get their covered wagons to Chicago without getting lost along the way, the Cardinals would then use a commanding victory in a much hyped "title" game as a springboard for an enormous season-ending payday against Grange and the crosstown Bears.

What O'Brien failed to realize was that the Maroons were not another collection of ratty old uniforms posing as brand-new jerseys. For starters, Doc Striegel was also negotiating with the Bears for the same finale that O'Brien craved. (In the context of the times, a championship banner in a fledgling league meant little next to the life-changing payday of a game against Grange.)

"The strangest part of the whole matter," Gordon Mackay recalled sometime later, "is how the Chicagoans hoodwinked themselves. They had never seen the Maroons in action and thought Pottsville had some sort of hick team, comprised of boys who carried straws stuck in the corners of their mouths and who had to currycomb their hair every morning to get the hayseed out."

Before a rousing send-off at the train station in Pottsville, even the self-deprecating Rauch confided that Mackay's "Perfect Football Machine" moniker might be coming true. In their current state, the Maroons were unbeatable. "We are playing good football and we've been doing it consistently since the Rochester game," said the coach. "All we need to do is play the same brand of ball and the championship is ours."

In a lengthy skull session on the train, Rauch unveiled his plan to the team. First, he wanted the Stein brothers to "spy" Driscoll throughout the game. This would take some getting used to since it was not a commonly used technique. Rauch, however, wanted the Steins to ignore everything else that was going on around them on the field and bracket Paddy like a couple of Al Capone's bodyguards. Tapping out his plan on the chalkboard, Rauch made his expectations clear. *I want you to stay so close to Driscoll that at halftime you can tell me what he ate for his pregame meal.*

In the meantime, Rauch was counting on the fact that word of Latone's legendary line-plunging skills had preceded the team to Chicago. In truth, Latone wasn't healthy enough to do anything more than act as a decoy. It was setting up to be a bittersweet trip for Tony. Seventeen years earlier, his father, Iggy, had succumbed to the very same streets of Chicago during a similar stretch of nasty winter weather. Latone was returning to the city as a star. Through his own fortitude, and the gift of football, he had extricated himself and his family from the clutches of the colliery and the death sentence his father had left for him. Latone would have liked nothing better than to close the circle for good with a triumphant performance against the Cardinals, but his arm just wasn't ready. He reacted to the disappointment in his usual fashion—by not speaking a word, turning it inward, letting it simmer into a raging broth that would be released on some poor, unsuspecting tackler at a later date.

At present, Rauch believed he could use Latone's injury to his advantage. He knew O'Brien would take them lightly—the Chicago papers were referring to his team as the "Pittsville Miners"—and his hope was that the Cards would spend their week reinforcing their interior defense in preparation for the Howitzer. He was right. News reports from Chicago indicated that "the Cardinals know all about the bone-crushing Latone and Wentz, and they have worked out a line defense which they think will hold the two powerful Pottsville backfield men." Rauch planned to counter this by using Flanagan's speed on the outside. That way, the snowy field conditions inside Comiskey might actually work in the Maroons' favor.

If nothing else, Rauch's idea of combining ice and speed would certainly provide a wild start to the game for the nearly 10,000 fans that had braved the blizzard. While this was about half the expected crowd, the idea that this many paying customers would risk hypothermia to watch pro football seemed every bit as monumental as the 70,000 Grange attracted in New York to become pro football's first great star. But lost in the grand shadow created by the Galloping Ghost's glorious ride through Manhattan was perhaps an even more vital creation to the health and growth of the league—the birth of the Maroons, the NFL's first great team.

On the first series of the game, with the Cardinals defense looking for Latone, Flanagan took off on a reverse around the right end. His legs flapping on the ice like a Charleston dance instructor, Hoot was just about to shake loose when he fumbled the frozen pigskin and Dunn recovered on the Pottsville 40. Four plays later, Driscoll twisted away from coverage and hauled in a pass from Dunn at the 12. It was the last bit of open field he would see all day. Backed up against their own goal line, the Stein brothers felt something awaken inside them. On the next play, they stuffed Cardinals fullback Bob Koehler on fourth and one, folding him in half like a cheap wallet, and the Maroons took over on downs. From that moment forward "on every play [Paddy] started there were two husky Eastern boys right on his heels or his neck and the dashing Paddy broke lose only three times during the afternoon's show," wrote the *Chicago Tribune*.

The rest of the first quarter continued like a fight between junkyard dogs; the two teams gnawed, scraped, and scratched in the crystallized mud for any advantage or angle. It was a stunning, versatile, and wildly entertaining display for fans used to the sledgehammer approach typically found in the NFL. Paid punting this was not. Flanagan hit on another reverse for 34 yards. Then the Maroons, forming a wedge behind Hathaway, partially blocked a dropkick by Driscoll. Chicago countered with a second interception by Koehler, who had just about made his way into the open field when Racis blindsided him, knocking him shin over chin and jarring the ball loose to preserve a 0-0 tie after the first 15 minutes of play.

His arm failing him miserably, the resourceful Ernst tried using his legs. On fourth down, the Bear retreated behind the line of scrimmage, snatched up the snap, then boomed a terrific punt that hit the frozen earth, bounced over Dunn's head, and traveled 67 yards, all the way to the 5-yard line, where Herb Stein was there to smother it. Driscoll tried one line plunge and then thought better of it, taking the next snap and punting the ball back to the Maroons. Ernst had seen this coming and dropped back deep enough to field the ball at the 50.

Rauch's obsession with the game's tiniest details, along with the camaraderie of the Maroons, combined for the first big play of the championship game. Punts may have been a meaningless procedural possession exchange to most everyone else at the time, but to Rauch, a man who identified birds from 100 yards away by a single variation on a lone feather, they were an unseen opportunity. Since their inception, punt returns had always been the game's toughest assignment, because they hinged on open-field blocking, a series of brutal, merciless, high-speed collisions in which 10 men sacrificed their bodies for the benefit of one. In other words, they required the commitment and teamwork not commonly found in the frontier era of pro football.

Yet when Ernst secured the ball in his lap and dug his cleats into the ground, he looked up to see a wall of teammates waiting to escort him. Inspired, and with a reckless abandon born of his passing struggles, the Bear rocketed up the left side of the field bouncing off tacklers, spinning, driving, and diving his frame to the 5-yard line. On third down, Wentz barreled in for the score, and back in Pottsville a deafening roar went up inside The Hipp.

It died just as quickly, however, when the news snapped across the telegraph that Flanagan was being assisted from the field with a limp arm. Running interference for Wentz at the goal line, he had snapped his collarbone on the grass end zone that was frozen hard as concrete.

The silence inside the Hipp said it all: The Maroons top two ball carriers were out of commission.

Rauch looked back at his bench. He had two options—neither one all that appealing. There was Walter French, the diminutive third-string back who tended to wilt in the face of such physical pursuit. Rauch's gaze moved from Little Walter and traveled down to the other end of the bench and his second choice, the team's bow-tied trainer, Eddie Gillespie, a gaunt-looking fellow with a sunken chest who had once held the Pennsylvania state high school record in the 100-yard dash. Rauch tried not to show any panic on his face, but he could hardly believe his luck. With the NFL championship on the line this was all he had left to work with: a guy who answered to "Little Walter" and a skeleton sporting a bow tie.

Rauch went with French and prayed for a miracle.

Down by seven but with the momentum clearly on their side, the Cardinals took a kickoff and marched right down the field to the Maroons' 30. Dunn then connected with Koehler at the 21, where he was stood up by a jolt from Osborn. Unglued by the injury to Hoot, Osborn continued to drive Koehler hard out of bounds and then headfirst into the Cardinals' dugout, where, had the back wall not been reinforced with concrete, he likely would have deposited the Cards fullback into the stockyards. A full-on donnybrook ensued, and when a wild-eyed Osborn was finally pulled from the melee, the Cardinals had the ball at the 6-yard line after an additional 15 yards were tacked on for unsportsmanlike conduct.

At this point, noted one observer, "the Maroons looked done for."

Dunn settled in under center, and the rest of the Cardinals took their spots with the swagger of a boxer waiting for his noodle-legged opponent to leave his corner stool.

Inside the Hipp, the standing-room-only crowd had fallen still.

Watching from a darkened wing of the theater, Fungy

Lebengood, who had not made the trip due to injury, hung his head, looking like he might become ill. Both Fungy and the fans had accepted the possibility of a defeat in Chicago.

But not like this, they thought.

The only thing that meant more to the citizens of Pottsville than their football team was the town's hard-earned reputation for standing tall under adversity. Founded by a hunter and forged by miners, the town's spirit had always been embodied by the "First Defenders"—the two companies of Pottsville soldiers who rushed in to protect Washington, D.C., at the outbreak of the Civil War. By 1925, the bronze monument to these men had been standing for almost 30 years in Garfield Square, on the way up to Minersville Park.

The crowd inside the Hipp grew silent, waiting for the telegraph to snap to life.

Not like this, they thought.

Not like this.

One by one Pottsville's defenders lined up, punching their fists into the mud just a few feet from the goal post. Said one observer, "The miners went into the fray bearing the ominous warning on their faces: 'If you want to know who's boss around here, just start something.'" On first and goal, Driscoll took the ball and shot to his right. Waiting for him there was Bucher, who put him in a bear hug and slammed him to the turf hard enough to rattle his fillings. On second down, Paddy tried again, this time on the other side of the line, where he ran right into the giant hands of Charlie Berry. Dunn attempted a forward into the end zone on third down that was angrily batted back into his face by Herb Stein. On fourth, Wentz, Osborn, Hathaway, and the Steins hammered through the wall of bodies at the line and nearly steamrolled Dunn, whose desperation pass into the end zone fell well short of the nearest receiver.

Pottsville's defenders had answered the call.

Among the packed crowd at the Hipp, "there was a howling and cheering and a tossing up of hats and even coats." On their first twelve chances from within the 12-yard line, the Cardinals managed a negative three yards from scrimmage. The Maroons had broken the Cardinals' spirit with a goal-line stand so fierce and physically overpowering that reporters noted a hearty round of applause coming from a throng of converted Cardinals fans. "Pottsville was invincible in her attack, stalwart in her defense," reported *The Philadelphia Inquirer.* "No eleven, East or West, has ripped asunder the Cardinals as did the Maroons today."

As Rauch feared, though, French's first carry was for just one yard and the Maroons were forced to punt the ball right back to the Cards. Rauch knew it was only a matter of time before Dunn and Driscoll got hot. And without a running game to chew up the clock and keep the ball out of their hands, Pottsville was far from victory. Rauch could afford to wait one more series for French to make something happen. If nothing did, he might just have to hand Little Walt's jersey over to Gillespie.

In the meantime, Dunn had grown weary of the Maroon-colored avalanche that was burying him after every snap. To avoid the rush, he tried to lob the ball over the Pottsville line on the Cardinals next series, only to have it picked off by Osborn at the Maroons' 37.

Rauch could see just how completely the Maroons were controlling the line of scrimmage on defense. Would it translate to the other side of the ball? When French was unsuccessful on yet another run to the outside, Rauch decided to find out. He called for a handoff right up the gut.

That was it. In one play Rauch would know the status of French's spine and the Maroons' entire season.

Little Walter gulped hard while settling into his three-point stance. Then he did as he was told, hitting the line right between the center and the guard with all the might his 155-pound frame could muster. Was the fear of letting his teammates down more powerful than the prospect of another neck injury?

The Maroons held their breath.

The Hipp fell still.

French disappeared into the wall of flesh and punched clear through to the other side of the interference. Emerging upright, his legs wobbling a bit from the shock of the whole thing, he nearly slipped in the snow. He quickly regained his footing and ripped off an amazing, whirling 30-yard run. French's mentality as a pinch-hitter—*Two on, two out, bottom of the ninth? Sure, Skip, send me in*—had finally kicked in. And you could tell from the bench, his body language had changed—from wallflower to man of the hour. French darted and dashed, started and stopped, turned and spun— he even buried his shoulder into a tackler or two. He zigged to the outside for 15 yards then zagged back toward the middle of the field for another 15, occasionally coming to a dead stop on his toes to let would-be tacklers slide on by.

The Maroons were positively giddy, and just as surprised as everyone else in Chicago.

Where had Giant Walter been hiding all year?

"The whole show," wrote the *Chicago Tribune*, "was centered around a slippery, cagey fellow named French. He bucked the line. He hurled passes. He caught passes. He ran the ends. He punted. He bobbed up in play after play and the yardage he gained would have made Red Grange sit up and check back in his notebook."

On his next carry, French floated with the ball toward the Maroons' bench looking like he was jogging off for a water break,

When Dr. John G. Striegel
became the owner of the
Maroons, he vowed to join
and dominate the nascent
National Football League.

To show NFL president Joe Carr that the
Maroons could deliver fans, Doc Striegel (seated
in the foreground in the black hat) and thousands
of Pottsville fans traveled to watch the team
defeat the Atlantic City Roses in 1924.

❁❖❁
Player-coach Dick Rauch
revolutionized the pro game
with his complex offenses,
his use of pregame scouting,
and his then-unique concept
of daily practicing.

Frankie Racis   Walter French

Barney Wentz   Duke Osborn

The Human Howitzer, Tony Latone: "That guy's
half Lithuanian and half nelson," recalled a fan.

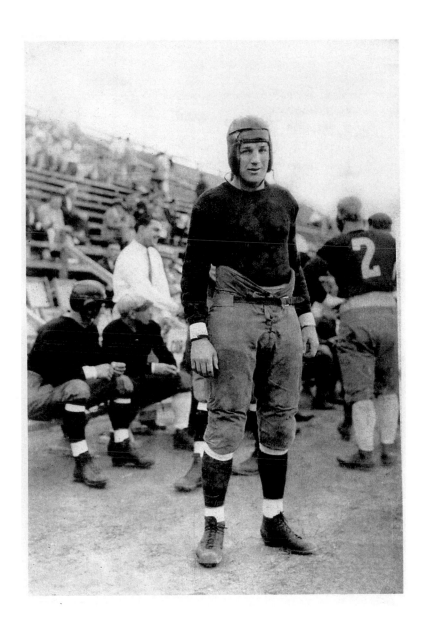

Quarterback Jack Ernst patrols
the sideline while Duke Osborn sits on the
bench in his "helmet"—a baseball cap.

❊⊰❊❊

The bard of Pottsville, sportswriter Walter Farquhar, chronicled most Maroons games with a poem; a Maroons cheer card reveals the pride Pottsville took in its team.

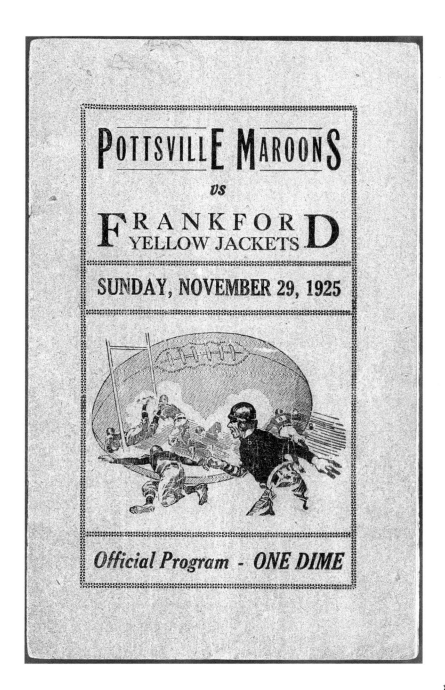

POTTSVILLE MAROONS

vs

FRANKFORD YELLOW JACKETS

SUNDAY, NOVEMBER 29, 1925

Official Program - ONE DIME

After being defeated by their Pennsylvania rival,
the Frankford Yellow Jackets, the Maroons returned
to Philadelphia two weeks later to hand the Yellow
Jackets their most humiliating loss of all time.

The Maroons' defeat of Notre Dame (and its legendary Four Horsemen) legitimized the NFL and ushered professional football into the modern era.

Sporting-goods store owner and Maroons patron Joe Zacko presented the team with gold championship pendants at the end of the 1925 season.

1925 WORLD CHAMPIONS

POTTSVILLE   MAROONS

REUNION
BANQUET

Saturday, June 29, 1963

LONGO'S   RESTAURANT
Pottsville · St. Clair Highway

By the time the Maroons reunited, in 1963, their
exploits were little more than coal country folklore.

Team captain Charlie
Berry, Joe Zacko, and
Walter Farquhar display
the bronzed version of the
shoe Berry used to kick
the winning field goal
against Notre Dame.

The official 1925 team portrait.

PHOTO

TBALL TEAM – 1925

CARDINALS, AT CHICAGO DECEMBER 6, 1925 – 21 to 7.

N MULES" OF NOTRE DAME, AT SHIBE PARK, PHILADELPHIA, PA.

AR" GAME PLAYED IN THIS COUNTRY.

NG GOODS, POTTSVILLE, PA.

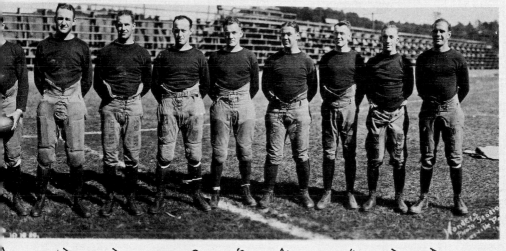

"RUSS" STEIN   "HERB" STEIN   "FUNGY" LEBENGOOD   "DENNY" HUGHES   "BARNEY" WENTZ   "EDDIE" DOYLE   WALTER FRENCH   DICK RAUCH COACH

Pottsville revisited: The Maroons reunited in the 1960s. Bottom row (left to right): Duke Osborn, Frank Bucher, Frankie Racis, Joe Zacko. Second row: Joe Hauptly (1924 Maroons), Fungy Lebengood, Russ Hathaway. Third row: Jack Ernst, George Kenneally (1926-28), Heinie Benkert (1926), and Tony Latone.

and then, just as the Cardinals committed fully to their lateral pursuit, he reversed field and bolted in the other direction. Left in a pileup by the sideline like a bottlenecked traffic jam, most of Chicago's defense could only stand and watch as French willed himself free of three tacklers before waltzing in for a 30-yard touchdown to put Pottsville ahead 14-0. "It was Mr. French, more than anyone on the Pottsville team, who wrecked the Chicago title hopes," wrote the *Tribune*.

With the first half winding down, O'Brien either benched, or tried to rest, Driscoll and the rest of his exhausted backfield. And with fresh receivers racing deep downfield, Dunn caught fire. He completed six passes in a row, moving the Cardinals 45 yards, all the way down to the 1, where Koehler plunged in from center to make it 14-7 at the half.

During the break the players tried to seek shelter from the storm wherever they could. Early in the third quarter, however, French's still-numb hands fumbled the ball back to Dunn, who quickly moved the Cardinals inside the 10. Close to the end zone, a short field squeezed Dunn's grand arm and athleticism into a space that made him an easy target for the Maroons' massive defensive line. Working either side of the center, the Steins were getting stronger by the down, devouring Driscoll and wreaking havoc on the aerial game plan. At the goal line, when Driscoll ran wide to avoid Herb—Berry or Bucher was there. And when Koehler ran right to avoid Russ—Osborn, Racis, Wentz, and Hathaway were there. It was as if the Maroons were playing defense with 15 men.

Chicago only needed a few more feet to tie up the game, but the Cardinals were turned away on four straight downs. Once again the Pottsville defenders stood tall.

The breaker boys would not be broken.

"Chicago discovered that all the brawn and brains of the football game are not located in the West," wrote the *Inquirer*. "The huskies from Pottsville gave a most entertaining exhibition of mopping up a muddy field with the limp forms of the Cardinals."

By the fourth quarter, Herb Stein was in the Cardinals' backfield so frequently that he should have changed into one of the team's striped jerseys. He was batting down almost every one of Dunn's harried pass attempts. With darkness approaching, temperatures plummeting, and time running out, Chicago had no choice but to continue trying for big advances through the air. Near midfield, Herb was finally able to get both hands on an offering from Dunn. He tucked the ball under his arm, lowered his stance, and shot 40 yards straight upfield, blasting would-be tacklers out of the way like a herd of sheep that had wandered into the path of a locomotive.

Then French hit center for six more, and Wentz took it the final three yards to make it 21-7.

Dunn continued heaving desperation passes all the way up until the final play of the game, but most of them were either batted down or intercepted by Herb Stein. The gun sounded after the final pick, and the crowd inside the Hipp exploded into the streets like an uncorked bottle of champagne, kicking off a citywide celebration that town elders said rivaled Armistice Day's.

"As far as the Chicago Cardinals are concerned," a reporter from the *Tribune* machine-gunned into his typewriter, "Pottsville, Pennsylvania, is the hub of the National Professional Football league wheel, and the sturdy football machine representing the Pennsylvania mining town is the champion of the league. In the face of a driving attack by the eastern eleven, the Cardinals curled up and were smeared in the snow on the gridiron at Comiskey park, 21-7."

As the teams shook hands and raced to the warmth of their locker rooms, a disheveled, delirious Chris O'Brien was spotted wandering about the field in a daze, bumping into people and sniffing
back tears, mumbling something about throwing away his chance
at an NFL title. "Who were these hicks from a jerkwater burg
named Pottsville who thought they could beat the great
Cardinals of the greatest city of Illinois?" asked Mackay. "Faugh!
Perish the thought! Well the Maroons went out to Chicago and
took the Cardinals just as the exalted General Grant took
Richmond. Didn't take the Maroons quite so long as it took
U.S.G. but it amounted to the same thing."

Nearby, in the dim light of a deserted press box, Walter
Farquhar cupped his hands over his mouth, warming his fingers
with his own breath, before typing what he believed to be the
final two stanzas of the Maroons epic:

> *Far in the future looking back,*
> *when the day seems dull and the prospect black,*
> *Inspiration we'll gain from the day that unfurled*
> *a champion team of the football world.*
> *For t'will always prove that there's one more fight*
> *in the little old Queen of the Anthracite.*

CHAPTER 17

OH, THE NOISE

T HE "NEWLY CROWNED FOOTBALL MONARCHS"
were a content but thoroughly battered team as their
Pullman car left Chicago for Harrisburg, Pennsylvania,
and then north to Pottsville. Hoot Flanagan's broken shoulder
was in a sling, and he was pale and somber from the pain.
Walter French had suffered a mild concussion, and his nose was
grotesquely disfigured, flattened and pushed over onto his
cheek. Tony Latone was still nursing his own injured wing, while
two other players had their hands wrapped in gauze bandages.
Everyone else seemed to be sporting a black eye, a split lip, or a
massive goose egg on his forehead. Mother Striegel did what
she could, but the players winced as a team after every bump in
the rails. And whenever someone walked past them in the aisle,
they all held their breath for fear of getting nudged slightly or
stepped on.

The day before, in New York, Red Grange, who was in the middle of a grueling 19-game, 67-day football tour, had been less than spectacular in a 19-7 win over the Giants. The Ghost had scored on a 35-yard interception return but had gained only 53 yards on 11 carries and tacked on just a meager 23 yards receiving. It hardly mattered. By some accounts, the game had attracted a crowd of nearly 70,000 and the astronomical gate receipts of $143,000 saved the Giants franchise from bankruptcy. The simple fact that professional football could attract such a massive crowd in a city that set the social agenda for the country meant that pro football had arrived.

The NFL was here to stay.

As a result, Grange had become the toast of the sporting world and was already being hailed as the savior of pro football. "It's always amusing to me when I read about how great some individual is," said a reluctant Grange. "Nobody's great in football. You're only as great as the other ten guys make you." Meanwhile, the actual NFL champions clacked home in pain and relative anonymity. The cruel irony was not lost on the Maroons, who joked that Grange was probably soaking in a hot bubble bath and sipping champagne with chorus girls in a luxury New York hotel suite.

Most of the players agreed that the frozen, unforgiving field at Comiskey had done more damage than the Cardinals. Had it been a clear, dry day, the Maroons were certain they would have won by two or even three more touchdowns. Accounts of the game seemed to agree. Banner headlines in morning newspapers from Chicago to Philadelphia declared the Maroons "CHAMPIONS" while using terms like "smeared," "humiliated," and "towered over" to describe Pottsville's dominance.

"Out of the East came a whirlwind arrayed in the Maroon of

the warriors of Pottsville, Pennsylvania, to swirl down upon the Cardinals, bury them 21 to 7 and take back eastward an unclouded title to the national professional football championship," began the story in the *Inquirer*.

Feeling good and in a particularly chatty mood, Rauch sat with the team for a spell, complimenting the defense on their play and stating that Wentz's lead blocking, or "line opening," as he put it, was the greatest he had ever seen. Though it hurt to laugh, the players couldn't help but chuckle a bit at the memory of O'Brien sobbing on the field after the game, walking around in a daze, while moaning to no one in particular that he had been a fool to challenge Pottsville.

All day on the train, as the team bumped east, rumors flew around the car: that Chicago officials had been bribed into extending the second quarter to allow the Cardinals their one face-saving score; that Driscoll might join the Maroons for the remainder of the season; that Red Grange and the Chicago Bears had offered an enormous payday to Striegel before he boarded the train; and that this game would be the first stop in a lucrative national tour for the new champs. A handful of Pottsville fans living in Chicago had boarded the train on a whim for a trip back home. Others riding on the train walked right past Philadelphia Athletics pitcher Jack Quinn as well as world-champion swimmers Johnny Weissmuller and Arne Borg just to get a glimpse into a window of the Maroons' private car.

Halfway home, after crossing the white wintry land of the Ohio plains, the train pulled into the Pittsburgh depot, where Osborn and the Steins disembarked. With ties to the area, they had agreed weeks earlier to play for the All-Pittsburgh team in an exhibition against Red Grange's All-Stars. The trio would take a crack or two at Red then jump on the train again to meet up with the Maroons in Philadelphia. Ernst also disembarked, to visit his mother.

Rolling east again, most of the team was asleep when they pulled into Harrisburg, where they had to switch tracks before heading north on a "flyer" that would speed them home toward Sharp Mountain. All day the numerous editions of the local papers were giving updates on the Maroons' travels, and by 6 p.m. the crowd waiting for the team in Pottsville had already swelled beyond the train platform and into the streets.

Football fans danced on the wooden train platform to music provided by the 75-piece Third Brigade Band and a local drum corps. Massive Maroons banners proclaiming their pro title, so big they required 10 men, snaked through the crowd. The fire and police chiefs met and mapped out an impromptu parade route, yelling to hear themselves above the roar of the crowd. Fans passed around late editions that reported the first news of a grand testimonial dinner being planned for the team on December 16 at the Hotel Allan. Merchants, shoppers, and curious visitors lined Centre and Mahantongo Streets, packed into every window, and onto every balcony and stoop, readying their flares, their team flags, and their red, white, and blue Roman candles.

Children climbed atop fire trucks, holding on to rungs of the metal ladders while craning their necks for the first glimpse of their heroes. "Here at last," Zacko wrote in his diary, "was the community spirit long promised and much needed."

Shortly after 7 p.m., the team's train crossed the Schuylkill, carved its way around a mountain pass and barreled into view. "That was the signal for an ear-splitting cheer which echoed and re-echoed throughout the station," according to one newspaper account. "The red candles and the waving flags, the drone of the fire sirens and the music of bands sent up a thrilling welcome to the returning gridiron heroes."

The sheer size of the crowd, the noise and energy, was like nothing Pottsville had ever experienced. Whatever reception Grange was treated to in New York, it could not have topped this. Shocked and embarrassed by the wild reception, some of the players tried to sneak off the train to avoid the commotion. But they were instantly caught by fans, hoisted up onto the shoulders of the crowd, and deposited on top of the fire trucks and police wagons for the parade.

"The noise, oh, the noise," remembered one fan. "It just seemed to grow and grow and build and build, and then it bounced everywhere around the town."

Yet the Maroons' reign as NFL champions would barely outlast that echo.

CHAPTER 18

FIGHT, FIGHT, ANTHRACITE!

THE LAST WISP OF ROMAN CANDLE smoke had barely cleared Centre Street when the phone rang early on Tuesday morning inside Doc Striegel's office. On the other end of the line was Shep Royle.

The Yellow Jackets' embarrassing loss to Pottsville had been hard enough to stomach, but apparently losing out on what was expected to be a massive payday at a packed Shibe Park, well, that had been driving Royle half-mad. After the 49-0 whitewashing, Royle had proposed a decisive third game between the two teams, which Doc eventually turned down. And since then Royle had been cooking up a scheme to punish Pottsville—something the NFL power structure back in Ohio seemed only too eager to support.

Over the phone, Royle was short and to the point as he laid out his position: Each NFL team has a designated "home territory" protected by the laws of the NFL. Shibe Park is within my protected territory. Therefore, if you go ahead with plans to play Notre Dame, I will file a formal protest with the NFL, and you will be suspended from the league. I have already received two telegrams from the league supporting my position and prohibiting the game. (Royle had gone so far as to schedule a last-second game with Cleveland on the same day just to bolster his claim.)

Striegel remained as calm as he could and asked Royle for a meeting in Philadelphia later that day. Royle agreed, and the two parties hung up amicably. Then Doc called the NFL offices in Columbus and demanded to speak to Joe Carr.

Why now, he wanted to know, waiting for the call to be put through.

Why was this 20-mile territory rule, something the league had never even bothered to put in writing, suddenly being enforced? And how could it possibly be taken seriously with the Cardinals and the Bears occupying the same city?

Doc had his suspicions. For starters, Notre Dame's quarterback, Harry Stuhldreher, had jumped his contract with the NFL's Providence Steam Roller and was therefore considered an outlaw pending a league investigation. (After one game with the Steam Roller, Stuhldreher asked for a substantial raise. When he was turned down, he jumped to an independent team in Connecticut, where he was allowed to name his price.) This protest by Royle would be Carr's first chance to punish Stuhldreher, albeit indirectly. But he was small potatoes compared with Striegel. Doc had been rubbing Carr and his cronies the wrong way for more than a year (starting in the summer of 1924, when he marginalized the president's authority by luring players intended for Cleveland to Pottsville). That injunction had been thrown out of court by a Schuylkill County judge.

Striegel's comeuppance was then supposed to take place all throughout the 1925 NFL season. But Carr and the rest of the NFL hadn't done their homework. Pottsville wasn't some small, disorganized semipro team. They had won the rugged Anthracite League in 1924. By the time Pottsville joined the NFL, they were loaded with talent, and before the rest of the league knew what had hit it, the Maroons had shot to the top of the NFL standings in their very first season. This only served to further vex the original owners in the Midwest who had created and nurtured the young league, only to watch as the power base slipped out of their hands and toward the East Coast.

Was this the time for Striegel's payback? Finally? It certainly appeared so.

The Notre Dame game had been announced publicly weeks earlier, and before signing the contract, Doc called the NFL offices as a courtesy to get permission to play the game. At the time, though, Carr was in the hospital recovering from what was believed to be appendicitis, so instead Striegel spoke with Jerry Corcoran, the manager of the Columbus Tigers. Corcoran was a close friend of Carr's and the man Striegel believed was filling in as the acting president.

Carr himself should have been thrilled by the proposition of a game against Notre Dame. Pro football had been floundering for nearly 25 years at this point, always a distant second to the college game. Just a week earlier, Pennsylvania attorney general George Woodruff, the former football coach at Penn, declared in a banner headline across the top of a Philadelphia paper: PROFESSIONAL FOOTBALL CANNOT SURVIVE MUCH LONGER—GAME TOO HARD. In the prior year alone, sports fans had spent $12 million on college football, while the NFL was said to be in such dire straits that the cost of a few new file cabinets for the president's office might have broken the league.

Unable to gain any ground in college football, Carr's league had suddenly been given a gift wrapped opportunity to showcase itself on a national stage. If the Maroons could even stay close to Notre Dame, the resulting national news reports would exponentially boost the credibility of and interest in the NFL.

Upon hearing talk of the game, the *Inquirer* wrote, "The Notre Dame team of a year ago was omnipotent in the college world. No 11 men could stand before them among the Simon Pures. What will they do against the outstanding professional team of the country is a question that will not be answered until the afternoon of December 12.

"One of the knotty problems that troubles football devotees is the relative strength of college and professional teams," the paper continued. "But in the very nature of things it is impossible to bring the money players together with the Simon Pures, and so it happens that the question has gone unanswered, and will, until December 12. Professional teams have been assembled all over the country, teams that have bristled with All-America Stars. The pro game has stepped ahead with strides of a Goliath. But never before has an all-conquering college team stepped into professional ranks as a unit to play together as they did when they wore the colors of their alma mater. It is absolutely unique.

"In effect, this will be a struggle between the champion college team of 1924 and the crack professional 11 of 1925. Is college football faster and more efficient than professional? Or is the gridiron sport as practiced by the money players more finished and more perfect than the game played within our great college stadiums?

"The result of this game will furnish practical evidence upon which a real opinion may be based."

Joe Carr's Victorian approach to building the league had always been that once he cleaned up the NFL's renegade image by strictly enforcing the rules, fans would begin to respect it and eventually, someday, in a decade or two, begin to pay attention. Doc Striegel argued that this was a brilliant marketing strategy—for 1910. In the old days, before the war, people wanted to see the cow, the feed, the grooming, the barn, and the butcher. In the 1920s, folks just wanted the fillet. Sports fans of the new era wanted to see and support the best. The methods, the costs, and the background hardly mattered. Just show us the best. Give us the best. Period.

At some point, as this controversy was unfolding, Carr surely must have realized that the Pottsville-Notre Dame game had provided the NFL with a golden opportunity to gain everything the league lacked in the public eye. By competing with Notre Dame, the Maroons would bring the NFL the national attention it so desperately needed to stay afloat. Afterward, upon reaping the publicity of the game, Carr could then prove to the skeptical fans who remained just what an upstanding league he was running by disciplining his best team. It was insidious and subversive, and it meant a town and a team would have to be sacrificed, but the league would come out light years ahead of where it had been just weeks earlier.

Carr never let on, but he knew it: The Pottsville-Notre Dame game, and Royle's subsequent protest, was the best medicine the sick president and his ailing league could have ever received.

Nevertheless, Carr was still indisposed when Striegel called Columbus a second time. Doc was hoping that an honorable Corcoran would confirm their previous conversation, and that would be that. But Corcoran's response was, in effect, "You got that in writing?" (Actually, he did. In separate sworn affidavits, both Rauch and Stahlman said that they had witnessed the original Striegel-Corcoran phone call and that "upon termination of the telephone call, Dr. Striegel ... said in substance, 'That's it, I just got Corcoran's okay to play the game.' " Rauch stated that not only did Corcoran give the league's blessing, he even wished Doc Striegel and the Maroons good luck before he hung up the phone.)

Corcoran's memory of the call became fuzzy once Royle hatched his plan. "It was evident," Doc would disclose later, "that [Royle] had wired the league about [our game]." Royle might have started out hoping only to scare the Maroons into canceling so that he could offer up his Yellow Jackets as a last-second replacement. But when Striegel balked, it left both Pottsville and the NFL in a terrible position: deadlocked and with no escape. Both sides were justified in their stances, and neither had a way to save face—even if they had wanted to back down. The NFL argued that it was simply enforcing its rules. Once the protest had been filed and made public, there was no going back; the league had to do something. There was simply no way Carr, Royle, Corcoran, and the rest of the league could allow Doc Striegel and the Maroons to make fools of them—*again*.

Meanwhile, Doc saw no reason to back down either since he had signed a contract to play the game only after getting what he believed was the league's blessing. He also desperately needed the payday to balance his books after a long, expensive season. Unless the NFL would cover his lost revenues and protect him against the lawsuits he was certain to face from promoters of the Notre Dame game, Doc couldn't cancel without the risk of bankrupting the team, his family, and his practice.

Corcoran said he would look into the matter. Then he reiterated the league's stance, warning the Maroons not to go ahead with the game. To which a cornered Striegel replied: "I have never backed out of a contract in my life, and I don't intend to do so at this stage of the game."

Locked in a stalemate, the conversation ended abruptly, with both sides underestimating the other's resolve as well as the seriousness of the divide. Doc figured there was no way the NFL would suspend its best team over a rule that wasn't even on the books, while the NFL couldn't imagine the Maroons throwing away a championship season for an exhibition game.

By this point, Rauch had shown up in Doc's office, and the two men drove south for their appointment in Frankford. The meeting began at 6 o'clock with the red-faced Royle threatening to band his 20-mile NFL territory with barbed wire and a Yale lock in order to keep the Maroons out of Philadelphia. When asked if he was just jealous of the Maroons and still smarting a bit from the spanking his team had received, the embarrassed Yellow Jackets owner bristled, "Oh no, not at all, we are only protecting our interests, and we are certainly going to do it."

But with time and reason, Royle's scheme began to unravel. By midnight, thanks to Doc's immeasurably persuasive skills and Rauch's unimpeachable character, along with the presence of several Philadelphia reporters, who saw right through the sour-grapes ruse, Royle was convinced to call off his protest. For the time being, at least. (He flip-flopped for the rest of the week, although it no longer mattered since the damage had been done and inside the NFL offices the wheels had already been set in motion.)

After the meeting, Rauch called Pottsville with the late-breaking news. As a result, the next morning's paper concluded, "A tempest that raged in a six-hour teacup over the question of whether the Maroons would meet the 'Four Horsemen' of the gridiron at Philadelphia on Saturday next was dispelled at midnight when it was announced that a Locarno Peace Pact had been arranged between Striegel and Royle over a friendly cup of tea. And as a consequence, the sale of tickets would start at Dory Schneider's drugstore this morning at 8 o'clock."

The next day, news of the accord with Royle and the impending world championship game gave Pottsville the feel of a college campus during homecoming week. "At no cost to the city at all," wrote one editorial, "the Maroons football team has advertised Pottsville as possibly no other agency could. North and south, east and west, Pottsville is today known as the greatest sports community in the country. Our gridiron heroes are at once our greatest publicity heralds. And if you ask the players what made the team great, they will tell you systematic practice and the loyalty of the fans."

Signs supporting this claim were everywhere: The message "NFL Champions" was soaped onto every storefront window. Banners that read "To Hell With Frankford" were on every car windshield. And "Beat the Four Horsemen" buttons were on every lapel and miner's cap.

Striegel knew he was taking a gamble with Carr, but great card player that he was, he never tipped his hand. By now most people had accepted the fact that Striegel, as one friend put it, "said a lot of things that were bigger than they sounded." And the town's newspapers, swept up in all the fervor, took him at his word, reporting with confidence that the Frankford protest was nothing but a toothless bluff.

On street corners, at cafés, speakeasies, church dinners, and barbershops, and inside the coal mines and country clubs alike, townsfolk talked about the Maroons, Notre Dame, football, their championships, and little else. Knowing Notre Dame would have a large, loud, and well-organized cheering section full of alumni, thousands of Pottsville fans actually attended "cheer rehearsals" at the Armory run by district attorney Bud Whitehouse and noted vocalist Dr. Tom Davidson. Reading from the thousands of flyers that had been distributed all over town, fans broke out into spontaneous cheers for their Maroons.

> *Whee-e-e-e-e-e;*
> *Site, Site, Anthracite;*
> *The very best Site in the Anthracite!*
> *Where?*
> *Pottsville, Pa.;*
> *P-O-T-T-S-V-I-L-L-E;*
> *Pottsville! Pottsville! Pottsville!*
> *POTTSVILLE!*

Said one eyewitness: "On practically every street corner, people would stop to gather and practice these cheers, giving the city a college campus atmosphere. Impromptu parades formed. Speeches were given on corners. Pottsville took on a holiday look."

Even at the outrageous prices of $2.50 for general admission and $3.50 for reserved seating, fans gobbled up all 2,000 ducats at Schneider's, and an order was immediately sent to Shibe Park for another 2,500 tickets. A special 8:15 a.m. train was also added to the Saturday schedule to handle the extra passengers headed down to Philadelphia. (The train ride itself had become just as entertaining as the games. For the first part of the trip, the tracks ran parallel to the road, and fans on the packed cars would hang out the windows and wave their straw hats and banners at the half-mile string of motorists who raced the locomotive to each crossing in a dangerous but breathtaking game of chicken.) After the success of the Cardinals broadcast, *The Republican* also announced plans for another direct telegraph wire, this time from Shibe Park, to the paper's offices. Fans who couldn't make the trip were invited to gather at the doorstep of the paper and listen as live results were broadcast via a telegraph and a megaphone. Homebound fans could dial up Pottsville 1,000 or Shenandoah 911 and hear game highlights from the operator. More tickets arrived on Thursday afternoon, and they sold out in 24 hours.

Doc should have been ecstatic, but instead he was reported to have been beleaguered and battered; the likely result of his final, devastating phone call with Carr that evening. The confrontation between the Maroons and the NFL, between Striegel and Carr, had become a metaphor for the times. The young, bombastic owner with delusions of grandeur and an enormous payday clouding his judgment was deadlocked against the stubborn, out-of-touch, and by-the-book old-time president. Neither was completely right. Neither was completely wrong. Yet their biggest mistake was that neither man was big enough to broker a deal, to compromise. It was all-or-nothing. And in the end, they all got nothing. Although Doc kept the call a secret, during their brief Thursday conversation, the president promised Striegel that the NFL would do everything it could, short of becoming a co-defendant, if he were to get sued by the Notre Dame promoters.

But for the second time in a week, he forbade the Maroons from playing Notre Dame.

Not knowing this, the team gathered for a short practice at their secret field behind the Silk Mill. With the Maroons' confidence and conditioning at an all-time high, Rauch did little more than limber them up, run through a handful of drills and a few basic plays, and give them one or two pointed reminders about Notre Dame's prolific passing attack. The Steins and Osborn, meanwhile, were still in Pittsburgh, preparing to face Grange.

And with Flanagan finished and French banged up from the Chicago game, Rauch could only hope that Latone would be able to summon the courage to play through the pain of his mangled arm. If he couldn't, it would be a long afternoon in Philadelphia. After an hour, a satisfied Rauch dismissed the team from practice. At this point, if he or any of the other team members were worried about or intimidated by the very real prospect of being humiliated by Notre Dame in a little more than 48 hours, they certainly didn't let it show.

Outside of Pottsville, however, few even entertained the idea that the Maroons could compete with Notre Dame, let alone win. According to one sportswriter on the East Coast, "The biggest name in American football in 1925 was Notre Dame, and it was generally assumed that professional players hadn't been born yet who could handle Notre Dame in head-to-head combat." The notion was reinforced by the promoters who guaranteed Notre Dame $25,000 to Pottsville's $6,000.

Philadelphia reporters who had seen the Maroons dismantle Frankford and Chicago tried to warn their readers, but to the average football fan, this matchup was like a contest winner in the stands of Yankee Stadium getting to pitch to Babe Ruth. The NFL champs were little more than expensive practice dummies, brought in to provide the best possible showcase for the world's finest football team. Few teams in any sport, on any level, and in any era were regarded with as much universal reverence as the 1924 Notre Dame Fighting Irish. This was the team, after all, that had begun the Notre Dame mystique. They were gods to some, stars to most, and heroes to all fans who believed that on Notre Dame's worst day, they could beat the best the NFL had to offer. (Inside the local speakeasies, John O'Hara won many a free rye because of his ability to recite the entire Notre Dame lineup.)

In 1924, Knute Rockne was already a living legend when he coached the Irish to an undefeated regular season. It was during this remarkable run, after Notre Dame's impressive victory over a talented Army team, that sportswriter Grantland Rice immortalized the Irish backfield—quarterback Harry Stuhldreher, right halfback Don Miller, left halfback Jim Crowley, and fullback Elmer Layden—with what would become a legendary passage in the *New York Herald Tribune*:

Outlined against a blue-gray October sky, the Four Horsemen rode again. In dramatic lore they are known as famine, pestilence, destruction, and death. These are only aliases. Their real names are Stuhldreher, Miller, Crowley, and Layden. They formed the crest of the South Bend cyclone, before which another fighting Army football team was swept over the precipice at the Polo Grounds yesterday afternoon as 55,000 spectators peered down on the bewildering panorama spread on the green plain below.

A cyclone can't be snared. It may be surrounded, but somewhere it breaks through to keep going. When the cyclone starts from South Bend, where the candlelights still gleam through the Indiana sycamores, those in the way must take to storm cellars at top speed. Yesterday the cyclone struck again, as Notre Dame beat Army 13 to 7, with a set of backfield stars that ripped and crashed through a strong Army defense with more speed and power than warring cadets could meet.

Notre Dame then traveled to play in the Rose Bowl. There they faced a Stanford team coached by Pop Warner himself, led by All-America quarterback Ernie Nevers and backed by 53,000 fans. The Irish prevailed with ease, 27-10, to capture the school's inaugural national championship. After the Rose Bowl, the

Louisville Post summed up the Irish's impact this way: "For the first time in the history of this country, it is possible to place a finger on a particular football team and say, 'This is the best.' The 11 from the University of Notre Dame have earned this indisputable distinction."

In the 30 games they played together, the Four Horsemen had lost only twice, both times to Nebraska. Rockne, a man not prone to hyperbole, or to smiling, for that matter, called his Horsemen a "product of destiny." Struhldreher was an extremely confident quarterback with unquestioned field command. He played almost the entire game against Stanford with a broken ankle and later went on to land the coveted head coaching job at Villanova. Rockne said Miller was the greatest open-field runner he ever coached. Crowley was a shifty, clever runner. And at 6'0", 162 pounds, Layden was the biggest, fastest, and most versatile of the Horsemen, doubling as a defensive back and a punter. The Four Horsemen were powered by the lesser-known Seven Mules, including the 200-pound All-America tackle Ed Garvey. "Pound for pound they stand alone," Rice later wrote. "What they lacked in poundage, they more than made up for in speed, spirit, smartness, and driving force. They worked with a rhythm that was unbelievably beautiful to watch, whether or not football happens to be your favorite game. If you consider such assets as speed, brains, heart, alertness, and rhythm important, then they had no equal."

By late in the week the Four Horsemen, along with five of the Seven Mules (and a handful of other former local college All-Americas), had made it to Philadelphia to prepare for the game newspapers were now calling the GREATEST FOOTBALL GAME EVER SEEN IN THE EAST. The All-Star team practiced twice inside Shibe Park. And they spent no time prepping for, or scouting, the Maroons. Most of them couldn't have located

Pottsville on a map. Instead they mostly just showed off for the fans who watched from nearby rooftops, thrilling them with their speed and technique along with a dizzying array of formations and complicated and intricately timed plays.

By contrast, for most of Friday afternoon, after a short workout on the 12th Street field, Rauch had his team in front of the chalkboard inside the Armory, breaking down the Notre Dame attack again and again and again. The strategy he had decided upon was, as usual, odd, advanced, and multidimensional. First, Rauch would wait until the second half before unleashing a fresh Latone on the Irish, which would confuse Notre Dame and safeguard against Latone's reinjuring his arm. That meant until Latone entered the game, Rauch needed the Steins, along with his other warhorses, up front to do damage in the trenches, wearing down the Mules and disrupting Stuhldreher's famous throwing rhythm and field vision.

On Sunday in Chicago, Herb and Russ had bullied All-Pro Red Dunn into throwing five interceptions. Word had just arrived from Pittsburgh that the Steins had done the same thing to Red Grange on Thursday, sending him to the sideline with a merciless pounding that resulted in a broken blood vessel in his arm and a torn ligament in his knee. (Debilitated by injuries piled up during his nonstop postcollege barnstorming, Grange would never be the same player in the NFL as he was for the Illini. And it all started, and ended, with a beating from the Stein brothers.) For Rauch's plan to work, the Steins would have to make Struhlhelder their third famous football victim of the week.

After an hour in front of the chalkboard, the players left the Armory, got cleaned up, and regrouped above Ginley's. With the town in a complete football frenzy, Ginley's was their last place of refuge. Doc Striegel's house was packed with fans, visitors, and well-wishers. Next door, the long, skinny basement bar of the Phoenix had become the team's unofficial hospitality suite. The town's hotels were all sold out, and crowds at Brushnars and Zacko's were overflowing to the point that their patrons were mingling in the middle of the street. Other fans gathered on street corners to practice their cheers and to debate the threat of a protest from Frankford.

Walter Farquhar, as usual, was busy at work on yet another one of his poems:

All the town's gone simply batty, Everyone's feeling chatty,
As they rave about the World Championship Game
And the factories are imposing. One by one are quickly
   closing;
There's no other thought than football today.
Each Policeman with his billy, Wishes he were down in
   Philly;
In the banks they can't distinguish goal from gold
And the lawyers in their pleading; Only know that
   Pottsville's leading
While the restaurants are serving food that's cold
Every Tom, Dick, and Jerry; Pulling hard for Charlie Berry
And the gang that keeps Pottsville to the fore
And the preacher's stern epistle; Waits for the referee's
   last whistle
Everybody's calling for the score
Every newsboy with his Journal; *Makes a din that's infernal*
As he sells his football extra on the street
And the old pal slaps his crony; As they give three cheers
   for Tony
And the team that swept Frankford off its feet
Everybody's acting phony, sure that Frankford is baloney

While the Maroons alone deserve full fame
And the Prince of Wales so regal; Wishes he was Doc Striegel
As he hears the Pottsville Four Horsemen Game.

Inside the frat room, the players were relaxed and confident. According to Zacko, the Frankford protest came up once or twice, but most felt assured that the NFL wouldn't follow through with such a flimsy argument. Even if it did, players like Berry couldn't imagine a scenario where, at a full hearing on a later date, the other owners wouldn't overrule Carr. Even those who didn't side with Berry believed in their hearts that history would judge the team by their accomplishments on the field—and nowhere else. If that was the case, then they simply couldn't pass up a chance at Notre Dame.

Beyond that topic of conversation, the players' main concern seemed to be getting enough tickets to the Saturday night showing of the musical *Rose Marie*, which was playing in Philadelphia. As the gathering at the clubhouse broke up around 10 p.m. Wentz promised to treat the team to the show, but only after a victory over the Irish.

The Maroons respected their opponent; many of them had known and played against the Four Horsemen in college. They weren't naïve or ignorant of the challenge they faced, but they had become a team of the Twenties: an embodiment of the ideal that no challenge was too great, no goal too high, no achievement too shocking. In the topsy-turvy world they now inhabited, the more Notre Dame was deemed unbeatable by the old guard and the gray-haired experts, the more confident the Maroons grew.

Around 10 p.m., the gathering at the clubhouse broke up with the appearance of Rauch who quietly poked his head into the room. In his usual soft-spoken but authoritative manner, the Maroons coach gave his final command of the season:

"Get a good night's rest, men."

CHAPTER 19

THE GREATEST GAME EVER SEEN

THE MAROONS ARRIVED IN PHILADELPHIA at 11 a.m. and enjoyed a light lunch of roast beef and tea at the downtown Elks Club before collecting their duffel bags and quietly stepping into a row of waiting cabs for the ride to Shibe Park.

The trip required taxis because the location of the park, on 21st and Lehigh, was so far north of downtown that when it was built in 1909, neighbors in the area still kept chickens, pigs, and other livestock fenced up in their yards. What it lacked in location, however, Shibe Park more than made up for in amenities and grandeur. Built for $300,000 by Benjamin Shibe for Connie Mack's Philadelphia Athletics, Shibe Park was one of the first stadiums made of reinforced concrete, and its steep double-decker grandstand allowed many of its 23,000 patrons to hover right above the action. (The park's capacity could be expanded by 10,000 with standing room only areas in the outfield next to the freestanding scoreboard. And for many years, several thousand more fans watched games for free from rooftops across the street—until the Athletics erected a 12-foot-high "spite fence" to block their view.)

The park's signature was its French Renaissance brick façade, featuring a four-story domed steeple entranceway behind home plate. The stadium extended out from either side of the main gate with long rows of massive, ornate archways and columns covered by a green slate roof trimmed with copper. Maroons fans marched up from the trolley station to the stadium. Protestants walked with Catholics, miners from the patches strode next to barons from atop Mahantongo, and the members of Pottsville's Jewish temple kept time to tunes from Ted Brushnar's Sauerkraut Band until, together, they all reached the awe-inspiring, state-of-the-art facility that seemed to be a fitting locale for a world championship.

An hour before kickoff, though, the game looked like it might never happen. In the shadows of Shibe's famous archways, as football fans poured in through stadium gates below, Doc Striegel, Irish captain Harry Stuhldreher, and the game's promoter, Frank Schumann, conducted a tense, last-minute contract renegotiation. Meeting here in the shadows to whisper surreptitiously about fees, rules, and guarantees was confirmation that Royle's plan had worked. Although Carr had not yet acted, he had already notified the league's other franchises not to play the "outlaw" Maroons and by the looks of the 10,000 or so below them, the Frankford-Cleveland game had managed to lure away almost half of Schumann's expected gate. (By contrast, Grange had drawn 36,000 fans to Shibe Park a week earlier.)

Anticipating that kind of crowd, Stuhldreher had been promised $25,000 for the game ($5,000 up front and another $20,000 to be placed in escrow by December 5), of which he had seen only $8,000. The self-assured quarterback and a man of growing import in the city of Brotherly Love, Stuhldreher made it simple for Schumann: pay us in full or we walk. And with the crowd below him full of mostly antsy Notre Dame fans, Schumann must have caved quickly, since shortly thereafter the Irish All-Stars trotted out onto the field to begin warmups.

For the next half hour, and well past the scheduled kickoff time of 2 p.m., Notre Dame remained the only team on the field while Striegel and Schumann haggled under the stands. The Maroons' advance was $6,000, a pitiful amount, Doc knew, compared to what they were risking by taking the field. In exchange, Striegel wanted Schumann to cover his losses should the NFL suspend the Maroons and take away their final two possible paydays in Providence and Chicago, where a game against the Bears was in the planning stages. Doc asked for an additional $2,000 for each missed game. Schumann balked. And Striegel waited. By now, fans and members of the press were getting restless. Schumann begged. And Striegel waited. His whole adult life he had never figured out if he should be insulted or grateful for the way people were constantly underestimating him because he was from Pottsville. Finally, in a huff, Schumann took out his checkbook and offered a compromise: full cover for the Providence game and half for the Bears game, since there were already reports that injuries would force Grange to hang up his cleats for the season. The two men agreed and Striegel raced down to the locker room, his wingtips tapping loudly down the cement steps, to give his team the okay to take the field.

Pottsville's bench was like a who's who of East Coast football. There was Rauch's mentor, Penn State coach Hugo Bezdek; Colgate coach Dick Barlow; Tim Mara, the owner of the New York

Giants; and Green Bay's Curly Lambeau. There were also rumors that Knute Rockne lurked among the overwhelmingly pro-Notre Dame crowd.

Maroons fans, some of them dressed playfully in full miner's garb, may have been outnumbered in the stands, but the team felt right at home on the field surrounded by Pottsville's color guard and the entire Third Brigade Band, which played the "Star Spangled Banner."

Already displaying what would become his trademark, a mastery of the quiddities that defined such social gatherings, John O'Hara set the electric pregame scene with a series of wires to *Journal* readers back in Pottsville:

> "The crowd at the box office bore a stronger resemblance to a collegiate crowd than any professional game seen this year by the writer ... Despite the October weather, fur coats were in the audience ... The players entered the press gate and hundreds paid homage to the Pottsville eleven ... The press box is sure to be the hottest place in Philadelphia in summer and the coldest in winter ... The entire team inspected the field before dressing. The ground is springy but dry ... A movie camera man is on the scene ... Reminiscent of the crowd on the bank of the creek at Minersville is a cluster of fans on housetops past right field ... Jack Bergen, millionaire automobile man, of Newark, called to congratulate the Pottsville team."

A few moments later Pottsville lost the coin toss, and the game proceeded in a similar direction for the sluggish and seemingly outmatched Maroons. Just as Rauch had feared, in the early going Notre Dame's multiple formations and complex passing attack neutralized the Maroons' advantages in size, strength, and conditioning. Pottsville was not used to such an intricate display.

The Horsemen were still running Rockne's famous "box" offense. They lined up in a conventional T formation backfield and then, after the call from Stuhldreher, shifted quickly into a trapezoid with one halfback behind center and another now out past the end. This allowed Notre Dame to run with an extra lead blocker, reverse the ball using the outside halfback's momentum, or send several backs wide to catch easy lateral passes with plenty of space to run. More than anything, though, the shifting confused and rattled defenses used to rudimentary running games. The rules decreed that all players had to hold their positions for a full second before the snap. But by using their reputation and the favor of awestruck referees, the Four Horsemen could shave that full-second pause down to less than a blink of an eye.

"Using the Notre Dame formations with which they conquered the college football world, Stuhldreher and his riding companions, Layden, Miller and Crowley, befuddled the Pottsville defense with a series of forward passes which were perfectly timed," wrote the *Philadelphia Public Ledger*. Stuhldreher, the Irish's All-America quarterback in 1924, picked apart the bigger, slower Maroons defenders. Using a passing game "bewildering in deception and amazing in execution" Stuhldreher was in mid-season form. Meaning, he was overconfident, talkative, and moving the ball at will, scrambling to his right and then using his tremendous arm strength to throw back across his body while confused Pottsville tacklers, looking like the Keystone Cops, knocked each other to the ground pursuing the play in both directions. Notre Dame so thoroughly dominated the first quarter that the game took on a vaudeville atmosphere. The Irish moved the ball up and down the field but never scored—much like a masked wrestler who pulls a beaten man off the mat in order to punish him some more. The lack of scoring was seen as nothing more the product of pity or gamesmanship on the part of the Irish.

Meanwhile, on offense, the lightning-quick French seemed listless and not fully recovered from the beating he took in Chicago or, perhaps, from the week he spent celebrating and convalescing. His feet repeatedly slipped out from under him deep in the backfield and he wasn't running away from tacklers or cutting up field with anything close to the same ferocity he had displayed a week earlier inside Comiskey.

Whether they were worried about Carr lowering the boom or suffering from whiplash after the Four Horsemen's eye-popping onslaught, most of the Maroons displayed a similar kind of apathy. As a result, Pottsville, a team used to physically dominating opponents to the point of humiliation, gained a mere 28 yards rushing in the first half. Only Osborn was playing with any kind of passion. Duke couldn't help it. He just had an innate enmity for the "pretty boys" he believed now populated college ball and especially South Bend. He also found all that fancy shifting and passing to be cowardly, as a way to go around defenders rather than face them straight up. And he wore his frustration openly. A caption under a photo taken of Osborn's angry, twisted visage during the game as he hunted down Layden in the open field, said, " … that's Osborn and he plays just as hard as he looks."

While French struggled, Latone barely moved from the bench. Covered in a heavy hooded canvas jacket, he stood periodically, causing the crowd to hold their breath in anticipation but it was only to stretch his massive legs or rub his sore arm which he held gingerly down against his torso. At the beginning of the second quarter, with the Maroons facing fourth-and-one at the Notre Dame 47, Pottsville fans had begun berating Rauch for leaving Latone on the sideline while the game, and their dreams of a World Championship, slipped away.

Predictably, French was turned back at the line of scrimmage and the Irish took over on downs. After two incomplete passes, Stuhldreher dropped back deep then shuffled to his right again, drawing the defense to him like a matador before unfurling a pass across his body to Crowley, who cradled it and raced to the 37. With the Maroons out of breath, Layden then rammed through the interference at the line, emerging into a wide-open secondary. He deked Ernst and headed for the end zone. French had charged up from behind only to get flattened by blockers escorting Layden, who then strutted the final 10 yards to paydirt.

Layden held the ball aloft and the "frenzied stands rose with a roar" according to one witness.

Alas, the sensational play was disallowed, the first of many to be recalled for illegal procedure. Linesman Eddie Bennis, a well respected football authority who led the 1904 Penn team to prominence, had been warned by Pottsville officials of the Four Horsemen's expectation that their popularity would allow them to bend the rules ever so slightly to their favor. Mainly, that referees would look the other way if during their many formation changes and pre-snap shifts a member of their backfield was in motion before the ball was snapped. (If this didn't work the Irish kept at it, hoping embarrassed refs would eventually just swallow their whistles.) Bennis was, to say the least, insulted by the assumption, and two plays later he again whistled for offsides, nullifying a 22-yard gain by Miller.

Until the Irish got the message—that the game was in Philadelphia and not South Bend—the drive continued to yo-yo on like this: 15 yards forward on a pass or run, 20 yards backward on a penalty. Bennis was not a homer but a stubborn and well-respected referee who refused to back down from either team. He flagged the Maroons twice on the same drive, the second penalty handing Notre Dame a first down at the Pottsville 1. "In one lunge, Layden made the distance and was across for the score," wrote the *Ledger*.

After the kick, Notre Dame led 7-0 in what local reporters were calling the most lopsided seven-point game they had ever witnessed. Just before the half, this realization began to hit home on the Notre Dame sideline where the Irish had stopped playing nice and started looking for opportunities to embarrass the no-name coal crackers across the field. "[Throughout the game], there was nothing gentle about the Horsemen and their compatriots," the *Ledger* reported. "They tackled fiercely and there was no hesitation about piling up or bringing their man down in a way to shake him from head to heel."

In particular, Notre Dame's frustrations with Bennis' officiating had begun to boil over. After another series of flags, players encircled him, bumping his chest and screaming at him nose-to-nose while the Irish crowd mercilessly hooted on the portly official. "I never was more booed in all my career as an official than at Shibe Park that Saturday by the Notre Dame crowd," Bennis later admitted. Egged on by the mob in the stands, the Horsemen began to argue with Bennis "so vigorously it was feared that the head linesman would be attacked," noted one reporter, "but intervention by the Pottsville players prevented the trouble."

Pottsville emptied its bench to protect the local ref, a man they did not know but still considered one of their own. And this one moment of valor changed the entire course of the game. Judging by their performance up until that point, the Maroons had been lulled into thinking the game was just a friendly exhibition. They wanted to win, of course, but with an NFL title in their hip pocket they had little left to prove. Even though they were only a hundred miles from home, it was obvious that most of the fans in Shibe Park were there to see the Four Horsemen roll over a team from the fledgling NFL. *Okay, fine*—the Maroons seemed to concede after the opening kickoff—*it's been a long season, we're tired, we're beat, we'll play along.*

Until, that is, players like Osborn, Racis, and the Steins grew tired of Notre Dame's cocksure attitude and sense of entitlement. Berry, meanwhile, was beside himself with the way his team was being run out of his home stadium, in front of sports fans who had come to respect him as the catcher for the A's. The ensuing uproar around Bennis only served to awaken the rest of the sleepwalking Maroons.

Now what? screamed the team's prickly, coiled body language during the fracas. *Now what's wrong? Are these royal princes of college ball too good to be flagged? Shall we just step aside? Are we playing football or dancing the Charleston? Enough. Enough. Let's play some ball.*

As the teams finally separated and repaired to their locker rooms for halftime it was clear that Notre Dame had just made a grave tactical error. The boys from South Bend had just royally pissed off the men from Pottsville.

The friendly exhibition was now a football game—a pro football game.

Whatever rage was simmering on the field ignited in full force inside the locker room when Doc Striegel was handed a telegram from Joe Carr. He didn't need to unfold the yellow parchment or read the black typeset message. He knew what it said. It was over. Carr had called his bluff. The league was fining the Maroons $500 and suspending them for playing the Notre Dame game inside Frankford's territory. An ashen-faced Striegel could barely speak the words: the Maroons were now "outlaws." Their recently scheduled game against Providence was now canceled and their annual trip back to Atlantic City would be little more than a scrimmage. The real punishment, he explained, was that they were no longer eligible for the championship they had won so convincingly a week earlier on the field in Chicago.

As the players sat in stunned silence, Striegel tried to argue that the suspension meant nothing since it would never hold up under the scrutiny of a full hearing before the entire league. He promised lawsuits. He promised injunctions. He waved his fists and pounded his feet and screamed to the rafters about justice. At best, though, Striegel had misled them about the severity of Carr's threat. At worst, he had lied right to their faces and tricked them into cashing in their championship for $6,000.

This was no longer a time for owners or league presidents or any other suits who wanted to debate the circular logic of the league's obtuse rules on territory, the way they were arbitrarily applied, or if the rules even existed in the first place. The Maroons had grown tired of all that. This was a time for players, for the men with the throbbing limbs and bloodied noses, the men who had stuck together through the heat of September, the hours inside the Armory, the threat of bankruptcy, the power of Canton, the speed of Green Bay, the size of Frankford, and the cold of Comiskey. "The NFL can go to hell," said Zacko. "And so can the rest of the league."

Osborn and Racis were frothing at the mouth wanting to get at the Horsemen. If the others stayed true to their personalities, their reactions to Carr's decision would have been easy to predict. Latone sat in silence, his arm in agony and his mind wandering back to his drunken father flashing that ruby ring and his grand plans all over Edwardsville. Thinking back to his first day in the mines as an 11-year-old child, he wondered if he had seen the last of the coal catacombs. Berry's mind returned to those pre-dawn hours delivering milk bottles before school. Ernst was back inside his childhood home, looking in on his ailing father reduced to skin over a skeleton by the Spanish flu. Wentz thought of all those Saturdays of his youth, sneaking out across his roof to play the game he loved but his father despised. The Steins traveled to the front porch of their family farmhouse, waiting behind the screen door for their father to grant them permission to play.

Latone. Berry. Ernst. Wentz. The Steins. They all knew what had to be done.

Without an NFL title there was one chance left to salvage the entire season and take their rightful piece of football immortality.

They would have to do the impossible and beat Notre Dame.

Once Striegel calmed down, Rauch addressed the team. In "his usual soft manner," according to one observer, he urged the line to take Osborn's lead and punish the less conditioned Irish until they cracked. He then nodded confidently to Latone and his lead blocker Wentz. *It's time,* he seemed to be saying. The coach was so calm, success seemed almost guaranteed. In the middle of this sordid mess, there remained something pure and honorable in Rauch that the team was seeing for the first time. Most coaches used fear or intimidation to motivate their players. Rauch was different, even revolutionary. He used disappointment. His players grew to think so highly of him that they were driven by an almost primal need not to let down the man who had become a father figure to them all. What should have been the lowest moment of their season evoked in the Maroons the most virtuous aspects of athletics: the paternal bond between players and coach and the moment a team becomes a family. With everything at stake—lawsuits, reputations, legacies, championships and hundreds of thousands of dollars—as officials called them back to the field at Shibe Park, this is what it came down to for the Pottsville Maroons: respect and love. For the game, their coach, and each other.

"To the man sitting quietly on the bench much of the victory was due," wrote one Pottsville reporter. "Rauch changed the entire style of play during intermission, put the fire back into his charges and saw them overcome the odds which were heavily against them and change the entire complexion of the game. Too much credit cannot be given Rauch for the unspectacular part he played in this and other wonderful victories of the year."

Explained one local paper, "Pottsville, emerging from the dressing room after the intermission, wore the aspect of a sorely chastened team. The miners were facing expulsion from the league and the loss of their championship emblems. They were faced with a $5,000 fine. Their game against the Steam Roller had been called off; there was the probability of a very small gate at Shibe Park, and, worst of all, they were facing probable defeat at the hands of the Four Horsemen.

"Yet it was a different team that trotted out onto the gridiron after the half. The players exhibited the gentle demeanor of Hyrcanian tigers during Lent; and Notre Dame, a trifle confident, owing to their fine showing in the first half, soon found that they had a bunch of wildcats to contend with."

The Maroons took the opening kickoff 44 yards, straight into Notre Dame territory as Wentz and Racis cleared the way with a series of crippling blocks that, two hours late, announced the Maroons' official arrival at Shibe Park. The last Notre Dame tackler managed to prevent a touchdown by grabbing the Pottsville return man by the collar of his sweater and holding him up until other tacklers could catch up. Seeming almost insulted by the Maroons' nerve to start with such an advance,

Notre Dame's coverage piled on excessively, resulting in an unsportsmanlike conduct penalty that advanced the ball to the Irish 22.

Suddenly, the entire Pottsville crowd stood on its feet, turning toward the Maroons' bench before letting out a thunderous roar. Rauch had relented. Latone was shedding his wool jacket and trotting toward the field. After replacing Little Walter in the backfield, The Howitzer needed a few skull-rattling hits to get his legs warmed up and his heart pumping at full throttle. The Maroons turned the ball over on downs on his first series. But the Pottsville defenders held and a weak punt gave the Maroons the ball right back, this time at the 38.

Then, with the slow, mesmerizing certainty of a tank, Latone simply took over the game.

"The hefty halfback could start faster than an electric train and he hit the line like a locomotive plowing into an automobile at a grade crossing with the same result and he would leave the wreck of the Notre Dame defense in his wake," noted one reporter. Rockne thought his Four Horsemen looked more like out-of-shape donkeys trying to keep up with the Human Howitzer.

On five of the next six plays, led by the cannonball blocking of Wentz, Latone began to pick away at Notre Dame's will with a series of ferocious line plunges. Apparently the time off had not affected Latone in the least. He ran with feral intensity, his head and shoulders so low it looked like he might knee himself in the face. The sickening noise of the resulting collisions made the Irish crowd wince in unison.

With the goal in sight, Ernst advanced for two yards and was then thrown for a four-yard loss by Ed Hunsinger. Those two plays near the goal line convinced Ernst that Notre Dame had switched to its own version of the Latone Special, with their center backs and wing backs cheating forward as reinforcements against Latone's onslaught. At first it looked like Ernst was at it again, trying to take over the game by himself. But the runs were a bluff. A spectacular, ingenious setup.

All the daily practice in Pottsville, all the endless chalk talk with Rauch inside the Armory, all the preparation that flew in the face of NFL convention, it was all about to pay off. "Behind the line, the Maroons held a parley," observed Mackay, "and the brain who devised the stratagem that followed is a field general, we'll tell the world. The Horsemen had ridden down the forward passes that were aimed at Berry, had scattered the aerial tosses chucked to everyone else. They evidently had figured that Signor Latone was only a bone crushing burly line breaker."

Ernst aligned himself behind center at the 18. And when the Notre Dame defense began cheating toward the line of scrimmage he tried hard not to let a wry smile unfurl across his face. Instead, he took the snap and rather than handing the ball to Latone as everyone suspected, continued to drop back deep behind the line of scrimmage. Taking the bait, relieved almost that Latone was not the ball carrier, the Irish raced after Ernst as The Howitzer slipped into the flat, unnoticed. Looking like a baseball pitcher in mid-windup, The Bear planted his right foot, reeled backward and heaved the ball skyward. During Ernst's drop, Latone had weaved his way to the 5, where he turned and waited, for what seemed like an eternity, while the fat round ball fell toward him.

"His big arms wrapped themselves about the ball as he was about to cross the goal," wrote the *Ledger*. "Another step ... and Latone scored."

After waiting almost three hours for something to cheer, the Pottsville crowd exploded. The celebration, however, was short-lived—Berry blasted the extra point low and straight into the crossbar. It hit the pole with a thud and bounced back onto the field, skipping, rolling and coming to rest right back at his feet as if it had been a boomerang. Incredulous, the Maroons captain hung his head and walked off the field.

The Maroons had come out of the locker room and counter-punched Notre Dame with everything they had and yet the Irish still led, 7-6.

Pottsville's defense dug back in and before the momentum could change on the very next series, the Steins and Osborn got the ball back by harassing Stuhldreher into an interception. "No one ever hit me harder," Stuhldreher later recalled. Rauch's instructions were once again spot on. The Irish were wilting and the Maroons were getting stronger as the game progressed. Behind Latone, who was now shooting through the line "so speedily, the secondary must have thought he was the interference," Pottsville drove quickly to the Irish 5. The Horsemen braced, stuffing Latone on the next play. Ernst then threw into the end zone for the sure-handed Berry, who watched helpless as the ball inexplicably dropped to the ground, just inches from his fingertips.

The normally dignified Berry was beside himself, knowing that an incomplete pass into the end zone meant a loss of possession for Pottsville. The Maroons' steadfast captain was having the worst game of his life on the one day Pottsville could least afford it—with a World Championship at stake, against the mighty Four Horsemen, and in front of his home crowd who would soon know of the team's embarrassing suspension from the NFL. With time ticking down in the fourth quarter and the sky over Shibe Park growing darker by the second, Berry began playing defense like a man possessed, desperately trying to redeem himself.

It was lucky, in a sense, that it was the universally beloved

Berry who was struggling. Because Berry was the only man on the team who could inspire every last Maroon—Irish, Lithuanian, German, Protestant, Catholic, coal miner, or college grad—to finish strong on his behalf. Berry's brethren saw that the captain was hurting and immediately picked up the cause. None more so than Latone, who remembered back to October and the shape they had been in before Charlie united the team on the eve of the Canton game.

Without Berry, the Maroons would likely have folded. The other men would have left town, gotten jobs in Philadelphia or Manhattan or a roster spot with another franchise. Not Latone. He was uneducated and, back then, still just a regional phenom with a large family to support. If the Maroons had gone under, Latone would have too. The very next day he would have been back below the earth swinging a pick, the feeling of the sun on his face at football practice a distant, dying memory.

"And at this point," recalled one witness, "the great drive began."

Layden hit a booming 60-yard punt that backed the Maroons up to their own 8-yard line with a few minutes remaining in the game. No one spoke to Latone as he shuffled slowly onto the field with footsteps that seemed to reverberate down to the building's steel pillars. His jaw was locked and his eyes had gone cold. In this state, even his teammates seemed afraid to look at him. The huddle broke and Latone took his place in the backfield, pushing his fingertips into the earth; the ones covered in thick smooth scars from the "red tops" he endured as a breaker boy. Just before the snap, he leaned forward ever so slightly, allowing the heel of his right foot to rise once again. The fuse was lit. In a moment of clarity all the hardship he had endured—his father's death, the coal mines, the injury at Frankford—suddenly made perfect sense. It was all for this moment.

The Four Horsemen knew exactly what was coming. But the will of the Golden Domers was gone, pummeled into dust by The Howitzer. "Something knocked me down and then it ran over me," recalled one defender. "I only learned later that it was Latone."

Some couldn't, and others simply wouldn't, continue to stand in his way.

Latone shot out of the backfield five times in a row, tearing into the bodies at the line not like The Howitzer he was but a Gatling gun, advancing the ball out to the 37. Wentz ran for four yards, then Ernst gave the ball right back to Latone, who knifed through the Irish defense for a first down at the 42. In three more carries—each one more beautifully brutal than the last—Latone took Pottsville down to the 21-yard line. It was Latone's fifth consecutive first down and, one reporter later noted, "one of the most remarkable exhibitions ever seen on a football field."

Backed up near their goal with the game on the line, Notre Dame stiffened. Wentz gained four yards, Latone was held for no gain, and Ernst lost a yard running off tackle. On fourth down at the 18, with time running out and the season leaking out of Pottsville's hands like cupped water, Rauch didn't hesitate, calling for his captain and kicker, Charlie Berry.

"The fourth period was fast ebbing, darkness was descending to mantle the warring legions," wrote Mackay. "Pottsville, with her kingly sway at stake, had become infuriated and through the sheer strength of her might had pushed the Horsemen and their Mules backward, backward until only eighteen yards away loomed the goal posts."

On bended knee, Charlie Berry groomed and patted the turf at the 30-yard line, where he wanted the ball placed. He stood abruptly as if called to attention, was joined by Ernst, the holder, and then he backed into position waiting for the ball with his head down and his arms at his side.

The stadium fell silent. The air was cool, dark, and calm.

Berry filled his lungs, then exhaled. And the crowd was so still he could hear the air pass over his lips.

Berry had made only three of his nine field goal attempts during the season and had missed badly on everything past the 29. Now, the vision of his earlier kick hitting the crossbar replayed itself inside his head over and over, each time the hollow, dead thump of the ball becoming more pronounced, echoing louder in the background as the rejected ball rolled up to his frozen, cursed feet.

It had all begun with the aerial display by Notre Dame, the near melee before the half, and the ensuing telegram from Carr, then continued on with the stalwart defense of Osborn and the Steins, the Herculean efforts of Latone, who finished with 139 yards (accounting for 75% of the Maroons offense), and the brilliant strategy of Rauch and Ernst. Now, with little time on the clock, the game offered the possible redemption of the local favorite, Charlie Berry, who was lined up to kick a potential game-winning field goal. At some point, the sportswriters and the rest of the crowd had come to an agreement: this was an epic, one of the few games that actually surpassed its hype.

Newspapermen sitting in the press box had already written their leads, describing the game as "without doubt the finest professional football game ever staged in this city."

The only thing left to type was the final score.

At center, Herb Stein gripped the ball in his hands, his thumbs nearly touching, before leaning over and looking back between his legs at his target, who from the center's unique perspective was now upside down. His hands squeezed and his biceps contracted.

The snap was straight and low and right on target.

Ernst caught it and poked the ball into the dirt as the avalanche of flesh at the line of scrimmage descended upon him.

Berry lunged forward and kicked clean through the ball. "He swung that agile hoof," wrote Mackay. "There was a crash of ball and foot and the crowd, awed into silence, held their breaths as the sphere soared and soared and skipped straight for the cross-bar ... "

This time, though, the ball continued to rise in what one observer described as "a graceful arc."

Up and up it went, end over end, floating toward the Notre Dame goal.

The crowd stood and remained perfectly still knowing exactly what was taking place—but not quite believing it. They stood there, frozen, dumbfounded, with their hands clasped atop their derby hats as if trying to contain the explosive, revolutionary images being processed inside their heads.

The ball continued on its historic trajectory, sailing right through the uprights and over the crossbar, and before the kick had even landed the football establishment had been turned upside down.

Most of the fans at Shibe Park, even the ones from Pottsville, had come out for a fun day of football and a glimpse at the famous Four Horseman. Instead, they were witness to a watershed moment in the history of American sports: the very moment that professional football surpassed college ball.

"Not until the referee lifted his arms up into the air," concluded Mackay, "were the gathered thousands sure the feat had been accomplished. Then Pottsville broke out into a frenzy of cheers."

Unaware of Carr's telegram and Pottsville's subsequent suspension, elated Maroons fans floated out of the stadium and into the street. They lingered in Philadelphia as long as they could, in hotel lobbies, restaurants, coffee shops, and train stations, carrying with them a newfound sense of civic pride that, for the first time, allowed them to puff out their chests and hold their heads high in this giant metropolis, or any other place in the world that their football team now ruled.

A spent Farquhar wrote that "the gain was a victory but no loyal Pottsville rooter wants to sit through another like it." Seated in the press box next to Farquhar and Mackay, local newspaper cartoonist Charlie Bell scribbled away frantically at a massive piece that would be part of the next day's coverage under the headline: YES, THE POTTSVILLE MAROONS WERE HORSE(MEN) OF ANOTHER COLOR. The portrait showed Berry with a giant cleat surrounded by dollar signs kicking Stuhldreher, Crowley, Miller, and Layden (along with the horse they rode in on) up over the field goal crossbar with the caption: "That will make you feel like the Four Horsemen of the Epileptics."

Finally, it was college football being lampooned and pro ball being held up in esteem—not the other way around.

There could be no doubt what the Maroons had accomplished. Their victory over Notre Dame legitimized the NFL.

It also destroyed the team and the town that made it all possible.

CHAPTER 20

A SAD PARTING

I T WAS PROPHETIC, in a way, that the final gathering place
of the 1925 Pottsville Maroons was inside the glamorous ballroom of a doomed structure. For the team's testimonial dinner,
the Pottsville Chamber of Commerce chose the grand old Hotel
Allan at the foot of Mahantongo Street. And although the Allan
still possessed high standards of civility and service, plans were
already under way to have the plain, four-story brick structure
demolished to make way for the grand archways, marbled
columns, and massive windows of the luxurious, nine-story Necho
Allen Hotel, named after the man who discovered anthracite coal.

Despite its impending date with the wrecking ball, the Allan
still put on a grand show for the Maroons. The lobby was steam-
cleaned and spit polished, and the entire structure, from its
cantilevered roof to its plain steel awning, was decorated with
the kind of red, white, and blue bunting normally reserved for

national holidays. All 300 tickets to the event had been sold out for days, and many more fans crowded the lobby and the sidewalk on Mahantongo Street. Visitors coming through the glass and brass front doors were immediately hit by the aroma of roasted chicken and stuffing and the dulcet sounds of an eight-piece orchestra and a quartet led by Bud Whitehouse, the town's singing district attorney.

"The occasion was one which has never seen its equal in this county and, for that matter, was equal to any staged within the confines of William Penn's land," wrote *The Republican*. "There were bankers, lawyers, physicians, druggists, butchers, bakers, and candlestick makers there, from near and from far. Never has the dining room of Pottsville's leading hostelry echoed and reechoed with such a din of cheering as was heard when the confined cheering from the 300 loyal fans broke loose at once. It is a good thing that a new hotel is contemplated on the site of the present Allan because just the least bit more cheering no doubt would have brought the ceiling tumbling down."

After making their way through the crowd, the Maroons took their seats at the head table at the front of the banquet hall, where the game ball from Chicago hung from the ceiling. Absent were Berry, Ernst, Flanagan, and Osborn, who on Monday had left by train for Coral Gables, Florida, where they had been invited to play in a series of exhibition games featuring Red Grange. Each player had sent a personal telegram with their regrets, and those were read out loud at the start of the banquet by the quirky toastmaster, E.S. Fernsler.

Sitting nearby were Doc and Neva Striegel, Rauch, Mackay, and preeminent team booster Dory Schneider. Pottsville mayor J. Owen Bearstler was also in attendance. He actually left the ongoing miners' strike talks in Harrisburg to attend the banquet, and his news that the standoff might be settled by Christmas was a relief for many of the attendees.

Gifts were then handed out to the players: gold fountain pens; leather traveling bags; the thick, wool sweaters popularized by Red Grange with the stitched inscription "Pottsville Maroons World Champions;" and tiny gold footballs engraved with their names, the Pottsville P, and "1925 NFL Champions and 1925 World Champions." Rather than wait for the league to award the players with traditional gold pendants, Zacko had made an overnight trip to New York to secure the honorary keepsakes. He explained that he had made it back to town with just enough time to clean up at the Pennsylvania & Reading station washroom before dashing over to the Allan. The players joked among themselves that unless they were about to receive traveling trunks as well, there was no way for them to carry home all their loot. A delighted Herb Stein exclaimed, "Did you ever see anything like it? I mean, I wouldn't expect anything like this from a college, but from a professional team—my goodness, it's wonderful!"

One by one the dignitaries paid tribute to the team, while the fans ate dinner and whispered in the smoky hall, waiting for the night's main event: speeches by Rauch and Striegel. There were many laughs and expressions of gratitude, but the words that resonated the most during the early portion of the program came from Eddie Bennis, the referee the team had protected from assault during the Notre Dame game. Turning around to look the players in the eyes, Bennis said simply, "I think you are true-blue, every one of you."

Bennis' heartfelt statement, filled with equal amounts of admiration and regret, served as the running theme of the evening: You Are True-Blue, Every One of You. And it could have been prefaced with the words "I don't care what Joe Carr and the rest of the NFL say ... "

But it didn't need to be, since that elephant in the room—the palpable anxiety over the fate of the Maroons' lost football crown—was so pronounced, it couldn't have been more conspicuous had it been wearing a tuxedo and sitting at the end of the head table.

Schneider then took the microphone and ribbed the players about how bad they looked during their first weeks of practice, with most of the town looking on from the bumpers of their Model T's in the parking lot at Minersville Park. At the time, the odds had been stacked against Doc and Rauch lasting until Halloween. Now look at them, Schneider said: "Here we are, the baby team of the league, the smallest city to have a franchise, facing the strike and such continuously bad weather, and we walk away with the championship? No one could have dreamed of such a thing!"

Mackay was also a hit, telling of how visiting sportswriters had complained to him that they lacked the language needed to describe the talents of Tony Latone. "Well, of course they did!" roared Mackay, well-versed in the punch-line-and-reverential-pull-back cadence of banquet speaking. "Because there isn't another back like him in the WHOLE WORLD! When your team faced Frankford, by god, it was as if someone yelled, 'TIME TO EAT!' And if you boys met the Horsemen again, YOU'D STEAL THEIR HORSES! You know, I wouldn't be half surprised to see a new, 15,000-seat stadium built in Pottsville for the following season, a throne in keeping with the dignity of the rulership. Because Pottsville is unquestionably the greatest team I ever looked at. They can't take the championship from you. No, they can't. You won it at Chicago. There is no question but that the

Maroons are the best team in football, and no edict will take the reputation from you. Because the newspapers of America say Pottsville is CHAMPION OF THE WORLD!!!"

Word of a new stadium, even though it had no basis in fact, along with the rose-colored tint of the speeches, had the crowd buzzing inside the hall and out. When it came time for Rauch to speak, hotel staff hurried to open the lobby windows so that the fans who had crowded outside on the street could listen in as well. Rauch then stood and, according to those in attendance, spoke in the soft, shy tone "of a schoolboy on grammar day," which made it difficult to hear even halfway back inside the banquet hall. Although much of the team's success could be attributed to Rauch's groundbreaking preparation, his in-game wizardry, and the sense of professionalism and pride he brought to the ragtag pro league, no one was surprised that the coach immediately deflected credit to those around him. "By the time I got here, Doc had already assembled the best talent ever," Rauch shrugged. "Doc and the players had the tough jobs, and they did all the work. The credit belongs to them and not me."

Echoing Bennis and Mackay, he then turned to the team and said, "You merit all you have earned, and all the edicts of Joe Carr cannot rob you of it." Rauch also paid tribute to Neva, murmuring into the microphone that "there is a time when the word of a woman helps with a fellow, and Mrs. Striegel is always there with a word or two for all the boys. When time is darkest ... she was on the job ... giving sunshine ... and ... her work means a lot."

The coach paused for a moment, then tried to go on. But overcome by emotion, he simply set the microphone down and walked back to his seat.

Fernsler then jumped up and quickly introduced the man of the hour: "Pottsville's foremost citizen today, a man who has made known the name of Pottsville from coast to coast entirely for the sake of sport and his old hometown, though it has cost him dearly—ladies and gentlemen, Doc Striegel."

Recalled a member of the audience: "Probably never has there been a reception given to a man as he rose to his feet to speak in this city as was accorded Dr. J.G. Striegel. Every person stood to praise him, and the applause and cheering was so prolonged that it was a minute before he could commence with his address."

By now word had spread among the crowd at the Allan that President Joe Carr had sent a telegram with his personal regrets about not being able to attend the banquet. It was nothing more than a polite gesture by a stern but thoroughly proper man. That didn't stop fans from thinking, in light of the scandal brewing with the Chicago Cardinals, that there was hope that the communiqué from Carr meant the Maroons were soon to be reinstated as NFL champions.

Pottsvillians seemed to talk of nothing else. Many of them noted that after losing to the Maroons, Cards owner Chris O'Brien used a quirk in the rules to attempt what the league categorized as an end around on the standings. Since the NFL champion was ultimately determined by winning percentage, O'Brien scrambled to line up two more opponents—the Hammond Pros and Milwaukee Badgers—before the official end of the season on December 20. His hope was that the Maroons would falter and the Cards could slip past them in the rankings by mere decimal points, winning the title on a technicality. It seemed ridiculous given that the Maroons had pummeled his team so thoroughly on their home field, but stranger things had happened.

For O'Brien, an NFL title was almost an afterthought. What he truly coveted was the right, as pro league champions, to face the Bears and Red Grange in a season-ending guaranteed moneymaker in the Windy City. (O'Brien had, in Mackay's words, hoodwinked himself again, because after a series of injuries, beginning in Pittsburgh at the hands of the Stein brothers, Grange had been ordered by doctors to stop playing real games.)

One of O'Brien's handpicked patsies, the Hammond Pros, had already disbanded for the season, but within a week they were able to get enough of their roster back together for a respectable contest inside Comiskey Park, where they played their part and lost to Chicago 13-0.

With Saturday filled, O'Brien tried to schedule the Milwaukee game. With little time to regroup, however, it was immediately apparent that the Badgers were not going to be able to field a team. A desperate Cardinals player named Art Folz then went back to his Chicago-area prep alma mater, Englewood High School, looking for replacement players. He eventually coerced four teenage players to fill out the Badgers roster, telling them the contest was nothing more than a practice game behind closed doors and would therefore have no bearing on their amateur status. Folz went so far as to drive the teenagers to the stadium and provide them with team jerseys. Predictably, the game was an embarrassing farce, with Chicago winning 59-0 in a contest so lopsided that the teams played shortened quarters and O'Brien refused to charge admission. "Touch football would have been termed rough compared to the exhibition staged," wrote the *Chicago Daily News*. "Neither team made any efforts to tackle, because the ground was frozen hard as a concrete sidewalk." It was, noted another reporter, "an odd game to base a championship on."

While Carr was disappointed with Pottsville's decision to go ahead with the Notre Dame game, he was incensed by the Cardinals and utterly beside himself about the corruption of four high school amateurs, something that only reinforced the notion of a mercenary, lawless league that the NFL was finally beginning to overcome. "Pro football has now forfeited all the prestige that Red Grange had given it," wrote one critic after the Badgers game. From his hospital bed in Columbus, Carr began an immediate inquiry into the Milwaukee scandal, promising swift, severe punishments, including lifetime bans and franchise forfeitures for anyone involved. Scared or embarrassed, the Milwaukee manager disappeared on the next train out of Wisconsin.

Meanwhile, back inside the ornate ballroom at the Allan, Maroons fans reasoned that in light of the seriousness of the Cards' violations, Pottsville's misdeeds seemed inconsequential—something Striegel tried to emphasize in the early portion of his speech.

"As to the championship," Striegel told the crowd, "if it depends on playing high school teams, well then, the Cards can have it. We can defeat any team the league picks as champions, and we are the real titleholders in the public's eye. I am not defying the league, but President Carr must give me a hearing before the whole league, and until that time, which will be in January, he can do nothing.

"Pro football, up until this year, used to be a defensive affair with scores of 3-0, 6-0, 6-3, et cetera," Doc continued. "Canton's largest score the year its club was champion was something like 10 points. They used to get 10 points and then kick the ball to death in defensive tactics. You see, it is no trick to get 11 men who can play fine defensive football. But it is a hard thing indeed to get an offensive club. Pottsville had a rare offensive club this season, one that piled up 327 points, which is not only a league record but a mark that will stand to be shot at for some time, despite the fact that the Maroons did not play high school teams such as the Chicago Cardinals did."

Doc continued on, strong, proud, and defiant. Even in the face of certain suspension he was empowered, at first, by the civic support at the Maroons' testimonial. The Maroons had made history, he said, and it was all embodied here inside this banquet hall. Not just their win-loss record, their eye-popping statistics, or their championship victories over the Cardinals and the Irish. But more so, the way they managed to profoundly change the game in a single season: by bringing an entire community together under the banner of pro football, by advancing the ideas of daily practice, scouting, and passing, and by using a roster that balanced local and imported players who assimilated into the community like a college team.

Even if they did end up losing their NFL title, as long as the league survived, then so too would the Maroons' influence and legacy.

That was Doc's hope, anyway.

Striegel paused for a moment to collect himself and his thoughts. All the banquet-style, rah-rah rhetoric was nice, but he knew it couldn't change the reality of the situation. Earlier in the day, he had been notified by the bank that Schumann had stopped payment on the extra check he had written before kickoff at Shibe Park. That double cross meant that the team and its owner were going to end the season just as they had begun it, teetering on bankruptcy. If the Maroons were $5,000 in debt by their third game, there was no telling how much of his own personal fortune Doc had spent to keep the team afloat since October. $10,000? $20,000? Whatever the total, most fans speculated that it was enough to break even the wealthiest men in Pottsville. And by the time Doc began to speak again, the strains of the season had begun to manifest themselves in his body language and speech.

"This team," he began, his head tilted downward and his shoulders rolled just slightly forward, "is too big for one man to handle. Somebody else must help. I shall remain the active head of the organization until such a time as I have fought out the battle now on my hands. But after I get it back, it is to be the property of the fans. I don't want it. It belongs to the fans who made it possible, and I don't want any part of it."

The gasp from the crowd quickly turned into a hushed silence. "There should be a true association," Striegel said flatly. "Make it a community affair. The franchise is yours. I will return it to you."

Standing before them was a man wholly unequipped to handle failure or public embarrassment or the dawning reality that, perhaps, he had misplayed the hand of his life and gambled away not only his own immortality but that of his team and his beloved hometown as well. The idea broke Doc's heart and his spirit. With eyes sunken and surrounded by dark circles, Doc looked out across the packed, spellbound crowd one last time and, in conclusion, said somberly, "All we want is football."

As with Bennis' speech, it was hard to tell if his remarks were filled with hope or regret.

Regardless, the next day's paper reported that Doc's final words were "greeted with an outburst of applause and cheers that echoed and re-echoed far out to the street [where] there were at least 100 fans that heard Striegel's offer and joined in the cheering."

Yet for Doc, the blissfully ignorant feeling of the testimonial dinner, despite what the team was facing, only reinforced what had become an unacknowledged, subversive theme of the free-for-all era they were living in. What if they were wrong? What if the good times were not going to last forever? What if, just like the gleaming and glamorous banquet hall they were in tonight, the Maroons were also soon to be reduced to rubble?

Was the team doomed? Was the town doomed? Was the era doomed?

Were they all?

After Striegel spoke, patrons and the guests of honor quietly ate pie and ice cream while listening to the string quartet and a handful of football song parodies by Bud Whitehouse. "The testimonial was then brought to a close by bidding farewell to the Maroons," reported the paper. The team dutifully lined up by the entrance of the hall and shook hands with fans and supporters as they filed out of the Allan and into the bone-chilling air and disorienting darkness of the street.

There was dignity and gratitude in the emotional exchanges between the Maroons and the citizens of Pottsville. There were plenty of firm, two-handed handshakes, pats on the back, and knowing nods, yet most of the exchanges seemed tinged by an underlying lament. The silent acceptance of their fate was disturbing. And during this somber farewell act—as players clutched the tiny gold footballs given to them, their thumbs drawn over the engraved words "1925 World Champions"— there were many misty eyes on both sides of the line. In the end, concluded one observer, the final act of the 1925 Pottsville Maroons was indeed "a sort of sad parting at that."

"You might say," O'Hara added, "there are mighty few teams in this vale of tears which are as good as the Maroons."

That same week, Pottsville newspapers reported for the first time on irregularities in the stock market.

CHAPTER 21

THE STOLEN CHAMPIONSHIP

MANY OF THE MAROONS PLAYERS, enjoying themselves on a barnstorming tour of Florida with Red
Grange, missed the postseason hoopla. Joe Carr,
however, wasted little time sorting out the controversies in his
league. On December 29, 1925, he fined the Milwaukee club
$500 and gave the Badgers management 90 days to dispose of
their assets and retire from the league. He also fined the
Cardinals $1,000 and placed O'Brien on probation for one year.
Chicago's game against the Badgers and the four high school
players was ordered to be stricken from league records, while Folz,
the player who admitted to recruiting the boys to the game, was
barred for life from the NFL. (The prep players suffered the
most, losing their amateur status and forfeiting any chance at
college scholarships.) Pottsville, meanwhile, was fined $500 and
suspended as a member of the NFL.

"Just when it seemed that our organization had gone fairly well," Carr stated to reporters through clenched teeth from the league offices in Columbus, "two events happened that threatened to tear the very foundation from under our league. First, Milwaukee and the Chicago Cardinals engaged in a game of football at Chicago in which four high school boys were permitted to play with the Milwaukee club. Then, over the positive orders of the president of the league, and against all of its rules and regulations, the Pottsville team invaded the territory of another club in the league and played a game with a team that was not a member of the league."

As he had promised, Doc and his brother, attorney George Striegel, traveled to the Hotel Statler in Detroit to plead their case at the NFL owners meeting. According to minutes of the meeting, during the first order of new business the Striegels asked for the president's report regarding the Pottsville suspension to be "laid on the table." The motion carried.

In it, Carr states: "In the case of Pottsville I had been apprised through reports of league members and the press that the Pottsville team intended to play a game in Philadelphia on Saturday, December 12. I immediately notified the management of the Pottsville club that the game should not be played, under all penalties the league could inflict. The Pottsville management wired me that they had signed a contract and that they desired the league to insure them against a damage suit. I advised that the league would give them every protection possible and again forbade them to play in the protected territory of another club, and with a team that was not a member of our organization. Three different notices forbidding the Pottsville club to play were given and the management elected to play regardless. Hence, I fined the Pottsville club $500 and suspended them from all rights and privileges, and declared their franchise forfeited in the league ... As to the hearing requested by the Striegel brothers, I advised them that under no consideration would I retract the penalties that had been imposed, unless instructed to do so by the league, and if it is the pleasure of the organization before we adjourn, the Pottsville club will be given a hearing and also the facts restated by your president. It will then be up to the organization to either sustain the president or give the Pottsville club a mitigation of sentence."

It was then moved by Frankford and Kansas City that the president's report be accepted as read regarding Pottsville's case. Before the vote could carry, however, a 10-minute recess was asked for and granted as a way to allow cooler heads a chance to prevail.

These were tumultuous, tenuous times for the NFL, when the league was still hanging on by a lace. One wrong move and pro football could have taken a much different path. The pro game's largest draw at the time was Grange, of course, but instead of coveting his services, when Grange and his manager C.C. Pyle asked for a franchise in New York, they were turned down by the NFL because Giants owner Tim Mara controlled the territory. (It was an odd way to thank Grange. Mara, after all, had been $40,000 in debt after the 1925 season until Grange and his Chicago Bears bailed him out by drawing 70,000 to the Polo Grounds.) Grange and Pyle responded by breaking away to form their own nine-team American Football League featuring Grange's New York Yankees football franchise.

With Grange's future uncertain, the NFL owners could not afford to lose the Maroons, their most talented, popular and successful team. What would it say to potential fans when the team that had just made national headlines by defeating the almighty Notre Dame Four Horsemen jumped to a rival league? At the same time,

Carr had made great strides in cleaning up the image of the NFL. By playing Notre Dame, the Maroons had clearly, and publicly, disregarded the rules of the league and violated the territory of another franchise. There was simply no way Carr could suspend the Maroons, brand them outlaws, and then two months later celebrate this rogue franchise as his league champions, the new, shining beacon of professional football. Trying to save the franchise and the championship, Doc Striegel laid himself bare before the NFL. I'm the culprit, he explained. I'm the one you want. Not the team. The players are innocent. Doc offered to sell the team and accept whatever fine or ban the league saw fit to hand down just as long as the Maroons could keep the honors they had won on the field. For a man like Doc Striegel it's hard to imagine a more humiliating—or heartfelt—gesture. And yet Carr refused.

But in order to keep the peace, and to prevent a string of defections to Grange's league, a private three-way settlement was apparently brokered among Chicago, Frankford, and Pottsville. It was this: Although they were clearly the best team in 1925, because they had been suspended from the league before the end of the season, the Maroons could not be named NFL champions. In turn, Striegel would accept this decision and stop demanding written proof of the territory law cited by Carr and Royle, a document that has never been produced and likely never existed. Doc would also reimburse Shep Royle $2,500 for lost gate receipts relating to the Notre Dame game (he had asked for $5,000) and in exchange Carr gave his word that by the summer the Maroons would be forgiven and re-admitted to the NFL. In addition, it appears O'Brien agreed not to stake a claim on the 1925 title and in exchange his hefty $1,000 fine for the Milwaukee debacle was rescinded.

For the second time in two months the Maroons would be

called upon to save the NFL from itself. And for some reason the Maroons agreed. Again.

It was a shrewd deal considering what would have been Striegel's perspective and motivation. At that moment, his No. 1 priority was not the 1925 NFL title but getting the Maroons back in the league and in good standing where, surely, with their talent they would win a handful of other championships and establish themselves as the Green Bay Packers of the East. A broke and desperate Striegel had weighed an NFL championship against a Notre Dame payday and others down the road, including a possible match with Grange or even a lucrative national tour—and he chose the money. At the time it was a wise decision. Striegel was warned at least once by Carr not to play the game in Shibe Park. But because he signed the contract based on what he thought was permission from the league, why should he back out and risk financial ruin? A game against Notre Dame could be a life-changing event while a championship crown in a league no one was sure would be around in a year or two didn't mean all that much. There was simply no way for Doc to understand that his team of pioneers would become lost in time and, that when they reemerged half a century later, an NFL title would be one of the most coveted sporting accolades on the planet.

Yet in everything except the official record book the Maroons were considered the 1925 champs. In brokering an accord with the NFL and not jumping ship to the AFL, Doc's only mistake was believing that the Maroons didn't need the official title to get the credit they deserved, that history would bequeath the crown to them after seeing what they had accomplished on the field. But it was a different time then, an era when results mattered—not honors. It was the Maroons' great misfortune to reemerge in an era when the exact opposite would be true.

The meeting was called back to order at 4:40 p.m., at which time the motion for the president's report to be accepted as read was carried.

Striegel, wisely, used the leverage of the AFL to insure that everyone kept his word. He traveled to Chicago to flirt with Grange and Pyle, and then took the AFL's offer straight to Carr's home in Columbus. Shortly thereafter, Carr began privately warning teams not to tamper with Pottsville's players because the Maroons were members of the NFL in good standing. Royle got his money and his petty revenge. O'Brien kept his team and avoided foreclosure. And it was agreed that the Milwaukee game would be stricken from the official record—leaving Pottsville and Chicago in a tie for first place.

Doc had vowed to restore the franchise for Pottsville. And at great financial loss and extraordinary embarrassment to himself, he had kept his word.

The more time Carr had to reflect, the more sympathetic the president became to the Maroons. Had he been manning his post at the league office when Striegel called for permission to play Notre Dame, none of this would have happened. Royle had also used the president's health problems and weakened state to railroad the league into action against Pottsville. In the grand scheme of things, Carr must have also realized that the Maroons' punishment for playing an exhibition that provided tremendous publicity for the league shouldn't be more severe than the Cardinals trying to manipulate the standings with games against teenagers. During the summer of 1926, Carr visited Pottsville, where he was given a tiny coal football fob with the inscription *Pottsville—J.F.C—1926*. The president showed no objection to the banners and team advertisements that proclaimed the Maroons the 1925 NFL champions. Zacko said he even received correspondence from the NFL addressed to "The Pottsville Maroons—1925 NFL Champions."

On this trip and during the rest of his time as NFL president, Carr wrote daily in a red-leather bound diary. Years later, when family members discovered the book they say it contained the notation: *Pottsville: All is forgiven—they are the true champions of 1925.* (The book was originally donated to the Hall of Fame. But after a disagreement with the Hall, Carr's family asked for it to be returned and it was apparently lost in the transfer.) Nevertheless, on July 12, 1926 at the Ben Franklin Hotel in Philadelphia, Carr essentially made the same proclamation when he reinstated the Maroons and, according to newspaper reports, gave them "a clean slate and all honors restored."

Carr also saw to it that O'Brien kept his word regarding the 1925 NFL title. In the end, the Cardinals owner became one of the Maroons' strongest advocates. So that it would remain in perpetuity as part of the league record, at the next owners meeting O'Brien again renounced the Milwaukee result, saying Chicago and Pottsville had finished 1925 in a tie for first place. And although pressured by other owners to bring closure to the season by accepting the title of NFL champion, the Cardinals' owner steadfastly refused to accept what he called a bogus title, saying his team could not claim ownership of something they had not rightfully won on the field.

As a result, the 1925 NFL championship was never officially awarded.

E PILOGU E

WATCHING AND WAITING

I N OCTOBER 1961, DICK McCANN, the original executive director of the Pro Football Hall of Fame, stepped to a
podium at the Schuylkill Country Club in Pottsville, looked
out across a packed audience of the Maroons' first team
reunion and pledged, "I will keep fighting until the 1925
National Football League championship is rightfully restored
to Pottsville."

Those were the words Pottsville had been waiting nearly four
decades to hear.

With a reworked roster, the 1926 Maroons went 10-2-2, losing
to the Chicago Bears, 9-7, and tying the Yellow Jackets, 0-0, in
the final two games of the season. The loss and tie dropped
Pottsville to third place behind the Bears and Frankford who, by
way of their 14-1-2, record were able to surpass the Maroons on
the final day of the season to claim the 1926 NFL championship.

The Maroons franchise never recovered from the two heart-wrenching near misses.

By the end of the 1927 season, a 5-8 campaign, there was considerably less excitement around the Maroons—many of the best original players had moved on and Striegel's heart was no longer in it. In 1928, he was so eager to distance himself from the franchise that Striegel leased the team to Osborn, Herb Stein, and Fats Henry for a nominal fee of $100. The team went 2-8 in front of sparse crowds. A year later, Doc sold the team to a group headed by George Kenneally, who moved the Maroons to Boston and renamed them the Bulldogs. The Boston Bulldogs brought Rauch back into the fold but could still do no better than 4-4.

On the verge of collapse, the franchise went out with a blaze of glory: traveling back home to Pottsville, where the team defeated the Buffalo Bisons and, two days later, the Orange Tornadoes in a swansong performance before a sold-out crowd at Minersville Park.

That very same day—October 29, 1929—the stock market crashed.

The Great Depression was particularly devastating to the coal region. The country's subsequent move away from coal and toward oil-based energy ensured that Pottsville, the Queen City of the Anthracite, would never regain the prominence or prosperity she had known during the Twenties. During the next three decades the Maroons were reduced to little more than a coal region folktale.

Disturbed that heroic, pioneering players like Tony Latone had become ghosts of the game, simple footnotes haunting the yellowing pages of football encyclopedias, Walter Farquhar reignited interest in the team in 1945 with the publication of an essay on the Maroons controversy titled "The Stolen Championship." It became the seminal piece of literature in Pottsville's fight to regain the title and is still being reprinted some 60 years later—mistakes and all. In it, an overzealous Farquhar claimed, falsely, that the Maroons had not been warned prior to the Notre Dame game and that Carr himself had ordered Chicago to play the two extra games to push them ahead in the standings. (This is untrue, although to be fair it had been included as fact in the NFL's own *Record & Fact Book* until 1986.) Regardless, Farquhar's piece stirred some regional interest and even motivated Zacko to produce 1,000 copies at his own expense to be distributed to the town's soldiers abroad during World War II.

For the next two decades the team survived by word of mouth as veterans of the war passed the legend of the Maroons and their saga down to their sons and grandsons as if it were a prized Pottsville heirloom. Like the First Defenders, the Molly Maguires, and the Battle of the Crater, the Maroons took their place in the pantheon of Pottsville lore. Then, in 1962, Zacko, who was 64, was leafing through his morning paper inside his store when he read a note about plans for the Pro Football Hall of Fame and the league's request for donated memorabilia.

Zacko rang up Dick McCann and told him he had the very size 9 shoe that Charlie Berry used to beat the Notre Dame All-Stars in 1925.

"Give us back the title that you stole," Zacko crowed. "And you can have the shoe. No title. No dang shoe."

McCann explained that he didn't have that kind of authority but he promised to get the Maroons' story to the men who did. Just like old times, Zacko and Farquhar sprang into action. A new series on the Maroons ran in *The Republican* and plans were made to host a team reunion dinner at the Necho Allen Hotel, on the same spot the team held its farewell testimonial in 1925. As RSVPs came back, organizers realized much of the sadness and regret from the saga had not dissipated. For starters, three of the major players from 1925 team would be unable to attend. After the stock market crash, with his social standing gone and his personal wealth depleted, a disgraced Doc Striegel left Neva and his four children behind and started a new life with his mistress outside of Philadelphia. His one-time nemesis, Joe Carr, had passed away in 1939 at the age of 59, a short while after being reelected to a 10-year term as NFL president, but not before making good on his promise to rid the league of nearly all its small-town teams. And by the 1960s, coach Dick Rauch, a retired and nationally recognized government ornithologist, was too ill to leave his home in Harrisburg to attend.

The players, all nearing retirement age, looked and acted like a band of long-lost brothers: identical black suits, gray hair, wire-rimmed glasses, rounded shoulders, thick necks, meaty forearms, and a collective laugh so hearty it shook the chandeliers. Just as they had suspected during their playing days, the memories the Maroons created in 1925 had indeed lasted a lifetime. All the great moments from the championship season were told and retold and, after another round of drinks, retold all over again.

There was Latone's gravity-defying line plunging against Notre Dame and Berry's world-changing kick that was only the captain's fourth field goal of the season; Rauch's dignity during halftime at Shibe Park; French's fantastic feet in Comiskey; the Stein brothers smothering Driscoll in the snow; the goal-line stands led by Hathaway, Racis, and Bucher, and Ernst's punt return against Chicago; Osborn handing the captaincy to Berry; Fungy's punted proposal; all those nights and days at The Phoenix and the scoldings from Mother Striegel; the train trips, the injuries, the gossip, and the star treatment.

"When we got back together at the reunion we acted like a bunch of young boys," recalled Latone.

The players were all given tiny gold replicas of Berry's famous cleat. Yet for nearly all the Maroons, the 1925 season turned out to be the least of their accomplishments.

Jack Ernst had become a lumber company executive in Williamsport. Charlie Berry was now the dean of American League umpires. Russ and Herb Stein used their football money to start a multimillion-dollar business in iron scrap and land development. Russ had also been elected sheriff of Niles, Ohio. Duke Osborn was now an executive with General Motors. Frank Bucher had become president of A&P foods, one of the largest grocery store chains in the country. Hoot Flanagan used his football money to start a dental practice back home in Martinsburg, West Virginia. Barney Wentz served out his term as a councilman in Shenandoah and became an auditor for the state of Pennsylvania.

Walter French had become the baseball coach at West Point. Fungy Lebengood and Mary Jane Reed were celebrating their 35th wedding anniversary. Frankie Racis remained a coal region legend, having played 18 years of pro football and retiring from the game in 1936 as one of the NFL's first great Iron Men.

Walter Farquhar was still the dean of Schuylkill County sportswriters. His protégé, John O'Hara, quit the *Journal* in 1926 because the editor wouldn't give him time off for a date. Just as he had promised, O'Hara moved to New York and with the publication of *Appointment in Samarra* in 1934, and his collection of stories about Gibbsville (which were based on his experiences growing up in Pottsville), he was being hailed as American literature's preeminent short story writer.

Tony Latone finished his football career in Providence. Shep Royle had tried to lure him to Frankford, but Latone retired rather than play for the Yellow Jackets. After his playing days, The Howitzer landed in Detroit where Bucher hired him to work in one of A&P's main warehouses. At A&P, Latone passed up several promotions to management because, his family says, he wasn't comfortable telling other men what to do. "I sure was glad to be back in Pottsville," Latone said upon his return to Sharp Mountain. "I am still sorry that I couldn't make a little better speech when it was my turn but words just wouldn't come out. I meant to tell of the best game I ever played, and you couldn't even guess that one, I bet. It was when I was with the Wilkes-Barre Panthers, when I played against Pottsville—because after that game, I became a Maroon. So, that is why I think it was my best game. The fans and the towns folk of Pottsville were the best."

Others rose to speak. Maroons supporters, like reunion committee president Dr. William C. Dorsavage, equated losing the title to having cancer eat away at his body. But to a man, the players all went to their graves having barely uttered a word about the team to even their closest friends and family. It was a different time then, an era when a breach in sportsmanship or comportment would have been far more embarrassing than a squandered NFL title. So as angry as some of the players were about the NFL's ruling and its treatment of the town, nearly all the Maroons remained silent. Although family members of the players contend that they all hoped, one day, the players would be remembered for what they achieved on the football field and for the way the confluence of the times, the town, and the talent came together in a magical way that altered the course of professional football.

After McCann's speech, Bucher spoke on behalf of the team. "The stolen championship was an insult to the great city of Pottsville, the Maroons, and their fans, and certainly a black mark against professional football and those who directed the league. Naturally, we players were disappointed; we felt cheated out of something we had earned the hard way. We were stunned and could not believe it to be true, yet we were powerless to do anything. However, we players can suffer it out if necessary. Many of our boys have passed on and in a few years there will be none of us left.

"In the heart of the anthracite region in Pennsylvania, tucked away in the hills, is the great little city of Pottsville," Bucher continued. "Small in number but big of heart: a community that has had to fight every inch of the way. In the Civil War days you were known as the First Defenders. In the days of the Pottsville Maroons, and today, you are known as the Proud Little Queen City of the Anthracite. You are the people who, by your loyalty, enthusiasm and never-say-die attitude, inspired the Maroons to a championship. You are the people who are still carrying the fight for plain and simple justice. You want no more and you will take no less.

"In Canton, Ohio, the National Professional Football Hall of Fame has its home and a monument to the sport is being erected. It would seem that depriving the Maroons of their championship violates the very basic concept of this great institution and failure to remedy this serious wrong only compounds the disgrace."

Spurred by the response to the reunions, in the summer of 1962, Zacko spearheaded a citizens' petition asking NFL owners for a vote to restore the 1925 title. Support rolled in from newspapers across the country, from the *Stars and Stripes* in Garmisch, Germany (where Berry was conducting a goodwill baseball clinic for the Army), to Portland, Phoenix, Birmingham, St. Louis, Chicago, Detroit and Philadelphia. "This should have been cleaned up long ago," Berry wrote in a letter to Bears owner George Halas. "No one could touch us."

In a bittersweet editorial the Wilkes-Barre *Independent* wrote, "The Maroons could very possibly have been the Green Bay Packers of the East were it not for the now infamous stolen championship." While the *Miami News* said: "Pottsville may have a short main street but it has a long memory and a long sense of justice. The mighty Zacko's campaign to have the 1925 NFL title taken away from the Chicago Cardinals—now the St. Louis Cardinals—and restored to Pottsville, its rightful claimant, he insists, has become a cause celebre. Little oppressed, mistreated men everywhere have identified themselves with little Pottsville in Pennsylvania's anthracite coal-mining region. Champions of the underdog from coast-to-coast have rallied to Pottsville's homemade banner."

Several prominent figures from inside the NFL also grabbed hold of that tattered flag. Art Rooney, owner of the Pittsburgh Steelers; Halas; Red Grange; Frank McNamee, president of the Philadelphia Eagles; and Milton King, vice president of the Washington Redskins, all publicly backed the Pottsville petition. Although his disdain for Pottsville was legendary, O'Hara still enlisted his friends in the media, including columnist Red Smith, to support the Maroons' cause. Pennsylvania governor William Scranton also sent a message to then-NFL commissioner Pete Rozelle informing him that the entire weight of the Commonwealth of Pennsylvania was behind the Maroons.

As the NFL's January 1963 meeting approached, Jim Kensil, then the public relations director for the league, called Zacko in Pottsville, pleading, "Pottsville is on the agenda for the meeting, Now, will you please call your friends out there and tell them to stop calling us and to stop writing us so the switchboard operators and the secretaries can get back to running the office?"

Everyone seemed to be in Pottsville's corner—everyone except the NFL. The Maroons lost the vote.

"I wanted the Maroons made champions at that meeting," insisted McNamee. "And I think that had they been recognized as champs it would have helped football tremendously. I, along with Art Rooney of the Pittsburgh Steelers, feel that you are entitled to the world championship which was fairly won on the field."

In the end, Pottsville couldn't overcome three major stumbling blocks. Although the basic facts supported the city's claim, the petition they submitted was flawed, unfocused, and abrasive to the point of being off-putting. Owners did not want to set a precedent that would force them to reexamine every league champion before a title game was instituted in 1933. But mostly, Pottsville's efforts were doomed by one man: Cardinals president Charles "Stormy" Bidwill Jr., whose family laid claim to the 1925 championship shortly after purchasing the franchise in 1932. (Up until 1985 the official NFL *Record & Fact Book* said the Cardinals had only been "proclaimed" the 1925 champs.)

Before a committee of Mara, Rooney, and others moved the issue to a vote, Bidwill Jr. wrote to sportswriter Red Smith to explain his family's position. "A recent newspaper article boasts of the determination of Pottsvillians engaged in an ex post facto battle for the 1925 championship," wrote Bidwill Jr. "It says: 'It would be well to note here that the men of Pottsville usually manage to get things done. When the Union Army laid siege to Petersburg, Virginia, it was a group of Pottsville miners who tunneled under the city with the famous Petersburg mine.' If this is an example of how Pottsvillians manage to get things done, I think they had best forget the whole thing. As you know, the Petersburg mine, which evolved into the Battle of the Crater, was one of the major Union fiascos of the Civil War. The

Pottsville effort to get a championship appears to fall into a similar category." Not quite done, Bidwill Jr. continued, saying, "the Cardinals do not intend to let one of their two NFL crowns go from their heads to the foot of one Charlie Berry."

And so the Hall of Fame opened as planned in 1963, but without Berry's bronzed cleat. Despite their pioneering efforts, not one player on the 1925 Pottsville team has ever come close to enshrinement. The Herculean Latone, whose courageous game against Notre Dame ranks as one of the sport's all-time great individual performances, was the unofficial leading rusher of the NFL for the 1920s and should have been a lock. While record-keeping was not nearly as exact as it is today, in six seasons, Latone played in 65 games and rushed for 2,648 yards and 26 touchdowns. By comparison, in 30 more games, the great Red Grange rushed for fewer yards (2,616) and touchdowns (21). Had Latone gone to college instead of the coal mines, George Halas once said, he "would certainly have been one of the greatest pro players of all time."

Berry, an All-Pro and the NFL's leading scorer in 1925, has not been elected to either the baseball or football Hall of Fame. The team captain, along with Herb Stein, Ironman Frankie Racis, the innovative Rauch, and Duke Osborn (the first man to captain four straight NFL championship teams), all deserve far more consideration from the Hall of Fame than they've received.

In the end, championship or not, the league chose to turn its back on some of the very men who helped create it. And while the controversy surrounding the 1925 NFL championship has helped keep the Maroons' saga alive, it often overshadows the accomplishments and influence of one of the most important teams in league history. Until the Maroons transferred all the qualities of college ball—innovation, preparation, teamwork, sportsmanship, and, most important, civic boosterism—the NFL had been destined for failure.

In the 1980s, *Republican* sportswriter Doug Costello took the baton from an ailing Walter Farquhar and began his own extensive series on the team. The *Journal of Sports History* said, "One of the greatest injustices in NFL history has been perpetrated." In response, the NFL's official historians Joe Horrigan, Bob Braunwart, and Bob Carroll countered Farquhar's "The Stolen Championship" with their own essay titled, "The Discarded Championship." While confirming that, by far, the Maroons were the best football team in the world that year, the treatise blames Doc Striegel for trading the team's glory for his own personal greed, even though Striegel lost significant amounts of money in 1925. What it does not mention, however, is Carr's empathy for the Maroons, the witnesses and affidavits supporting Striegel's claim that he got permission from the league office to play Notre Dame, or the fact that the league has never produced the "territory" rule that Shep Royle used to begin the entire mess. In the end, the NFL's official version ended up being no more— or less—accurate than the town's. The main difference was that this time all the questionable elements were bent in favor of the league's perspective by three of its employees.

In the eight decades since the original standoff between Striegel and Carr, neither side has managed to gain any ground. Are the Pottsville Maroons the rightful 1925 NFL champions? It's the worst of all conceivable arguments because you can theoretically stand for either side and be both correct and justified.

"Every decade, some ink-stained Quixote sallies forth to save fair Dulcinea from the nasty windmill," wrote Carroll. "In the football version of the classic tale, the time has been updated to 1925, Dulcinea is called Pottsville, Pennsylvania, and the windmill is the

National Football League. 'Tis a story to break your heart."

By insulting and angering the town and the team's supporters with this kind of language, and therefore solidifying the David versus Goliath angle of the debate, the NFL only stoked the flames of a controversy that could have been extinguished decades ago. Instead, it's remained white hot. "It's one thing not to give the team the title it won and deserves," says Kevin Keating, the current Pottsville High School football coach, a lifetime resident and the son and grandson of coal miners. "But there's no excuse for the way the NFL has treated this town. It wasn't necessary. It's beneath a league that prides itself on class and professionalism. Whether the league gives the title up or not is irrelevant. The NFL should have more respect for the men who played the game, the men who paved the way, and for the fans who helped make it what it is."

ALMOST AS AN APOLOGY, in 1985 Pottsville became the only city to earn the NFL's prestigious Gladiator statue for contributions to the game. In 1995, the Hall of Fame also included a tribute to the Maroons as part of its 100 Years of Football exhibit. The centerpiece is a football carved from a chunk of shiny black anthracite and etched with the words: *Pottsville Maroons, NFL and World Champions.* As the millennium ended, that black ball appeared to be the only prize Pottsville would ever receive. Then, one more grassroots push caught the attention of Pennsylvania governor (and football fanatic) Ed Rendell. And at the owners meetings in May 2003 came a sign that pressure over time might finally transform the city's lump of coal into a championship trophy.

As Steelers owner Dan Rooney, Eagles owner Jeffrey Lurie, Pottsville mayor John Reiley, and Governor Rendell waited to plead

Pottsville's case to an NFL owners meeting—in Philadelphia, no less—they decided upon a remarkably simple compromise that received then-commissioner Paul Tagliabue's blessing.

Let the Maroons and the Cardinals share the title.

As Reiley remembers, "the commissioner turned to me and said, 'Mayor, when we get this championship for you, the four of us are coming to Pottsville to present it to you personally.' I thought for sure it was finally over.' "

The giant wood conference doors swung open. Once again, after nearly 80 years, all that stood between the Maroons and an NFL crown was the Cardinals. This time, though, it wasn't a fair fight. Not even close. Since the 1925 season, the Cards have won only one NFL championship, in 1947, and both Reiley and Rooney believe that drought has caused current owner Bill Bidwill to stick to his grandfather's wish and tighten his grip on his bogus claim to the 1925 title.

Although his franchise remains something of a laughingstock, with one playoff win during the last 59 years, the 76-year-old Bidwill remains a powerbroker in the league. Somehow, despite his clear bias, he was named as a member of the three-man committee appointed to look into the Maroons controversy. Bidwill, who worked as a ball boy for his grandfather's team when it was still in Chicago, then used his influence to squash the Maroons.

"What's been done to this town and this team—it's not right," said an angry Rooney. "It needs to be fixed."

When the owners gathered again in October 2003 they voted 30-2 against even discussing the issue—a moratorium Bidwill has kept to this day.

Now, in a league that practically legislates parity and success, fans in the Arizona desert have begun to wonder if the Cardinals' inexplicable failings are the result of a curse borne of their owner's treatment of the Pottsville Maroons. Fans of the team, which has had double-digit losing seasons in 13 of the past 18 years, have gone so far as to call members of the Pottsville Maroons Memorial Committee to ask for The Cards Curse to be lifted. Their request has been denied.

After the 2003 vote, sheepish NFL owners announced plans to present Pottsville with the Daniel F. Reeves Pioneer Award at the 2004 Hall of Fame festivities. The city, however, wasn't interested in any more consolation prizes. The ceremony was canceled. "That award is a slap in the face and it would be a disgrace to the players to accept it," says Nick Barbetta, 91, one of the few remaining eyewitnesses of the team and a founding member of the Pottsville Maroons Memorial Committee in the mid-1970's. "If we take it, the NFL would think the matter is closed. It isn't. It never will be, until justice is served."

The widowed Barbetta lives by himself in a split-level walkup in Schuylkill Haven just five miles south of Pottsville. The tiny but tidy home is cluttered with golf trophies, pictures of his grandchildren, intricate metal toy car models, including the Model T he rode to Maroons games in, and, of course, a whole stack of team memorabilia. Barbetta grew up in Pottsville and lived on a street where several of the players boarded during the season.

"Oh, they were rugged men," he says. "Rugged and tough, but honorable." Barbetta sold newspapers as a teenager for two cents a copy and he can still recall the wonder of walking into the city's ornate hotel lobbies, walking among the crowds of men in three-piece suits and wing-tipped shoes who always seemed to be talking of the next Maroons game and coal prices and nothing else. When Grange played in Pottsville, Barbetta, on a dare from his friends, snuck up behind him at the train depot and tugged on his trademark raccoon coat. Barbetta was startled at how fast the giant Ghost managed to twist around and catch him in the act. Red then palmed his head and messed up his hair before gently shooing him away. Later, Barbetta and his friends snuck under a hole in the fence at Minersville Park to watch the Maroons flatten the great Grange.

As an adult, while working for the Pennsylvania Chamber of Commerce, Barbetta traveled the region signing up businesses while spreading the legend of the Maroons. He's written, repeatedly, to every owner and to each of the last four commissioners. He drove to New York to confront Pete Rozelle but was turned away. Undeterred, he has since helped secure an historical marker for the team across the street from what used to be Schneider's Drug Store. Barbetta and the Maroons Memorial Committee also got a portion of the highway leading to the site of Minersville Park renamed the Pottsville Maroons Highway. "But the title," he says bowing his head, "we've just never been able to quite get our hands on the title."

The players are all gone now. The coach, the owner, the fans, all gone. (Joseph "Duke" Marhefka, the last known surviving Maroon, died in 2003 at the age of 101.) There's a strip mall where Minersville Park used to be; an Italian restaurant sits on the 50-yard line. Yuengling still brews a very popular line of beer from the top of Mahantango Street, although the company has remained largely absent from the Maroons' fight. The Armory is still standing, as is the town's glorious courthouse, and the brick prison where the Molly Maguires were hung in 1877. The Phoenix Hook & Ladder station house is still in operation. Next door, Doc Striegel's home is now a rundown apartment building. Schneider's name can still be seen in the custom bricks at the top of what is now a florist shop. The Hipp is an office for an insurance company. Zacko's is a dusty, abandoned storage space for a local artist who occasionally places large, colorful paintings of angels in the massive display window.

Looking out at the city's current panorama from Striegel's rickety, weather-worn porch, it's still easy to imagine this once bustling city; it's a feeling that hits visitors as uplifting and sad all at once.

Berry's bronzed cleat from the Notre Dame game sits in a small, nondistinct glass case just inside the lobby of the Historical Society of Schuylkill County. Next to it rests the Gladiator statue and several pictures of the team. Walter Farquhar is gone, as is Doug Costello. When Zacko died in 1975, his son Russ took up the fight. Now he's gone, too.

One of the town's last remaining connections to the team is a faded, haunting, black and white photo of the 1925 Maroons that hangs in the doorway of the Pottsville High School football locker room.

In the photograph, the team stands shoulder-to-shoulder, tall and proud, with their hands clasped behind their back. The few fans who understand the impact and influence of the Maroons approach the photo with reverence, moving slowly toward the image in the same way one might study a rare painting in a museum. It was a single moment in time captured more than 80 years ago yet many little details still stand out: like the unmistakable chiseled chin and dark eyes of Tony Latone; the wavy jet-black hair of Jack Ernst; the cockeyed stare of Duke Osborn; the sheer size of the Steins; the purposeful positioning of Charlie Berry holding the ball in the exact center of the team; the calm, dignified grin of Dick Rauch; and the certainty that Doc Striegel must have been just out of the frame, orchestrating everything.

In the glare of the setting sun, the players all squint slightly into the camera, bravely facing the dimming light, as if seeking an answer to the same question. And until that day comes, the Maroons will remain here, watching and waiting.

Over the past few decades Barbetta has stood by as well and watched as the team's players and supporters have passed away, one after the other, without realizing their dream: to get back the 1925 title and answer the question that haunts this team and this town. He suspects that was the NFL's intention all along, to simply outlast them all. And it has worked. When it hits, this realization stops Barbetta in midsentence.

There is sadness in his silence, a hint of bitterness and defeat. The deep creases that crisscross his face like a road map fall still, giving a brief but startling glimpse at the human toll this controversy has taken on the proud people of Pottsville.

After a long stretch of silence, Barbetta says that through the decades of disappointment he has tried to find peace with the one untouchable, untainted, undisputed fact regarding his beloved team.

"We'll always have those six days between the Chicago and Notre Dame games," he says. "And for those six glorious days, no one can deny that the Pottsville Maroons were champions of the world."

1925 POTTSVILLE MAROONS
Roster

DR. JOHN G. STRIEGEL (University of Pennsylvania) owner
DICK RAUCH (Penn State) coach/G-C
EDDIE GILLESPIE trainer

CLARENCE BECK, 5'11"/200, 30 (Penn State), **T-DL**
CHARLIE BERRY, 6'0"/185, 22 (Lafayette) captain, **E-PK**
FRANK BUCHER, 5'11"/190, 24 (Detroit Mercy), **DE**
HARRY DAYHOFF, 5'9"/180, 29 (Bucknell), **WB-FB-TB**
EDDIE DOYLE, 5'9"/173, 27 (Army), **DE**
JACK ERNST, 5'11"/180, 26 (Lafayette), **QB-DB-P-PR**
HOOT FLANAGAN, 6'0"/169, 24 (West Virginia-Wesleyan, Pittsburgh), **TB-WB**
WALTER FRENCH, 5'7"/155, 26 (Rutgers, Army), **WB-TB**
RUSS HATHAWAY, 5'11"/238, 29 (Indiana), **T-DL**
DENNY HUGHES, 5'11"/185 (George Washington), **C**
TONY LATONE, 5'11"/195, 28 (no college), **FB-WB-TB-LB**
FUNGY LEBENGOOD, 5'11"/175, 23 (Villanova), **WB-P**
ARMIN MAHRT, 5'11"/182, 27 (Dayton, West Virginia), **TB-DE**
BOB MILLMAN, 5'11"/178, 22 (Lafayette), **WB-LB**
DUKE OSBORN, 5'10"/188, 28 (Penn State), **G-DL**
FRANKIE RACIS, 6'0"/200, 25 (no college), **G-T-E**
ED SAUER, 5'10"/246, 26 (Miami Ohio), **T-DL**
HERB STEIN, 6'1"/186, 27 (Pittsburgh), **C-DL**
RUSS STEIN, 6'1"/210, 29 (Washington & Jefferson), **T-DE**
BARNEY WENTZ, 5'11"/204, 24 (Penn State), **FB-DL**

1925 POTTSVILLE MAROONS
Results

September 20	**COLWYN-DARBY**	48-0	**W**
September 27	**BUFFALO BISONS**	28-0	**W**
October 4	**PROVIDENCE STEAM ROLLER**	0-6	**L**
October 11	**CANTON BULLDOGS**	28-0	**W**
October 18	at **PROVIDENCE STEAM ROLLER**	34-0	**W**
November 1	**COLUMBUS TIGERS**	20-0	**W**
November 8	**AKRON PROS**	21-0	**W**
November 14	at **FRANKFORD YELLOW JACKETS**	0-20	**L**
November 15	**ROCHESTER JEFFERSONS**	14-6	**W**
November 22	**CLEVELAND BULLDOGS**	24-6	**W**
November 26	**GREEN BAY PACKERS**	31-0	**W**
November 29	**FRANKFORD YELLOW JACKETS**	49-0	**W**
December 6	at **CHICAGO CARDINALS**	21-7	**W**
December 12	**NOTRE DAME ALL-STARS** (at Philadelphia)	9-7	**W**

BIBLIOGRAPHY

Allen, Frederick Lewis. *Only Yesterday: An Informal History of the 1920s*. New York: First Perennial Classics, 2000.

Baughman, Judith S. *American Decades (1920-1929)*, Michigan: Thomson Gale, 1995.

Carroll, Bob, Michael Gershman, David Neft, and John Thorn. *Total Football II (The Official Encyclopedia of the National Football League)*. New York: HarperCollins, 1997.

Cope, Myron. *The Game That Was: An Illustrated Account of the Tumultuous Early Days of Pro Football*. New York: Thomas Y. Crowell, 1974.

Daly, Don, and Bob O'Donnell. *The Pro Football Chronicle*. New York: Macmillan, 1990.

Dumenil, Lynn. *The Modern Temper: American Culture and Society in the 1920s*. New York: Hill and Wang, 1995.

Jennings, Peter, and Todd Brewster. *The Century*. New York: Doubleday, 1998.

Leonard III, Joseph W. *Anthracite Roots: Generations of Coal Mining in Schuylkill County, Pennsylvania*. Charleston: The History Press, 2005.

Leuchtenburg, William E. *The Perils of Prosperity 1914-32*. Second edition. Chicago: The University of Chicago Press, 1993.

Neft, David S., et al. *Pro Football: The Early Years (An Encyclopedic History 1892-1959)*. United States: Sports Products Inc., 1978.

Peterson, Robert W. *Pigskin: The Early Years of Pro Football*. New York: Oxford University Press, 1997.

Poliniak, Louis. *When Coal Was King: Mining Pennsylvania's Anthracite*. Lancaster: Applied Arts Publishers, 2004.

Pottsville Bicentennial Committee. *Pottsville Bicentennial, Volume III (1906-1955)*. The Republican and Herald. Pottsville, 2006.

Smith, Robert. *Illustrated History of Pro Football*. New York: Madison Square Press, 1972.

Ward, Leo L. and Mark T. Major. *Pottsville in the Twentieth Century*. Charleston: Arcadia Publishing, 2003.

Ward, Leo L. and Mark T. Major. *Schuylkill County*. Volume II. Charleston: Arcadia Publishing, 1998.

Warren, Scott. *Pottsville Maroons Private Archives*. Wilkes-Barre, Pa., 2006.

Wolff, Geoffrey. *The Art of Burning Bridges: A Life of John O'Hara*. New York: Alfred A. Knopf, 2003.

Zacko, Joe. *Pottsville Maroons NFL Champions*. Pottsville, Pa., 1963.

Ziemba, Joel. *When Football Was Football: The Chicago Cardinals and the Birth of the NFL*. Chicago: Triumph Books, 1999.

SOURCE NOTES

Prologue: The Ghost Speaks

Red Grange agreed to speak: "Greatest Football Star? Could Have Been Latone," *Grit Magazine*, 1954.

Lycoming Hotel: "The Genetti Hotel, A Rich History," The Genetti Hotel—Williamsport, Pennsylvania. Website, 2006.

Grange had been offered: "Champ was a Star," Mahanoy City (Pa.) newspaper, 1975.

Grange stepped off the train: Nick Barbetta, interview, June 2005.

In Pottsville: Ward, Leo L., *Pottsville in the Twentieth Century*, Charleston: Arcadia Publishing, 2003.

"Everybody ... let their hair down": Cope, Myron, *The Game That Was: An Illustrated Account of the Tumultuous Early Days of Pro Football,* New York: Thomas Y. Crowell, 1974, pp. 41-42.

'The Perfect Football Machine': "Says Maroons Greatest Ever," *Philadelphia Inquirer*, December 2, 1925.

Angry citizens shot up the team's train: Jack Lebengood, interview, May, 2006.

Greatest Football Game: advertisement, *Philadelphia Inquirer*, December 12, 1925.

Volunteered to play: "The Stolen Championship of the Pottsville Maroons," *Journal of Sports History*, Spring, 1982, p. 56.

Minersville Park: Daly, Dan, *The Pro Football Chronicle*, New York: Macmillan, 1990, p. 6.

Crowds grew so big: "Pottsville Overwhelms Frankford Yellowjackets," *Philadelphia Public Ledger,* November 29.

On the first snap from scrimmage: "Champ was a Star," Mahanoy City (Pa.) newspaper, 1975.

"Four men and a horse ... ": MacCambridge, Michael, *ESPN College Football Encyclopedia,* New York: ESPN Books, 2005.

A performance that inspired: Peterson, Robert W., *Pigskin: The Early Years of Football,* New York: Oxford University Press, 1997, p. 85.

Grange got up: "Champ was a Star," Mahanoy City (Pa.) newspaper, 1975.

"The Pottsville Maroons were the most": Frank Bucher, Interview Reunion Program, 1961.

an homage Grange repeated: Stan Latone, interview, May 2005; "How Many Deserving Will Miss Hall?" *Pro Football Illustrated*, March 1963, p. 12.

unofficial leading rusher of the 1920s: "Lost in Time," *ESPN The Magazine*, February 28, 2005, p. 68.

"transferring his own mantle": "Greatest Football Star? Could Have Been Latone," *Grit Magazine*, 1954.

"When you talk about the birthplace of football": Dan Rooney, interview, December 5, 2004.

got his face slapped: Jack Ernst Jr., interview, March 2006.

a White House function: Cope, *The Game That Was,* p. 41.

smallest town to ever host a team: "Lost in Time," *ESPN The Magazine*, February 2005, p. 68.

One: Buried Alive

Ignatius Latone: Stan Latone, interview, May 2006.

At 300 feet: Lakawanna Coal Mine, reporting, April 2006.

More than 12,000 miners: Lakawanna Coal Mine, interviews, April 2006.

"slaughtered": Leonard III, Joseph W. *Anthracite Roots: Generations of Coal Mining in Schuylkill County, Pennsylvania.* Charleston: The History Press, 2005. p. 41.

only advertised employment: Ibid., p. 20.

Latones emigrated: Latone family letters, February 2006.

Necho Allen: Poliniak, Louis. *When Coal Was King: Mining Pennsylvania's Anthracite.* Lancaster: Applied Arts Publishers, 2004, p. 2.

Most other coal veins: Leonard, *Anthracite Roots,* p. 25.

deepest in the country: Wolff, Geoffrey, *The Art of Burning Bridges, New York:* Knopf, 2003. p. 17.

Anthracite is a rare: "Schuylkill was built on Anthracite," *Schuylkill County Chronicles,* December 11, 1997, p. 4.

He saw nothing special: Anthracite Heritage Museum (Scranton, Pa.), reporting, April 2006.

He was a dreamer: Latone family letters, February 2006.

Kingston Coal Company: Luzerne County Historical Society, archives, 2006.

The coal patches: Poliniak, *When Coal Was King,* pp. 26-27; Anthracite Heritage Museum (Scranton, Pa.), reporting, April 2006.

'monkey' coal: Ibid.

Four foot steel drill ... dynamite: Ibid.

Dead miners: Lakawanna Coal Mine, interviews, April 2006.

prescribed alcohol: Leonard, *Anthracite Roots,* pp. 19-34.

The town was home to: "Edwardsville: 100 Years," Luzerne County Historical Society, 2006.

Elizabeth took in: Stan Latone, interview, May 2006.

Her one respite: Latone family letters, February 2006.

Comerford's: "Edwardsville: 100 Years," Luzerne County Historical Society, 2006.

One morning: Latone family letters, February 2006.

Drank himself into a stupor: Ibid.

Coal company policy: Stan Latone, interview, May 2006.

two other infants: Latone family letters, February 2006.

Two: The Breaker Boy

80 million tons: Poliniak, *When Coal Was King,* p. 2.

200,000 workers: "Principal Mineral Production (table No. 5)", The Mineral Industry, webpage, December 6, 2006.

hundreds of boys: Poliniak, *When Coal Was King,* p. 14.

10-12 hours a day: "Virtual Field Trip", Pennsylvania State Historical Sites, Eckley Miners Village, website, September 18, 2005.

"red tops": Poliniak, *When Coal Was King,* p. 12.

his mother's child: Stan Latone, phone interview, March 2006.

"mule boys or 'drivers'": Poliniak, *When Coal Was King,* p. 19; Leonard, *Anthracite Roots,* p. 41; Ward, Leo L., and Mark T. Major, *Schuylkill County,* Volume II. Charleston: Arcadia Publishing, 1998, p. 16.

joined the Navy: Stan Latone, interview, May 2006.

coal car pushing: "Sportitorial: Leg Drive and Crouch," *Pottsville Republican*, October 15, 1961.

"I found myself": Ibid.

played sandlot football: Anthracite Heritage Museum (Scranton, Pa.), photo displays, April 2006.

Latone could make: "Greatest Football Star? Could Have Been Latone," *Grit Magazine*, 1954.

down in position: Scott Warren photo collection, Wilkes-Barre, Pennsylvania, 2006.

better plug your ears: Nick Barbetta, interview, May 2006.

"Tony was": "Greatest Football Star? Could Have Been Latone," *Grit Magazine*, 1954.

"Everything comes natural": Tony Latone, letter (from the collection of Scott Warren), January 15, 1967.

carried the ball oddly: "Pottsville Maroons Pushing Tony Latone for Berth in Pro Football Hall of Fame," *Sunday Independent*, June 27, 1965; "Sporting Snapshots" by Tom Heffernen, paper unknown.

nicknames: Zacko, Joe, *Pottsville Maroons NFL World Champions 1925,* unpublished manuscript (from the collection of Scott Warren), October 1963.

back in school: "Pottsville Downs Shenandoah," paper unknown, 1924.

"He would have certainly been": "Tony Latone, the Hero of Pottsville," *The Coffin Corner*, Vol. 9, 1987.

more than 100 yards: "Lithuanian Knights smother Steelton in Football Game," paper unknown, 1924.

"We never kicked": "Greatest Football Star? Could Have Been Latone," *Grit Magazine*, 1954.

"the dashing new halfback": "Pinebrook too Good for Speedy Plains Grid Team," Scranton dateline, paper unknown, October 23, 1923.

$75 a game: "Latone Remembers Being a Champ," *Houghton Lake Resorter*, August 28, 1975, p. 11.

Fritz Pollard: *Old Leather,* NFL Films, 1976.

without dropping: "Latone Plays Great Game for Panther Eleven," paper unknown, 1923.

The Latone Special: Nick Barbetta, interview, April, 2006; "Panthers End Up With Victory," *Wilkes-Barre*, Dec. 3, 1923; "Latone Praised by Grid Critics for Fine Playing," *Wilkes-Barre*, November 1929.

a safe year: Anthracite Heritage Museum, fatalities chart, April 2006.

Three: The Golden Glow

East Norwegian Street: "The John Striegel Mystique," *Republican*, September 23, 1991, p. 12.

Geographically and economically: Pottsville town website, March 2006; Ward, Leo L., and Mark T. Major, *Pottsville in the Twentieth Century,* Charleston: Arcadia Publishing, 2003, p. 2.

statue of Henry Clay: Ibid., p. 15.

Mahantongo Street: Ibid., p. 30.

railroad station: Ward, Leo L., and Mark T. Major. *Schuylkill County,* Volume II. Charleston: Arcadia Publishing, 1998, p. 88.

rail service: "Centennial edition," *Journal,* May 1925.

Schuylkill Trust: Ward, *Pottsville in the Twentieth Century, p. 39.

$100,000 YMCA: "Lost in Time," *ESPN The Magazine*, February 2005, p. 68.

town hall: Ward, *Pottsville in the Twentieth Century,* p. 60.

a single wall: Ibid., p. 78.

risen to a place: Budd Schulberg, (foreword), *Gibbsville, PA: The Classic Stories,* New York: Carroll & Graf, 1992, p. 26.

an imposing figure: Bios, Reunion Program, Pottsville Maroons Memorial Committee, June 1963, p. 8.

Doc was considered: Ibid.

A few years later: "City sent celestial message to NFL in '24," *Republican,* September 23, 1991, p. 12.

He inhaled: Ford Dolin, interview, April 2006.

Monte Carlo: Ibid.

Doc's brother: Ibid.

Molly Maguires: Ibid.

Organized pro ball: "The Pottsville Maroons: their games and tribulations of 1925," *Republican,* August 12, 1985, p. 6.

By 1922 Pottsville's team: Ibid.

the other owners: Ibid.

Canton Bulldogs: Carroll, Bob, et al., *Total Football (The NFL Encyclopedia)* (New York: HarperCollins, 1997), p. 92.

Striegel swooped in: "City sent celestial message to NFL in '24," *Republican,* September 23, 1991, p. 12.

The petition: Ibid.

rang up Joe Zacko: "Lost in Time," *ESPN The Magazine,* February 2005, p. 68.

Saturday morning: Zacko, *Pottsville Maroons NFL World Champions 1925,* p. 51.

Pottsville's population: "The Stolen Championship of the Pottsville Maroons," *Journal of Sports History,* Spring 1982, p. 58.

the first time in history: Dumenil, Lynn, *The Modern Temper: American Culture and Society in the 1920s,* New York: Hill and Wang, 1995, p. 11.

socio-economic triad: Dumenil, *The Modern Temper,* p. 4.

every 10 seconds: Baughman, Judith S., *American Decades (1920-1929),* Michigan: Thomson Gale, 1995, p. 268.

the Golden Glow: Ibid.

earning $2,000 a year: Ibid., p 437.

leisure spending: Ibid., p. 269.

easier to get a drink: Nick Barbetta, interview, May 2006.

radio sales/car purchases: Ibid., p. 268.

installment purchasing: Leuchtenburg, William E., *The Perils of Prosperity 1914-30,* Second edition. Chicago: The University of Chicago Press, 1993, p. 197.

Pomeroy's: Pottsville Bicentennial Committee, *Pottsville Bicentennial, Volume III (1906-1955)*, The Republican and Herald, Pottsville, 2006, p. 49.

Hippodrome and Hollywood Theatre: "The Roaring Twenties," Charles A. Strange, Historical Society of Schuylkill County file, May 23, 1999, pp. 4-5.

First Defenders: "Patriotic Duty Has Always Been a Priority," *Schuylkill County Chronicles*, December 11, 1997, p. 33.

famously collapsed: Ibid.

Rather than miss kickoff: "Pottsville Overwhelms Frankford Yellow Jackets," *Philadelphia Public Ledger*, Nov. 29.

ran close to the ground: "Leg Drive and Crouch," *Republican*, October 15, 1961.

"Wilkes-Barre's home product": Maroons game story (headline unknown), *Republican*, October 5, 1924.

a heavy rain: Ibid.

transfixed by the smell: Stan Latone, interview, May 2006.

Doc made a bee-line: Zacko, *Pottsville Maroons NFL World Champions 1925*, pp. 18-19.

tin-roofed structure: Jack Lebengood, photos, March 2006.

sealing the deal: Zacko, *Pottsville Maroons NFL World Champions 1925*, pp. 18-19.

Four: A New Faith

Construction: Munsell, W.W., *History of Schuylkill County*, New York, W.W. Munsell & Co., pp. 194-213.

Father William Sullivan: "Centennial edition (church directory)," *Journal*, May 1925.

Father Sullivan himself: Zacko, *Pottsville Maroons NFL World Champions 1925*, pp. 28-29.

had obliterated: "Maroons," *Ghosts of the Gridiron*, Geocities.com website, February 11, 2005.

"I can get this team": "The John Striegel Mystique," *Republican*, September 23, 1991, p. 20.

4,000 football fans: Ibid., p. 1.

William Riddle: Atlantic City Free Library, acfpl.org.; Zacko, *Pottsville Maroons NFL World Champions 1925*, p. 29.

wood plank bleachers: Atlantic City Foto Service, photograph (from the collection of Scott Warren), November 9, 1924.

gathered at the 50: Ibid.

best non-NFL teams: "The John Striegel Mystique," *Republican*,

September 23, 1991, p. 20.

grown up on a farm: "The Pottsville Maroons: their games and tribulations of 1925," *Republican*, August 12, 1985, p. 6.

first pair of brothers: Ibid.; Bios, Reunion Program, Pottsville Maroons Memorial Committee, June 1963, p. 29.

W.W. Giffen: "The Pottsville Maroons: their games and tribulations of 1925," *Republican*, August 12, 1985, p. 6; "Steins featured," Niles newspaper, date unknown.

a compromise: Ibid.

finished 9-1: "The Early Years (of Niles football)," Niles Historical Society, date unknown, p. 61.

canceled: Ibid.

went on to play: "Herbert A. Stein, football star," obituary, Niles newspaper, October 26, 1980.

(Russ) played: Bios, Reunion Program, Pottsville Maroons Memorial Committee, June, 1963, p. 20; "Herb, Russ Stein Put City On The Map, All-Americans," Sesquicentennial program, August 1984.

Harry Robb and Fats Henry: "The Pottsville Maroons: their games and tribulations of 1925," *Republican*, August 12, 1985, p. 6; Carroll, Bob, et al., *Total Football (the NFL Encyclopedia)* (New York: HarperCollins, 1997), player bios.

Lafayette College: Football program, Lafayette College website (goleopards.cvst.com), 2006.

had already signed: "Maroons in Fine Shape," *Republican*, September 27, 1925.

a teenager: Brooks Reese, phone interview, May 2006.

Jack Ernst Sr.: Jack Ernst Jr., interview, March 2005.

Spanish flu: Ibid.

two weeks: Ibid.

the steel mills: Jack Ernst Jr., interview, May 2006.

scholarship fund: Ibid.

the scam: Jack Ernst Jr., interview, March 2005.

"Ernst was a very good passer": George Kenneally, interview with Maroons reunion committee (from the collection of Scott Warren), 1963.

Bear: Brooks Reese, phone interview, May 2006.

"Jack was about as cool": "Just Horse Sense Needed ... Jack Ernst of the Pottsville Maroons," *Republican,* September 1924.

the Maroons bench: Atlantic City Foto Service (from the collection of Scott Warren), photograph, November 9, 1924.

"A football regime": "Pottsville Invited in Big League," *Journal,* December 19, 1924 from John O'Hara Papers, 1923-1991, quoted with permission of the Special Collections Library, the Pennsylvania State University Libraries.

Five: "We're In."

Zacko's Sporting Goods: Zacko, *Pottsville Maroons NFL World Champions 1925,* p. 57.

Farquhar: "Walter Farquhar Extra," *Republican*, October 11, 1967, p. 1.

Farquhar was mentoring: Wolff, *The Art of Burning Bridges,* pp. 58-59.

crafted a column: Zacko, *Pottsville Maroons NFL World Champions 1925,* p. 31.

Zacko dispatched: Ibid., p. 34.

O'Hara: Wolff, *The Art of Burning Bridges,* pp. 58-59.

"there's no telling": "A Cub Tells His Story," *Journal,* May 1925 from John O'Hara Papers, 1923-1991, quoted with permission of the Special Collections Library, The Pennsylvania State University Libraries.

in their underwear: Wolff, *The Art of Burning Bridges,* p. 59.

"The ultra-conservative character": John O'Hara Papers, 1923-1991, quoted with permission of the Special Collections Library, the Pennsylvania State University Libraries.

"a God awful town": Wolff, *The Art of Burning Bridges,* p. 9.

League was born: Carroll, *Total Football,* p. 14.

At the APFA's next meeting: Carroll, *Total Football,* p. 15; Peterson, Robert W., *Pigskin: The Early Years of Pro Football,* New York: Oxford University Press, 1997, p. 69.

a fifth-grade education: "Joe Carr," Professional Football Researchers Association, 1984, Vol. VI, p. 1.

At 13: Ibid., p. 2.

Carr proposed: Peterson, *Pigskin: The Early Years of Pro Football,* p. 77; "The Man Who Had a Dream," NFL Game Program, September 18, 1977, pp. 119-120.

kicked them out of the league: Peterson, *Pigskin: The Early Years of Pro Football,* p. 77.

Blue Laws: Leo Ward (Historical Society of Schuylkill County), interview, May 2006; "The Pottsville Maroons: their games and tribulations of 1925," *Republican*, August 12, 1985, p. 6.

two checks: "In Historic Season the Maroons Were Mighty," *Republican*, September 24, 1991, p. 1; "1925 Pottsville Maroons,"

Professional Football Researchers Association, 1981, p. 2.

below $2,000: *The Pro Football Chronicle*, New York: MacMillan, 1990, p. 17.

a profit of $7: Peterson, *Pigskin: The Early Years of Pro Football*, p. 79.

40 NFL teams: Carroll, *Total Football*, p. 16.

40,000 in losses: Ibid.

Oorang Indians: Peterson, *Pigskin: The Early Years of Pro Football*, pp. 81-82.

coal strike looming: "United Mine Workers Leaders Met Secretly," *Republican*, August, 1924, p. 1.

team boosters: Zacko, *Pottsville Maroons NFL World Champions 1925*, p. 35.

"we have the money": Ibid.

supporters had raised: Ibid., p. 34.

"sirens screamed": Ibid, p. 35.

Six: The Mad Doctor

Asylum Field: *Old Leather,* NFL Films, interview, 1976.

15 points: Carroll, *Total Football,* p. 92.

went bankrupt: Ibid.

"paid punting": *The Pro Football Chronicle*, New York: MacMillan, 1990, p. 8.

Beck had begun consulting: Zacko, *Pottsville Maroons NFL World Champions 1925*, p. 39.

of Harrisburg: Bios, Reunion Program, Pottsville Maroons Memorial Committee, June 1963, p. 9.

a classic: Alison Rauch Dudley, interview, March 2006.

"spending time with Dick Rauch": Alison Rauch Dudley, personal letters, 2003.

an ornithologist: "Dick Rauch the Coach," *Republican*, November 11, 1925.

previous summer: Notes for bios (submitted by subject), Reunion Program, Pottsville Maroons Memorial Committee, June 1963, p. 9.

Limnodromus griseus: "Short-billed Dowitcher," birdweb.org, November 11, 2006.

told Doc: Zacko, *Pottsville Maroons NFL World Champions 1925*, pp. 45-47.

taking a room: John Youngfleish, e-mail interview, March 23, 2006.

shelled out $300: "Russ Hathaway's honor elicits memories of Triangles," *Dayton Daily News*, April 22, 1960, p. 13; Russ

Hathaway, personal letters (from the collection of Scott Warren), May 24, 1961.

Frank Bucher/Hoot Flanagan: Bios, Reunion Program, Pottsville Maroons Memorial Committee, June 1963, pp. 15 and 17.

open-field running style: Nick Barbetta, interview, May 2006.

Barney Wentz: "It's Now Councilman Wentz," *Republican*, 1925.

coached a semi-pro football team: "Must Beat Frankford, Racis," *Republican*, 1925.

concrete trowels: Frank Racis Jr., interview, March 2006.

'red tops': "The way it was," *Shenandoah Evening News*, Sept. 29, 1978.

one punch: Frank Racis Jr., interview, March 2006.

"I was determined and conditioned": *Old Leather,* NFL Films, interview, 1976.

alma mater: Frank Racis Jr., interview, March 2006.

$7 a game: "A 'father' of trench warfare," *Voice,* November 24, 1975, p. 3.

"I realized that they were college men": "Must Beat Frankford, Racis," *Republican,* 1925.

"To defeat Frankford": Ibid.

$75 a game: "The way it was," *Shenandoah Evening News*, September 29, 1978.

Fungy Lebengood: Bios, Reunion Program, Pottsville Maroons Memorial Committee, June 1963, p. 16; "Native Son With Maroons," *Republican*, November 2, 1925.

Duke Osborn: Bios, Reunion Program, Pottsville Maroons Memorial Committee, June 1963, p. 13; "Sock 'Em, Says Osborn," *Republican*, October 29, 1925.

petitioned Carr: Duke Osborn, personal letter (from the collection of Scott Warren), June 1, 1971.

Striegel offered: Ibid.

running guards: "Two Fetes for Osborn," Ohio newspaper, June 1962.

Falls Creek: Bios, Reunion Program, Pottsville Maroons Memorial Committee, June 1963, p. 16.

"looked like a good game": "Sock 'Em, Says Osborn," *Republican,* October 29, 1925.

baseball cap: "Tribute to Duke Osborn," *Courier-Express,* November 6, 1976, p. 9; Zacko, *Pottsville Maroons NFL World Champions 1925,* October 1963, p. 80.

tobacco: Ibid.

cleats chugging: *Old Leather,* NFL Films, interview, 1976.

"Duke played": Blood McNally, *Old Leather,* NFL Films, interview, 1976.

call out plays: Bio notes, Reunion Program, Pottsville Maroons Memorial Committee, June 1963.

attack on sight: Ibid.

"I loved to play": *Old Leather,* NFL Films, interview, 1976.

tossed him: Duke Osborn, personal letter (from the collection of Scott Warren), June 1, 1971.

The Kid: Ibid.

team captain: "Sock 'Em, Says Osborn," *Republican,* October 29, 1925.

training under the Phoenix: Cope, *The Game That Was,* p. 46; Leo Ward, Historical Society of Schuylkill County, interview, June 2004; "Lost in Time," *ESPN The Magazine,* February 2005, p. 69.

preseason regiment: "First Practice for Maroons," *Republican,* September 14, 1925.

drove the men: Nick Barbetta, interview, May 2006.

the town's most popular pastime: "First Practice For Maroons," *Republican,* September 14, 1925; Nick Barbetta, interview, May 2006.

sign with Canton: "Robb & Henry Not Coming," *Republican,* August 15, 1925.

Dick Stahlman: Zacko, *Pottsville Maroons NFL World Champions 1925,* p. 61.

"Doc Striegel": Ibid., p. 56.

wagering: Ibid.

Seven: Iodine and Whiskey

18 fatalities: Peterson, *Pigskin,* p. 45.

soldier's skull: "Be a sports equipment expert!" Rawlings Sporting Goods Company, articles 2-4-5-8-9.

to abolish: Peterson, *Pigskin,* p. 46.

rules changes: Ibid., p. 47.

a follow-up study: "Football Toll Heavy on Players," *Philadelphia Public Ledger,* November 29, 1925.

a splash of iodine: Ziemba, Joel, *When Football Was Football: The Chicago Cardinals and the Birth of the NFL,* Chicago: Triumph Books, 1999, p. 89.

for protection: Beau Riffenburgh, et al., *Total Football II* New York: HarperCollins, 1997, p. 34-38; "A History of Football

Equipment," *The Official NFL Encyclopedia*, date unknown, pp. 540-543; "Be a sports equipment expert!" Rawlings Sporting Goods Company, articles 2-4-5-8-9; "Evolution of the Football," Pro Football Hall of Fame Feature, pp. 64-66; Robert W. Peterson., *Pigskin: The Early Years of Pro Football,* New York: Oxford University Press, 1997, pp. 47 and 74.

Osborn insisted: Zacko, *Pottsville Maroons NFL World Champions 1925,* October 1963.

average player: "Lost in Time," *ESPN The Magazine*, February 28 2005, p. 69.

rules established by college football: Carroll, *Total Football,* pp. 1,583-1,592.

the field was: Ibid.

hash marks: Ibid.

waste a play: Ibid.; Peterson, *Pigskin,* p. 70.

four placements kicks: David S. Neft, *The Sports Encyclopedia: Pro Football (The Early Years)*, New York: Sports Products Inc., 1978, p. 52.

the ball had to be thrown: Carroll, *Total Football,* p. 1,587.

reduced by four inches: Ibid., p. 398.

28 inches long: "Evolution of the Football," Pro Football Hall of Fame feature, pp. 64-66.

drop kick: Zacko, *Pottsville Maroons NFL World Champions 1925,* pp. 24-25.

defensive formations: Carroll, *TOTAL FOOTBALL*, p. 413 (figure 2).

single wing: Ibid., Peterson, *Pigskin,* p. 71.

instruction: Ibid.

to signal plays: Ibid., p. 412.

best shape of their lives: "First Practice for Maroons," *Republican*, September 14, 1925.

double wing: Carroll, *Total Football,* p. 398.

a funnel: "Lost in Time," *ESPN The Magazine*, February 2005, p. 68.

"the Maroons showed one thing": "Maroons Delight Fans and Win by 28-0 Score," *Republican*, September 28, 1925.

Chicago Bears game: Cope, *The Game That Was,* pp. 42-43.

his own solution: Zacko, *Pottsville Maroons NFL World Champions 1925,* October 1963.

Ginley's furniture: "Maroons' Four-Horsemen Game Ball Is Property of City Man," *Sunday Independent*, January 6, 1963, p. 5.

Eight: Bison Hunting

5,000 fans: "Maroons Delight Fans and Win by 28-0 Score," *Republican*, September 28, 1925.
Minersville Park: Pottsville Bicentennial Committee, *Pottsville Bicentennial, Vol. III (1906-1955),* The Republican and Herald, Pottsville, 2006.
for $2.20: "Sale Season Tickets Open," *Republican*, September 9.
to avoid ticket cost: Nick Barbetta, interview, May 2006; "Maroons Delight Fans and Win by 28-0 Score," *Republican*, September 28, 1925.
10 cents: Maroons-Bulldogs game program, October. 11, 1925, p. 1.
in the steep hills: Nick Barbetta, interview, May 2006; "Maroons Delight Fans and Win by 28-0 Score," *Republican*, September 28, 1925.
Walter Koppisch: "Walter Koppisch," Coffin Corner, Vol. 23, No. 6.
youngest coach: "Don Shula," Pro Football Hall of Fame biography, 2003; "Youngest NFL Coaches (modern era)," Pro Football Hall of Fame, 2007.
signing Koppisch: "Walter Koppisch," Coffin Corner, Vol. 23, No. 6.
physically removed him: Ibid.
Ernst dropped back: "Maroons Delight Fans and Win by 28-0 Score," *Republican*, September 28, 1925.
his trademark pose: Brooks Reese, phone interview, May 2006.
from the five: "Walter Koppisch," Coffin Corner, Vol. 23, No. 6.
his habit: Zacko, *Pottsville Maroons NFL World Champions 1925,* p. 70.
booming punt: "Maroons Delight Fans and Win by 28-0 Score," *Republican*, September 28, 1925.
two first downs: Ibid.
Buffalo players were spotted: Zacko, *Pottsville Maroons NFL World Champions 1925,* p. 71.

Nine: Dark Skies

holding back six starters: "Potts Squad Is Crippled," *Republican*, October 3, 1925.
an infected arm: Ibid.
had gone AWOL: Ibid.
Providence boasted a line: "Wrestlers Are on Providence," *Republican*, October 3, 1925.

Zacko announced: Zacko, *Pottsville Maroons NFL World Champions 1925,* pp. 73-75.

tongue hanging out: "Steamrollers Who Are Here," *Republican,* October 2, 1925.

volunteers would gather: "Fans Cleaned Off the Snow," *Republican,* November 27, 1925.

few thousand fans: "Fumbles Cost Maroons Game; Steam Rollers Outplayed," *Republican,* October 5, 1925.

Latone ripped through: Ibid.

kick was low: Ibid.

own goal line: Ibid.

first-down advantage: Ibid.

final two pass attempts: Ibid.

Striegel appeared: Zacko, *Pottsville Maroons NFL World Champions 1925,* p. 79.

Miner rep John Lewis: "AFL Endorses Anthracite Strike After Lewis Speech," *Republican,* October 14, 1925.

a public offering: "Football Club Needs $5,000," *Republican,* October 14, 1925.

$5 for common: "Football Club Gets Offer of Support From Fans," *Republican,* October. 14, 1925

if $5,000 was not raised: Ibid.

25 straight victories: David S. Neft & Richard M. Cohen with Robert Carroll and John Hogrogian, *Pro Football: The Early Years (An Encyclopedic History, 1892-1959),* United States: Sports Products Inc, 1987, pp. 28-41.

"these Canton boys": Zacko, *Pottsville Maroons NFL World Champions 1925,* p. 81.

an unconditional release: "Maroons Can Be Best in Land," *Republican,* October 22, 1925.

Ten: In Berry's Hands

national championship: Football program, Lafayette College (website), 2006.

elbowed his head: Lafayette alumni program, player feature, 1950.

bartered the ball: Jack Ernst Jr., interview, March 2006.

Berry grew up: Charlé Reiber, interview, June 2006.

to deliver milk: Ibid.

admittance to Princeton: Ibid.

the first med school: Ibid.

class ring: Ibid.

first-team selection: Football program, Lafayette College (website), 2006.

elected captain: "Pro Ball Here to Stay," *Republican*, November 6, 1925.

"As successful as he was": Charlé Reiber, interview, June 2006.

drop-kicking: "Walter French To Get Going," *Republican*, October 1925.

screen pass: "The Battle of Pottsville," *Newark Ledger*, January 27, 1963.

"Then we have ourselves a picnic": Ibid.

After starring at Army: "From Back Lot to Army Start," *Republican*, November 2, 1925; "Walt French Reaches Pinnacle of Sports Stardom in Playoffs," *The Caduceus*, April 1980, p. 3.

5'7", 155 pounds: Carroll, *Total Football*, p. 722.

new formations: "New Offensive for Maroons," *Republican*, October 1, 1925.

resigned his captaincy: Zacko, *Pottsville Maroons NFL World Champions 1925*, p. 80.

captained the last three: "Tribute to Duke Osborn," *Courier-Express*, November 6, 1976.

$50 extra: George Kenneally, interview, 1963.

unanimously elected: Zacko, *Pottsville Maroons NFL World Champions 1925*, p. 80.

under 1,000: "Maroons Made Short Work of Canton Bulldogs," *Republican*, October 12, 1925.

"Oh boy did Henry": "Berry Recalls Athletic Heydays," Canton newspaper, 1968.

cross midfield only once: "Canton Sustains Worst Defeat in History at Hands of Maroons," *Journal*, October 12, 1925, p. 1; "Maroons Made Short Work of Canton Bulldogs," *Republican*, October 12, 1925.

a single rushing first down: Ibid.

bracketed fats: Ibid.

seven passes: "Statistics of Victory," *Journal*, October 12, 1925, p. 1.

"Ernst asked me": "Berry Recalls Athletic Heydays," Canton newspaper, 1968.

Berry did manage: "Canton Sustains Worst Defeat in History at Hands of Maroons," *Journal*, October 12, 1925, p. 1; "Maroons Made Short Work of Canton Bulldogs," *Republican*, October 12, 1925.

Eleven: A Million Rumors

Captain Berry's boys: "Football Club Gets Offer of Support From Fans," *Republican*, October 14, 1925, p. 1.

On Tuesday: "Do Not Believe Maroons Will Leave Pottsville," *Republican*, October 15, 1925.

$2,400 for the Maroons: Ibid.

Striegel's plan: "Striegel Will Take Over Team," *Republican*, October 16, 1925.

guaranteeing salaries: Ibid.; Zacko, *Pottsville Maroons NFL World Champions 1925*, p. 90.

to celebrate: "Maroons to Providence," *Republican*, October 16, 1925.

fans followed: Zacko, *Pottsville Maroons NFL World Champions 1925*, p. 86.

fans had lined up: "He Could Carry Every Time," *Republican,* May 10, 1963.

at 1:27 p.m.: "Parade for the Maroons," *Republican*, October 19, 1925.

"someone captured": Ibid.

Twelve: A Town's Soul

After starring: Bio notes, Reunion Program, Pottsville Maroons Memorial Committee, June 1963.

Ernst handled: Neft, *Pro Football: The Early Years*, p. 49.

knocking her out cold: Jack Lebengood, interview, May 2006; "One Fan Really Knocked Out by Lebengood," *Reading Eagle*, 2003.

forced to admit: "The Pottsville Maroons: Their Games and Tribulations of 1925," *Republican*, August 12, 1985, p. 6.

The Protestants came: Pottsville Bicentennial Committee, Pottsville Bicentennial, Vol. III (1906-1955), The Republican and Herald, Pottsville, 2006; Ward, *Pottsville in the Twentieth Century*, pp. 27-29, 78.

cover their faces: Nick Barbetta, phone interview, 2004.

$1.65 for each seat: "Maroons Can Be Best in Land," *Republican*, October 22, 1925.

a strong base of: "The Stolen Championship of the Pottsville Maroons," *Journal of Sports History*, Spring 1982, p. 56.

almost a third: Ibid.

Molly Maguires: Poliniak, *When Coal Was King*; Wolff, *The Art of Burning Bridges,* p. 16.

the 1924 DMC: Lynn Dumenil, *The Modern Temper: American Culture and Society in the 1920s*, New York: Hill and Wang, 1995.

large marches: Anthracite Heritage Museum, Scranton, Pennsylvania, photo displays, April 2006.

"schwackies": Wolff, *The Art of Burning Bridges,* p. 105.

mixed marriages: Ibid.

"better be a bit conservative": "Mount Those Steeds, Horsemen!" *Philadelphia Inquirer*, December 11, 1925.

"thrown up the sponge": "Maroons Can Be Best in Land," *Republican*, October 22, 1925.

"pushing ones and fives": George Kenneally, interview with Maroons reunion committee, 1963.

darted backward: "Maroons Beat Columbus 20-0," *Republican*, November 1, 1925.

"as pretty a run": Ibid.

more long runs: Ibid.

pro football experience: Carroll, *Total Football,* p. 722.

severe neck injury: "From Back Lot to Army Star," *Republican*, November 2, 1925.

"The back who is to cover": "Mount Those Steeds, Horsemen!" *Philadelphia Inquirer*, December 11, 1925.

thwarted a late comeback: "Maroons Slide to Victory Over Akron 21-0 in Mud as Thousands Defy the Storm," *Republican*, November 9, 1925.

"pitching forward": "Mount Those Steeds, Horsemen!" *Philadelphia Inquirer*, December 11, 1925.

"the best end in the United States": Ibid.

was so feared: "Tony Latone, the Hero of Pottsville," *The Coffin Corner*, Vol. 9, 1987.

dressed to the nines: "The Famous Back of the Pottsville Maroons," newspaper photo (paper unknown).

chewing gum: "Sport Screen," Edwardsville newspaper, 1963.

"we remember seeing him": "Greatest Football Star? Could Have Been Latone," *Grit Magazine*, 1954.

"You can teach a man": "Sport Screen," Edwardsville newspaper, 1963.

a security agent: "Maroons Can Be Best in Land," *Republican*, October 22, 1925.

envy of her peers: "John Striegel Bore His Crosses in Silence," *Republican*, September 21, 1991, p. 8.

fans would yell: Maroons cheer card (from the collection of Scott Warren), May 2006.

volunteered to tidy up: Duke Osborn, personal letter (from the collection of Scott Warren), June 1, 1971.

off until Wednesday: "Maroons Get Back to Work," *Republican*, October 21, 1925.

even a rumor: Alison Rauch Dudley, interview, March 2006; John Youngfleish, e-mail interview, March 2006.

Maroons were invited: "Maroon Football Players See Harold Lloyd at The Hipp and Meet Crowd of Cheering Fans," *Republican*, October 27, 1925. p. 1.

a member of the audience: Ibid.

the rival Yellow Jackets: "The Frankford Yellow Jackets, Part 2: The Good Years," *The Coffin Corner*, Vol. IX, 1987.

Thirteen: A Savage Sting

Philadelphia annexed: "Fond of Frankford," *Northeast Times*, March 16, 2006.

Royle was: "The Frankford Yellow Jackets, Part 1: Pre-NFL," *The Coffin Corner*, Vol. IX, 1987, p. 2.

first-class stadium: Ibid.

led the league: Carroll, *Total Football*, p. 776.

bowed out: "Pottsville Invited In Big League," *Journal,* December 19, 1924 from John O'Hara Papers, 1923-1991, quoted with permission of the Special Collections Library, the Pennsylvania State University Libraries.

midget football: "The Frankford Yellow Jackets, Part 1: Pre-NFL," *The Coffin Corner*, Vol. IX, 1987, p. 2.

20,000 fans: "20,000 See Locals Turn Back Foemen," *Philadelphia Inquirer*, November 14, 1925.

parading on the grounds: Zacko, *Pottsville Maroons NFL World Champions 1925*, pp. 110-114.

incomplete pass: "Forward Passes and Field Goals Caused Downfall of Maroons," *Republican*, November 14, 1925.

"most savage attacks": "Maroons Were Outsmarted and Outplayed by Frankford Team," Frankford paper, November 14, 1925.

began heaving forward: "20,000 See Locals Turn Back Foemen," *Philadelphia Inquirer*, November 14, 1925.

a sure six points: "Forward Passes and Field Goals Caused Downfall of Maroons," *Republican*, November 14, 1925.

Fourteen: Shadows of Defeat

six games: "The Frankford Yellow Jackets, Part 2: Pre-NFL," *The Coffin Corner*, Vol. IX, 1987, p. 7.

Eddie Gillespie: Bios, Reunion Program, Pottsville Maroons

Memorial Committee, June 1963, p. 26; Zacko, *Pottsville Maroons NFL World Champions 1925*, p. 121.

"the defeat should not": Zacko, *Pottsville Maroons NFL World Champions 1925*, p. 116.

a vibrant, striking woman: "The John Striegel Mystique," *Republican*, September 23, 1991, p. 12.

changing role of women: Dumenil, *The Modern Temper*; Allen, Frederick Lewis, *Only Yesterday: An Informal History of the 1920s*, New York: First Perennial Classics, 2000; Leuchtenburg, William E., *The Perils of Prosperity 1914-32*, Second edition. Chicago: The University of Chicago Press, 1993.

Neva had become: "Lost in Time," *ESPN The Magazine*, February 2005, p. 69.

"Mother Striegel": "Mother Striegel's Influence Aids Pottsville Maroons," *Journal*, December 22, 1925.

started in the mines: "The way it was," *Shenandoah Evening News*, September 29, 1978.

feet ached: "A 'father' of trench warfare," *Voice,* November 24, 1975, p. 3.

straw derby: Player bios, Reunion Program, Pottsville Maroons Memorial Committee, June 1963.

original iron men: A 'father' of trench warfare," *Voice,* November 24, 1975, p. 3.

"Finally I yells": *Old Leather,* NFL Films, 1976.

"I'd just charge": A 'father' of trench warfare," *Voice,* November 24, 1975, p. 3.

a flattened halfback: "The way it was," *Shenandoah Evening News*, September 29, 1978.

several spectacular runs: Game summaries 1925, Elias Sports Bureau and PFRA Line Score Committee, p. 12.

in the fourth: Ibid.

NFL standings: Ibid., p. 1.

Against Cleveland: "Maroons Crush Cleveland 24-6 in Spectacular Game," *Republican*, November 23, 1925.

he whispered: "Cleveland Praises Team," *Republican*, November 23, 1925.

"unanimous opinion": Ibid.

a local prep legend: "Earl (Curly) Lambeau," member profile, Pro Football Hall of Fame, September 18, 2005.

founded the Packers: Ibid.

shoveling off the field: "Fans Cleaned off the Snow," *Republican*, November 27, 1925.

all 24 points: "Pottsville Swamps Green Bay by Score of 31 to 0,"

Republican, November 27, 1925.

league scoring title: Carroll, *Total Football,* p. 527.

"Berry puts such fire": "Notre Dame '24 Meets Maroons," *Republican,* December 1, 1925.

"Charlie gets half": "Maroons on Deck in Fine Shape for Fray," *Republican*, December 5, 1925.

"Why shouldn't Red Grange": "Why Shouldn't Red Make a Fortune?" *Journal*, November 20, 1925 from John O'Hara Papers, 1923-1991, quoted with permission of the Special Collections Library, the Pennsylvania State University Libraries.

Ernst liked to: "Mount Those Steeds Horsemen!", *Philadelphia Inquirer*, December 11, 1925.

Russ Stein out: "Russ Stein is out of Game," *Republican*, November 25, 1925.

Latone ran through: "Pottsville Swamps Green Bay by Score of 31 to 0," *Republican*, November 27, 1925; "Green Bay Swamped," *Journal*, November 26, 1925.

62% of his throws: Ibid.

"a sweet moving machine": Ibid.

Fifteen: The Perfect Machine

trees were already filled: "Pottsville Runs Wild," *Philadelphia Public Ledger*, November 29.

The Allan hotel was filled: "All Ready for Yellow Jackets," *Republican*, November 22, 1925.

VIPs: Zacko, Joe, *Pottsville Maroons NFL World Champions 1925*, p. 136.

11 extra Pullman: Ibid.

advance ticket sales: "All Ready for Yellow Jackets," *Republican*, November 22, 1925.

tickets up for sale: Zacko, *Pottsville Maroons NFL World Champions 1925*, p. 137.

clogged for miles: "Pottsville Overwhelms Frankford Yellow Jackets," *Philadelphia Public Ledger*, November 29, 1925.

more than 11,000: "Pottsville Runs Wild," *Philadelphia Public Ledger*, November 29, 1925.

sea of supporters: "How Stage Was Set for Game," *Republican*, November 30, 1925.

gold-colored jerseys: Ibid.

padded his roster: "Maroons Practiced in Secret and Outwit Scouts," *Republican*, November 28, 1925.

Ladies Home Journal: Zacko, *Pottsville Maroons NFL World Champions 1925*, pp. 139-140.

New uniforms: Ibid.

Latone had no choice: "Sport Ed's Confession," *Journal,* May 2, 1925 from John O'Hara Papers, 1923-1991, quoted with permission of the Special Collections Library, the Pennsylvania State University Libraries.

pack up your trunks: "Four Horsemen Know Something in Name," *Philadelphia Inquirer,* December 10, 1925.

frenzy of barnstorming: Dan Rooney, interview, December 5, 2004.

promoters in Philadelphia: "In Historic Season the Maroons Were Mighty," *Republican,* September 24, 1991, p. 1; "Mixing 'Em Up," *Philadelphia Inquirer,* December 2, 1925.

moved practice: "Maroons Practiced in Secret and Outwit Scouts," *Republican,* November 28, 1925.

rumors flourished: Ibid.

four games: "The Frankford Yellow Jackets, Part II," *The Coffin Corner,* Volume IX, 1987.

"each play was gone over": "Maroons Practiced in Secret and Outwit Scouts," *Republican,* November 28, 1925.

wheelbarrows full of sawdust: "How Stage Was Set for Game," *Republican,* November 30, 1925.

game details: "Pottsville Runs Wild," *Philadelphia Public Ledger,* November 29, 1925; "Maroons Crush Frankford," *Republican,* November 29, 1925; "Yellow Jackets Eleven Annihilated by Pottsville Cyclone," *Philadelphia Record,* November 29, 1925.

Latone went limp: "Yellow Jackets Eleven Annihilated by Pottsville Cyclone," *Philadelphia Record,* November 29, 1925.

sick on the sidelines: Ibid.

Flanagan saw this: Ibid.

seven passes: "Maroons Crush Frankford," *Republican,* November 29, 1925.

extra wood benches: Zacko, *Pottsville Maroons NFL World Champions 1925*, p. 140.

would be suspended: "The Frankford Yellow Jackets, Part II," *The Coffin Corner,* Volume IX, 1987.

by mutual agreement: "In Historic Season the Maroons Were Mighty," *Republican,* September 24, 1991.

five times in a row: "Must Beat Frankford," Racis, *Republican,* 1925.

running the wrong way: "Yellow Jackets Eleven Annihilated by Pottsville Cyclone," *Philadelphia Record,* November 29, 1925.

every fourth down: "Pottsville Runs Wild," *Philadelphia Public Ledger,* November 29, 1925.

21 to 4 advantage: "Maroons Crush Frankford," *Republican*, November 29, 1925.

worst defeat: "Jackets Get Severe Jolt," publication unknown, November 1925.

Perfect Football Machine: "Mixing 'Em Up," *Philadelphia Inquirer*, December 2, 1925.

rubber match: "This is the way it came down," *Republican*, August 15, 1985, p. 7.

wasn't broken: "Maroons Start Practice Wed," *Republican*, December 1, 1925.

the game was scheduled: "Maroons May Tackle Cards," *Republican*, December 1, 1925.

Frank Schumann, the promoter: "This is the way it came down," *Republican*, August 15, 1985, p. 7.

Sixteen: Giant Walter

would draw: Carroll, *Total Football,* p. 16.
official title game: Ibid., p. 121.
nasty snow storm: "Maroons Win Championship Whip Chicago Cardinals," *Republican*, December 7, 1925.
a wash boiler: "Fans Enjoyed Game at Home," *Republican*, December 7, 1925.
telegraph wire: "Play by Play Story of Game at Chicago from Stage at Hipp," *Republican*, December 3, 1925.
trip to Chicago: "50 Locals to See Big Game," *Republican*, December 4, 1925.
drove the 30 hours: "Go to Game on Motorcycle," *Republican*, December 4, 1925.
test the equipment: "Fans Enjoyed Game at Home," *Republican*, December 7, 1925.
Berry had stood: "Maroons Work to Train Time," *Republican*, December 4, 1925; "Players Sole Mind—to Win," *Republican*, December 8, 1925.
two light workouts: Ibid.
Cardinals began: Ziemba, Joel. *When Football Was Football: The Chicago Cardinals and the Birth of the NFL,* Chicago: Triumph Books, 1999, p. 11.
Chris O'Brien: Ibid.
purchased used jerseys: "Chicago Cardinals," sports e-cyclopedia (website), October 26, 2006, pp. 1-2.

disbanded in 1906: Ibid.

$300 a game: Ziemba, *When Football Was Football,* p. 74.

50-yard bombs: "Eastern Champs Invade City For Pro Title Tilt," *Chicago Tribune,* December 5, 1925.

pre-game sales: "Cardinals Keyed for Title Tilt with Pottsville," *Chicago American,* December 5, 1925.

Comiskey: "Comiskey Park, 1910," Encyclopedia of Chicago, October 26, 2006.

also negotiating: "Shall Pottsville Bring Red Grange Here?" *Republican,* November 26, 1925; "Proud and Happy Maroons En Route Home," *Republican,* December 7, 1925.

"we are playing good football": "Maroons Work to Train Time," *Republican,* December 4, 1925.

"Cardinals know all about": "Players Sole Mind—to Win," *Republican,* December 8, 1925.

10,000 fans: "Maroons Win Championship Whip Chicago Cardinals," *Republican,* December 7, 1925.

Chicago game details: "Maroons Win Championship Whip Chicago Cardinals, 21-7," *Republican,* December 7, 1925; "Cards Drop Game to Pottsville, 21-7," *Chicago Daily News,* December 7, 1925; "Pottsville Wins Over Cards and Takes Pro Title, 21-7," *Chicago Tribune,* December 7, 1925; "Maroons Conquer Cards, Take Crown," *Philadelphia Inquirer,* December 7, 1925; "Pottsville Gains Pro Grid Honors," *Philadelphia Public Ledger,* December 7, 1925; "Cards Beaten by East in Pro Title Game," *Chicago American,* December 7, 1925.

"on every play": "Maroons Conquer Cards, Take Crown," *Philadelphia Inquirer,* December 7, 1925.

snapped his collarbone: "Proud and Happy Maroons En Route Home," *Republican,* December 7, 1925.

Eddie Gillespie: Bios, Reunion Program, Pottsville Maroons Memorial Committee, June 1963, p. 26

Fungy Lebengood: "Fans Enjoyed Game at Home," *Republican,* December 7, 1925.

bronze monument: Ward, *Pottsville in the Twentieth Century.*

"there was a howling": "Fans Enjoyed Game at Home," *Republican,* December 7, 1925.

"went into the fray": "Maroons Conquer Cards, Take Crown," *Philadelphia Inquirer,* December 7, 1925.

converted Cardinals fans: Ibid.

picked off by Osborn: "Maroons Win Championship Whip Chicago Cardinals," *Republican,* December 7, 1925.

whirling 30-yard run: Ibid.

20-yard touchdown: Ibid.

Dunn caught fire: "Pottsville Wins Over Cards and Takes Pro Title, 21-7," *Chicago Tribune*, December 7, 1925.

inside the 10: "Pottsville Gains Pro Grid Honors," *Philadelphia Public Ledger*, December 7, 1925.

the Hipp exploded: "Fans Enjoyed Game at Home," *Republican*, Dec. 7, 1925.

O'Brien was spotted: "Proud and Happy Maroons En Route Home," *Republican*, December 7, 1925; "Pottsville Is King," *Philadelphia Inquirer*, December 18, 1925.

two stanzas: Zacko, *Pottsville Maroons NFL World Champions 1925*, October 1963.

Seventeen: Oh, the Noise

thoroughly battered: "Proud and Happy Maroons En Route Home," *Republican*, December 7, 1925.

east for Harrisburg: Ibid.

French had suffered: Ibid.

67-day tour: "Red Equals Green (1925 recap)," Pro Football Researchers Association, 2006.

only 53 yards: "Classic Moments," ESPN Classic (espn.com), 2006.

nearly 80,000: Carroll, *Total Football*, p. 16.

gate receipts of $143,000: Ibid.

"always amusing to me": Cope, *The Game That Was,* p. 38.

players agreed: "Proud and Happy Maroons En Route Home," *Republican*, December 7, 1925.

greatest he had ever seen: Ibid.

Pottsville fans: Ibid.

rumors flew around: Ibid.

Halfway home: Ibid.

crowd waiting for the team: "Lost in Time," *ESPN The Magazine*, February 2005, p. 70; "Fans! Meet Team Train 7 O'clock," *Republican*, December 7, 1925, p. 1.

testimonial dinner: "The Dinner to the Football Team," *Journal*, December 11, 1925.

"That was the signal": "Pottsville Gives Rousing Welcome to Maroon Eleven," *Journal*, December 8, 1925.

caught by fans: Ibid.

"the noise": Nick Barbetta, interview, June 2005.

Eighteen: Fight, Fight, Anthracite!

the phone rang: "Just Where the Maroons Stand," *Republican*, December 14, 1925, p. 5.

laid out his position: Ibid.

jumped his contract: "Four Horsemen for Hire," *Republican*, September 1991.

spoke with Jerry Corcoran: "Maroons Will Play at Philly," *Republican*, December 9, 1925; "Chamber of Commerce Banquets Pottsville Maroons Football Champions of the World for 1925," *Journal*, December 17, 1925.

close friend of Carr's: Carroll, *Total Football*, p. 93.

spent $12 million: "Sports shorts," *Journal*, November 1925.

"got that in writing?": "Chamber of Commerce Banquets Pottsville Maroons Football Champions of the World for 1925," *Journal*, December 17, 1925.

sworn affidavits: "Richard Rauch Affidavit," notarized December 1, 1966; Richard Stahlman affidavit, notarized April 6, 1967.

"it is evident": "Chamber of Commerce Banquets Pottsville Maroons Football Champions of the World for 1925," *Journal*, December 17, 1925.

the lawsuits: "Just Where the Maroons Stand," *Republican*, December 14, 1925, p. 5.

the meeting: "Maroons Will Play at Philly," *Republican*, Dec. 9, 1925; Zacko, *Pottsville Maroons NFL World Champions 1925*, October 1963.

"Oh, no, not at all": Ibid.

he flip-flopped: Ibid.

signs supporting this claim: Zacko, *Pottsville Maroons NFL World Champions 1925*, October 1963.

"said a lot of things ... ": "Sportitorial," *Journal*, December 17, 1925.

thousands of flyers: Zacko, *Pottsville Maroons NFL World Champions 1925*, October 1963.

whee-e-e-e-e: Maroons cheer card (from the collection of Scott Warren), July 2006.

"every street corner": Zacko, *Pottsville Maroons NFL World Champions 1925*, October 1963.

tickets: "Special Train to Phila. Sat.," *Republican*, December 9, 1925.

8:15 a.m. train: Ibid.

raced the locomotive: Zacko, *Pottsville Maroons NFL World Champions 1925*, October 1963.

live results: "Follow the Championship Maroons with the Republican News Service," *Republican*, December 11, 1925, p. 1.

Thursday conversation: "The Shaky Legend of 'The Stolen Championship,'" *Republican*, September 1991.

short practice: "Maroons Out to Practice," *Republican*, December 9, 1925.

Notre Dame $25,000: "The Shaky Legend of the Stolen Championship," *Republican*, September 1991.

O'Hara won: Wolff, *The Art of Burning Bridges,* p. 94.

undefeated regular season: "The Four Horsemen," University of Notre Dame Football Supplement, 2005, p. 157.

"product of destiny": "Knute Rockne Was Notre Dame's Master Motivator," ESPN Classic (website), 2006.

confident quarterback: "The Four Horsemen," University of Notre Dame Football Supplement, 2005, p. 157.

broken ankle: "Knute Rockne Was Notre Dame's Master Motivator," ESPN Classic (website), 2006.

greatest open field runner: "The Four Horsemen," University of Notre Dame Football Supplement, 2005, p. 157.

Seven Mules: "Four Horsemen Know Something in Name," *Inquirer*, December 10, 1925.

practiced twice: Ibid.

inside the Armory: Zacko, *Pottsville Maroons NFL World Champions 1925,* October 1963.

Rauch would wait: "Pottsville Stages Rally to Beat Horsemen," *Philadelphia Record*, December 13, 1925.

merciless pounding: "Maroons Help Down Grange," *Republican*, December 11, 1925.

Rose Marie: Zacko, *Pottsville Maroons NFL World Champions 1925,* October 1963.

Nineteen: The Greatest Game Ever Seen

Maroons arrived: "Maroons Cheered as They Face Four Horsemen," *Republican*, December 12, 1925.

Shibe Park: "Shibe Park," Ballparks of Baseball (website), March 22, 2006; "Shibe Park," alanluber.com, March 22, 2006.

Maroons fans marched: Zacko, *Pottsville Maroons NFL World Champions 1925,* October 1963.

contract renegotiation: "Easy Riders, holdups, holdouts, outlaws, chaos," *Republican*, August 14, 1985, p. 1.

more than 30,000: Game summaries 1925, Elias Sports Bureau and

PFRA Line Score Committee, p. 15.

$5,000 up front: "Easy Riders, holdups, holdouts, outlaws, chaos," *Republican*, August 14, 1985, p. 1.

Striegel and Schumann haggled: Ibid.; "Just Where the Maroons Stand," *Republican*, December 14, 1925, p. 5.

offered a compromise: Ibid.

a Who's Who: Zacko, *Pottsville Maroons NFL World Champions 1925*, October 1963.

Rockne lurking: "The Stuhldreher Connection," *Republican*, August 14, 1985; "The Stolen Championship of the Pottsville Maroons," *Journal of Sports History*, Spring, 1982, p. 56.

in full miner's garb: Ibid.

O'Hara set the scene: "Maroons Get Warm Reception," *Journal*, December 12, 1925 from John O'Hara Papers, 1923-1991, quoted with permission of the Special Collections Library, the Pennsylvania State University Libraries.

multiple formations: "Pottsville Stages Rally to Beat Four Horsemen," *Philadelphia Record*, December 12, 1925.

'box' offense: Carroll, *Total Football*, p. 413.

a full second: Ibid.

Game details: "Maroons Cheered as They Face Four Horsemen," *Republican*, December 12, 1925; "Pottsville Tumbles Four Horsemen," *Philadelphia Public Ledger*, December 13, 1925; "Berry's Field Goal in Closing Quarter Unseats Four Riders," *Philadelphia Inquirer*, December 12, 1925; "Pottsville Stages Rally to Beat Four Horsemen," *Philadelphia Record*, December 12, 1925.

28 yards rushing: "Pottsville Tumbles Four Horsemen," *Philadelphia Public Ledger*, December 13, 1925.

"that's Osborn": photo caption, *Philadelphia Inquirer*, December 13, 1925.

fourth and 1 at the 47: "Pottsville Tumbles Four Horsemen," *Philadelphia Public Ledger*, December 13, 1925.

berating Rauch: Zacko, *Pottsville Maroons NFL World Champions 1925*, October 1963.

raced to the 37: "Maroons Cheered as They Face Four Horsemen," *Republican*, December 12, 1925.

Linesman Eddie Bennis: "Pottsville Tumbles Four Horsemen," *Philadelphia Public Ledger*, December 13, 1925; "Wonderful Testimonial to the Champions," *Republican*, December 17, 1925.

frustrations with Bennis' officiating: Ibid.

telegram from Carr: "Pottsville Tumbles Four Horsemen," *Philadelphia Public Ledger*, December 13, 1925; "The Doc Was Doing Fine," *Republican*, September 1991.

$500: Meeting minutes, NFL archives, Pro Football Hall of Fame, 2005.

"outlaws": "Pottsville Maroons Lose League Franchise; Called Outlaws for Game Here," *Philadelphia Inquirer*, December 12, 1925.

was canceled: "Why No Game in Providence," *Republican*, December 13, 1925.

Striegel tried to argue: "Wonderful Testimonial to the Champions," *Republican*, December 17, 1925.

Rauch addressed the team: "Maroons Cheered as They Face Four Horsemen," *Republican*, December 12, 1925.

"To a man sitting": Ibid.

collar of his sweater: Ibid.

"The hefty halfback": "Pottsville Tumbles Four Horsemen," *Philadelphia Public Ledger*, December 13, 1925.

out-of-shape donkeys: "The Stolen Championship of the Pottsville Maroons," *Journal of Sports History*, Spring 1982, p. 56.

next six plays: "Maroons Cheered As they Face Four Horsemen," *Republican*, December 12, 1925.

at the 18: Ibid.

Berry's feet: "Pottsville Tumbles Four Horsemen," *Philadelphia Public Ledger*, December 13, 1925.

"no one ever hit me harder": "They Remember Russ Stein," *Canton Repository*, June 7, 1970.

"so speedily": "Berry's Field Goal in Closing Quarter Unseats Four Riders," *Philadelphia Inquirer*, December 12, 1925.

inches from his fingertips: "Pottsville Tumbles Four Horsemen," *Philadelphia Public Ledger*, December 13, 1925.

"the great drive began": Ibid.

60-yard punt: Ibid.

"Something knocked me down": "Sportitorial: Leg Drive and Crouch," *Republican*, October 15, 1961.

"one of the most remarkable": "Pottsville Stages Rally to Beat Four Horsemen," *Philadelphia Record*, December 12, 1925.

just beyond the 30: "Pottsville Tumbles Four Horsemen," *Philadelphia Public Ledger*, December 13, 1925; "Maroons Beat Four Horsemen 9 to 7," *Journal*, December 12, 1925 from John O'Hara Papers, 1923-1991, quoted with permission of the Special Collections Library, the Pennsylvania State University Libraries.

replaced by Ernst: "Berry's Field Goal in Closing Quarter Unseats Four Riders," *Philadelphia Inquirer*, December 12, 1925.

139 yards rushing: "Pottsville Tumbles Four Horsemen," Philadelphia Public Ledger, December 13, 1925.

"without a doubt": "Pottsville Stages Rally to Beat Four Horsemen," *Philadelphia Record*, December 12, 1925.

Herb Stein gripped the ball: "Berry's Field Goal in Closing Quarter Unseats Four Riders," *Philadelphia Inquirer*, December 12, 1925.

a graceful arc: "Pottsville Tumbles Four Horsemen," *Philadelphia Public Ledger*, December 13, 1925.

cartoonist Charlie Bell: "What Appealed to Bell at Shibe Park Yesterday," *Philadelphia Inquirer*, December 12, 1925.

Twenty: A Sad Parting

plans were underway: "Wonderful Testimonial to the Champions," *Republican*, December 17, 1925.

all 300 tickets: "Chamber of Commerce Banquets Pottsville Maroons Football Champions of the World for 1925," *Journal*, December 17, 1925.

roasted chicken: "Wonderful Testimonial to the Champions," *Republican*, December 17, 1925.

Bud Whitehouse: Ibid.

game ball from Chicago: "Banquet Briefs," *Journal*, December 17, 1925.

absent were: "Wonderful Testimonial to the Champions," *Republican*, December 17, 1925.

Pottsville mayor: Ibid.

gifts were handed out: "Pottsville Celebrates Victory," Reunion program, 1963, p. 40.

an overnight trip: Zacko, *Pottsville Maroons NFL World Champions 1925*, October 1963. "Banquet Briefs," *Journal*, December 17, 1925.

"Did you ever see": "Pottsville Is King," *Philadelphia Inquirer*, December 18, 1925.

"you are true blue": "Sportitorial," *Journal*, Dec. 17, 1925.

"the baby team": "Wonderful Testimonial to the Champions," *Republican*, Dec. 17, 1925.

roared Mackay: Ibid.; "Chamber of Commerce Banquets Pottsville Maroons Football Champions of the World for 1925," *Journal*, December 17, 1925.

shy tone: Ibid.

"By the time I got here": Ibid.

"never has there been": Ibid.

sent a telegram: Ibid.

two more opponents: "Editorial," *Chicago Tribune*, December 11, 1925; "Cards Hope to End Year in Tie for Pro Grid Title," *Chicago Daily News*, December 8, 1925.

lost to Chicago, 13-0: "Cardinals Win 13-0 from Hammond and Claim Pro Crown," *Chicago Daily News*, December 12, 1925.

coerced four teenaged players: "Pros Banish Prep Scandal Leaders," *Chicago Tribune*, December 30, 1925; "Pros Version of Grid Tangle," *Chicago Tribune*, December 17, 1925.

an embarrassing farce: "Cardinals Beat Milwaukee Team by Score of 58-0," *Chicago Daily News*, December 10, 1925; "Cards Wallop Milwaukee 58 to 0," *Chicago American*, December 10, 1925; "Four Preps Confess Pro Grid Charge," *Chicago Tribune*, December 16, 1925.

an immediate inquiry: "Cardinal Owner to Assist in Clearing Boys," *Chicago American*, December 17, 1925; "Pro League Head Sifts Scandal of Milwaukee Game," *Chicago Tribune*, December 18, 1925.

Milwaukee manager: "Pro League Head Sifts Scandal of Milwaukee Game," *Chicago Tribune*, December 18, 1925.

"as to the championship": "Chamber of Commerce Banquets Pottsville Maroons Football Champions of the World for 1925," *Journal*, December 17, 1925.

stopped payment: "Easy Riders, holdups, holdouts, outlaws, chaos," *Republican*, August 14, 1985, p. 1.

teetering on bankruptcy: "In the end, this is the way it came down," *Republican*, August 15, 1985, p. 7.

pie and ice cream: "Wonderful Testimonial to the Champions," *Republican*, December 17, 1925.

"You might say": "Punts and Passes," *Journal*, November 13, 1925 from John O'Hara Papers, 1923-1991, quoted with permission of the Special Collections Library, the Pennsylvania State University Libraries.

"a sort of sad parting": "Wonderful Testimonial to the Champions," *Republican*, December 17, 1925.

Twenty-One: The Stolen Championship

barnstorming tour: "Maroons Go to Florida," *Republican*, December 16, 1925.

he fined: "Football League Punishes Three Clubs," *New York Times*, December 30, 1925; "Pros Banish Prep Scandal Leaders," *Chicago Tribune*, December 30, 1925.

stricken from the record: Ibid.; "In Pottsville, They're Still Champions All the Way," *Washington Post*, December 16, 2000, p. D12.

"In the case of Pottsville": NFL Owners meeting minutes, Pro Football Hall of Fame document, January 1, 1926.

they were turned down: Carroll, *Total Football,* p. 17.

responded by breaking away: Ibid.

save the franchise: "The Intrigue and Games of 1926," *Republican,* September 1986; "Two Seasons That Might Have Been One," *Republican,* November 23, 1987.

three-way settlement: "NFL Changes Words but Not Its Message," *Republican,* October 13, 1986.

reimburse Royle: "NFL Changes Words But Not It's Message," *Republican,* October 13, 1986.

$5,000: NFL Owners meeting minutes, Pro Football Hall of Fame document, January 1, 1926.

was rescinded: "NFL Changes Words but Not Its Message," *Republican,* October 13, 1986.

order at 4:40 p.m.: NFL minutes, Pro Football Hall of Fame document.

used the leverage: "The Intrigue and Games of 1926," *Republican,* September 1986; "Two Seasons That Might Have Been One," *Republican,* November 23, 1987.

not to tamper: "NFL Changes Words But Not It's Message," *Republican,* October 13, 1986.

coal football fob: "Joe Carr of the NFL: tales about him, by him," *Republican,* October 24, 1991.

red-leather diary: "Joe Carr of the NFL: tales about him, by him," *Republican,* October 24, 1991.

O'Brien again renounced: Ziemba, *When Football Was Football,* p. 89.

refused to accept: Ziemba, *When Football Was Football,* p. 89; "In Pottsville, They're Still Champions All the Way," *Washington Post,* December 16, 2000, p. D12.

Epilogue: Watching and Waiting

In October 1961: "Hall of Fame Director Urges Fans to Keep Up Fight for '25 Title," *Republican,* October 15, 1961.

1926 Maroons: David S. Neft, *Pro Football,* pp. 56-71.

1927 season: Ibid.

in 1928: Ibid.

leased the team: "Maroons," Ghosts of the Gridiron (Geocities.com), February 11, 2005; "The John Striegel Mystique: '60s were great years for the old Maroons," *Republican,* September 28, 1991, p. 1.

Sold the team to George Kenneally: telegram, J. G. Striegel, May 27, 1929.

traveling back home: David S. Neft, *Pro Football,* pp. 56-71.

The Stolen Championship: "The Stolen Championship," *Journal,* December 21, 1945.

included as fact: "NFL Changes Words but Not Its Message," *Republican*, October 13, 1986.

produce 1,000 copies: "The Anthracite Antic," Jerry Izenberg (publication unknown), 1966.

Zacko rang up McCann: Ibid.

size 9 shoe: Ibid.

Doc Striegel left Neva: Ford Dolin, interview, April 2006.

passed away in 1939: "The Man Who Had a Dream," NFL Game program, September 18, 1977, pp. 119-120.

Dick Rauch: Alison Rauch Dudley, interview, May 2006.

gold replicas: Zacko, *Pottsville Maroons NFL World Champions 1925,* October 1963.

the players: reunion photos, *Republican*, September 1991.

"When we got back together": "Sportitorial," *Republican*, Fall 1963.

player careers: "Lost in Time," *ESPN The Magazine*, February 2005, p. 68; Jack Lebengood, interview, May 2006; Jack Ernst Jr., interview, March 2006; Stan Latone, interview, May 2006; Russ Stein III, interview, June 2006; Frankie Racis Jr., interview, March 2006; Charlé Reiber, interview, June 2006.

Hoot Flanagan: "Dr. William Flanagan (Obituary)," *Washington Post*, February 4, 1975.

Barney Wentz: "'60s were great years for the old Maroons," *Republican*, September 28, 1991, p. 10.

Walter French: "Walt French Reaches Pinnacle of Sports Stardom in Playoffs," *The Caduceus*, April 1980, p. 3.

John O'Hara quit: "Famous Author Writes of His Early Days," *Journal,* 1950 from John O'Hara Papers, 1923-1991, quoted with permission of the Special Collections Library, the Pennsylvania State University Libraries.

Lure him to Frankford: "Latone Remembers Being a Champ," *Houghton Lake Resorter*, August 28, 1975, p. 11.

"I sure was glad": "Sportitorial," *Republican,* Fall 1963.

reunion committee president: "Hall of Fame Director Urges Fans to Keep Up Fight for '25 Title," *Republican*, October 15, 1961; Reunion speeches, recording (from the collection of Scott Warren), 1963.

"The stolen championship": "Frank Bucher," reunion program, June 1963.

newspaper across the country: "Maroons special edition," *Republican*, 1963.

"This should have been": Charlie Berry, letters (from the collection of Scott Warren), 2006.

Several prominent figures: "testimonials," Maroons reunion program, June 1963.

O'Hara enlisted friends: "Red Smith Column," *Philadelphia Inquirer,* 1963.

Governor William Scranton: "The Anthracite Antic," Jerry Izenberg (publication unknown), 1966.

"Pottsville is on the agenda": Ibid.

lost the vote: "In Pottsville, They're Still Champions All the Way," *Washington Post*, December 16, 2000, p. D12.

"I wanted the Maroons": "Testimonials," Maroons reunion program, June 1963.

"proclaimed": "NFL Changes Words but Not Its Message," *Republican*, October 13, 1986.

"A recent newspaper article": "Bidwill's History Just Isn't in Cards," *Philadelphia Inquirer*, February 17, 1963.

In six seasons: Neft, *Pro Football,* p. 102.

Gladiator statue: "Lost in Time," *ESPN The Magazine*, February 28 2005, p. 72.

a football carved: Ibid.

grassroots push: Ibid.

simple compromise: Ibid.

Bill Bidwill: Ibid.

Reeves Pioneer Award: Ibid.

The widowed Barbetta: Nick Barbetta, interviews, June 2005 and May 2006.

Zacko died in 1975: "The Long Crusade (and lament) of Joe Zacko," *Republican*, September 30, 1991.

black-and-white photo: Kevin Keating, interview, October 2006.

sadness in his silence: Nick Barbetta, interviews, June 2005 and May 2006.

ACKNOWLEDGMENTS

After spending the last several years on this project, there are myriad moments to choose from as a jumping-off point for these acknowledgements: the day I spent 400 feet below the earth in the clammy confines of a Scranton, Pennsylvania, coal mine; my time on the shores of a choppy lake in northern Michigan, inside a one-room cabin built by Tony Latone; an entire day lost in the cold, marble catacombs of a Philadelphia public library; my research on the ornithology of the Canadian Arctic; my discovery of Charlie Berry's cracked wooden steamer chest in the dark recesses of his daughter's basement; reading the accusation by a curmudgeonly NFL historian that I was an ink-stained Quixote sallying forth to save the new Dulcinea, Pottsville; or my final research trip to Penn State, where I stole a moment sitting at the writing desk of John O'Hara.

But in truth, it would be absurd to begin anywhere else than with my heartfelt appreciation for the sacrifices made by my wife and family during this long, bizarre journey. Many times, whether at our own dinner table or out with friends, I would zone out, my mind wandering back to the book and the team. Yet this always solicited from Kim nothing more than a gentle nudge or a warm, half-joking invitation for me to leave the 1920s: "Say goodbye to your friends in Pottsville and join us back here in the 21st century."

I don't know anyone who isn't a writer who understands writing—mainly, the constant mental churning and the random and repeated cycles of euphoria and exasperation—as well as my wife does. This book is a testament to her selfless spirit, tender heart, and gifted mind, as well as to her flawless and steadfast support.

Matching Kim in that regard are my daughters, Ally and Kate. They never failed to raise my spirits or correct my perspective. Recently, when I dramatically announced that I was going to do them the great honor of including them in the dedication of the book, Ally and Kate formed their own football huddle for a moment, whispering back and forth with their arms around each other and the crowns of their heads touching, before responding in unison that while that was nice and all, what they really wanted were some new Crocs. Talk about a deal.

The truth is, I feel similarly indebted to nearly everyone associated with this book. I am deeply appreciative of the children and families of the Maroons. Alison Rauch Dudley, Stan Latone, Frank Racis Jr., Jack Lebengood, Ford Dolin, Charlé and Art Reiber, Russ Stein III, and Jack Ernst Jr. were extremely gracious with their time and personal treasures while honoring me with the safekeeping of the memories of their amazing fathers. Despite the NFL's treatment of the Maroons, none of the descendants have broken with the legacy of dignity and grace created by the Maroons some 80 years ago.

Prior to that first NFL season, when he was asked to comment on his profession, the estimable Pottsville sports editor Walter S. Farquhar wrote in the centennial edition of the *Pottsville Journal:* "Another fine principle, I think, is to remember that you really are writing sports history, and that the game you are telling about may be harked back to many years in the future. Thus it becomes living literature and, if told properly in the first place, will seem fresh and interesting if picked up 20 years from now." Farquhar was a loyal son of Pottsville who secretly longed to make his mark outside of both sports writing and the coal region. I, for one, am grateful he stayed put. Eighty-two years later, this book is, in part, the result of the saga that he first reported, nurtured, protected, and passed along like a priceless heirloom.

Also working to preserve the Maroons legend were sports editor Ed Zweibel and his staff at *The Pottsville Republican*, as well as Joe Zacko (owner of the Pottsville landmark Zacko's Sporting Goods), who organized the first team reunion in the 1960s and the first petition to the NFL. Some 50 years ago, Zacko had the great sense to annotate his memories of the Maroons, and the Zacko Papers, as they are called, were a tremendous resource. When Joe passed away, his son Russ took up the fight, and he was joined by *Republican* reporter Doug Costello, who produced an epic and exhaustive series in the 1980s. From there Nick Barbetta, of Schuylkill Haven, and the rest of the Pottsville Maroons Memorial Committee carried the banner with the help and support of Leo Ward, the president of the Historical Society of Schuylkill County, and Pottsville mayor John Reiley.

To the countless number of citizens, fans, and members of the media who kept the team's legacy (and this book) alive: Thank you.

I believe Myron Cope, the legendary voice of the Pittsburgh Steelers, put it best when he said in the preface to his book *The Game That Was:* "It is only right that I plead guilty, immediately, to having camped upon ground broken by another." I wholeheartedly share in his sentiment, and to the distinguished list of the "Keepers of the Maroons" I must add Scott Warren of Wilkes-Barre, Pennsylvania. As the preeminent private collector of Maroons data and memorabilia, Scott not only opened his entire collection to me but tirelessly aided me in my research. Remarkably, during this entire process, Scott did not turn down a single one of my pleas for help. He asked for nothing in return, motivated only by his fondness for the Maroons and his dedication to their quest. Scott also graciously donated from his collection the photo that appeared on the cover and the lithograph that decorates each chapter.

The first editor I pitched this story to at ESPN rejected it flatly. It was my—and the Maroons'—great fortune that Gary Belsky, my friend and an editor of *ESPN The Magazine*, saved it from the dust heap. Gary not only championed this project but also lent his vast expertise and keen eye to everything involving the Maroons over the last four years. Gary is also a loyal, lifelong fan of the football Cardinals, and I would argue that his work on behalf of the Maroons just might be enough to get the residents of Pottsville to lift their dreaded Cardinals Curse from the current team in Arizona. (Though I highly doubt it.) Executive editor Sue Hovey shaped and guided the original magazine story that I used as a blueprint for the book, while editor in chief Gary Hoenig, along with deputy editor Chad Millman, provided me with the support and time needed to complete the book.

From there it was placed in the capable care of my agent, Byrd Leavell, and then into the hands of my editor at ESPN Books, Michael Solomon. Michael took the entire project to another level with his deft literary touch, his creativity, and his overall passion for the book, the team, and the cause. He is also the one who pushed me to explore the life and works of Pottsville's prodigal son John O'Hara, which turned out to be one of the unexpected joys of the project.

Along the way, I also received a great deal of research help in re-creating the Maroons' saga. Many, many thanks to the staff at the Historical Society of Schuylkill County; to Audrey John of the Niles (Ohio) Historical Society; the Pro Football Hall of Fame archives, as well as Sandra Stelts and Tim Babcock of the special collections library at Penn State University. I'm also indebted to

ACKNOWLEDGMENTS

Chris Sprow in Chicago; Abby Farson in Davidson, North Carolina; Keith Brey of Llewellyn, Pennsylvania; and Joe McClain of WBT radio in Charlotte. Special thanks to Doug Mittler, the fastidious and tireless researcher charged with fact-checking a tale with practically no eyewitnesses, huge gaps in the paper of record, and, oftentimes, multiple versions of the same events—to say nothing of my dangerous attempts at math.

Finally, regardless of the outcome of the quagmire surrounding the 1925 NFL championship, the league's overall neglect of this honorable team of pioneers—not to mention its treatment of Pottsville and many generations of Maroons fans—is simply inexcusable. It is, of course, my supreme hope that this work will help facilitate that change: to reclaim for the Maroons the honor and place in history that men like Tony Latone earned on the field.

There could be no greater legacy for a book and no higher honor for the people mentioned in these pages, who made it all possible.

—David Fleming, July 2007

About the Author

DAVID FLEMING is a senior writer for *ESPN The Magazine,* a columnist for ESPN.com's Page 2, and the author of Noah's Rainbow. Before joining ESPN in 2000, he covered the NFL for six seasons as a staff writer at *Sports Illustrated.* He and his wife, Kim, live in North Carolina, with their daughters.